Mit herzlichem
Gruß !
Jürgen Rüttel
12.7. 06

Alfred Thomas Barton

GVLIELMI SHAKESPEARE CARMINA QUAE SONNETS NUNCUPANTUR LATINE REDDITA

Latin Elegies after William Shakespeare's Sonnets
Newly edited with a commentary and a revised text of Shakespeare's
Sonnets by Ludwig Bernays. With an essay by Markus Marti.

Lateinische Elegien nach den Sonetten Shakespeares
Neu herausgegeben und kommentiert, mit revidiertem Text der
Sonette Shakespeares, von Ludwig Bernays. Mit einem Essay von
Markus Marti.

VERDANKUNGEN

Wir danken der Jubiläumsstiftung der Thurgauer Kantonalbank und einem ungenannt sein wollenden Freund der Shakespearschen Dichtungen für ihre finanzielle Unterstützung bei der Herausgabe dieses Werks.
Dem Anglisten Jürgen Gutsch in München danken wir für die Beschaffung von Grundlagenmaterial und seine kompetente Beratung. Ohne ihn wäre dieses Werk nicht zustande gekommen.

Herausgeber und Verlag

Cover von Belinda Oetterli
Herstellung: Heer, Grafisches Druckzentrum
CH-8583 Sulgen | TG

Bestellungen über den Buchhandel oder direkt bei
EDITION SIGNAThUR CH-8580 Dozwil/TG
Tel. oder Fax 0041 (0)71 411 00 91 oder E-Mail an
signathur@gmx.ch | Siehe auch www.signathur-schweiz.org |

Preis: 24 CHF | 15 Euro | 18 US-Dollars
ISBN-10: 3-908141-43-5 | ISBN 13: 978-3-908141-43-3

Alfred Thomas Barton (1840 – 1912)

INHALTSVERZEICHNIS / CONTENTS

Dem Buch sind auf den Seiten 10, 168, 207 und 227 frühere Fassungen aus Manuskripten Bartons beigegeben, die der Erstpublikation von 1913 vorangingen.

VORWORT

Shakespeare-Sonette in lateinischer Nachdichtung – soll das wohl ernst gemeint sein? Man kennt die humoristische Wirkung des würdevoll-steifen Lateins und die lustigen lateinischen Versionen von Kinderbüchern wie Max und Moritz, Asterix, Harry Potter – aber Shakespeare auf Lateinisch? Und wenn schon Shakespeare, warum dann nicht eines seiner Lustspiele, sondern ausgerechnet die Sonette, deren nicht selten verworrene Gedankengänge und dunkle Andeutungen schon in ihrem altertümlichen Englisch schwer genug verständlich sind?

In der Tat sind die vom englischen Altphilologen Alfred Thomas Barton (1840–1912) in jahrzehntelangen Bemühungen nach den Sonetten Shakespeares verfassten lateinischen Elegien (d.h. aus alternierenden Hexametern und Pentametern bestehende reimlose Gedichte) ohne Zweifel – auch wenn sie ursprünglich in eher spielerischer Absicht entstanden sein mögen – ernst gemeint.

Darüber hinaus ist Bartons Werk wohl unbestreitbar ein Glanzstück nicht nur der Übersetzungskunst, sondern überhaupt der neulateinischen Literatur. Diese Literatur, die die Werke fast aller europäischen Geistesgrössen vom Mittelalter bis in die Spätrenaissance umfasst, erfreute sich gerade in England besonders sorgfältiger Pflege; so schrieb Shakespares Zeitgenosse Francis Bacon wie auch noch der etwas jüngere John Milton sowohl englisch wie lateinisch. Barton mag sich die Frage gestellt und zu beantworten versucht haben, wie Shakespeares Sonette etwa hätten klingen können, wenn sie in dem zu ihrer Entstehungszeit noch durchaus lebendigen Latein anstatt im eher barbarischen Idiom der Angelsachsen verfasst worden wären. Jedenfalls ist es Barton gelungen, manche Unklarheiten und Unebenheiten des Shakespeare-Texts – der uns nicht in seiner authentischen Gestalt, sondern lediglich in der unautorisierten, mit zahlreichen Fehlern durchsetzten Edition von Thomas Thorpe (1609) überliefert ist – zu vermeiden.

5

Allerdings ist auch Bartons Text nicht in einer vor der Drucklegung vom Verfasser selber durchgesehenen Fassung überliefert. Sein hier vorgelegter Text stützt sich auf die von John Harrower 1923 herausgegebene, längst vergriffene Zweitauflage,[1] die ihrerseits auf dem von Schülern Bartons kurz nach dessen Tod herausgegebenem Erstdruck von 1913 beruht.

Jürgen Gutsch hat schon in einer Publikation von 2003 auf die „gewaltige Sprachleistung" Bartons hingewiesen, deren sich „ein des Lateinischen *und* der Shakespeare-Sonette Kundiger" einmal annehmen sollte.[2] Ebenfalls Gutschs Idee war es, dem neu edierten Barton-Text einen neu revidierten Shakespeare-Text gegenüber zu stellen, in welchem Anregungen Bartons verarbeitet und weitere, vom Thorpe-Text abweichende, möglicherweise zutreffendere Lesarten zur Diskussion gestellt würden. Dieser Doppelaufgabe hat sich der Unterzeichnete mit Begeisterung unterzogen. Dass die von ihm da und dort vorgeschlagenen Neuformulierungen des englischen Texts kaum endgültige Lösungen sein können, versteht sich von selbst; sollten sie die Diskussion um den ‚richtigen' Text fördern und befruchten, so wäre ihr Zweck erfüllt. Unberechtigt ist wohl auf jeden Fall die gerade heutzutage nicht seltene, auf falscher Pietät beruhende kritiklose Haltung gegenüber dem Thorpe'schen ‚Urtext', einem offenbar mit wenig Sorgfalt und Verständnis hergestellten Raubdruck. Im Folgenden sind allen neu vorgeschlagenen Lesarten die entsprechenden Versionen des Thorpe-Texts (Th.) gegenübergestellt, während bereits bekannte Emendationen meist kommentarlos übernommen wurden.

Zürich, im Juni 2006   *Ludwig Bernays*

---

[1] Ausserdem standen uns teils handschriftliche, teils gedruckte und noch von Barton eigenhändig korrigierte frühere Fassungen einiger Elegien dank der Freundlichkeit des Pembroke College, Oxford [Oxford Universities Imaging Service], zur Verfügung.

[2] *„...lesen, wie krass schön du bist konkret",* William Shakespeare – Sonett 18 vermittelt durch deutsche Übersetzer, Dozwil 2003, S. 23. ISBN 3-908141-28-1.

PRAEFATIO

Vorwort zu ersten Ausgabe von 1913

GVLIELMI SHAKESPEARE CARMINA
QUAE SONNETS NUNCUPANTUR LATINE REDDITA

ALVREDVS THOMAS BARTON, cujus memoriam veneratione ac desiderio colentes haecce carmina in lucem edenda curavimus amici, Birminghamiae tribus et septuaginta abhinc annis natus, ibidem in Schola Grammatica puer doctrinae elementis imbutus est: mox Collegii Corporis Christi apud Oxonienses Exhibitionarius adscitus, postquam spatia Academica fauste et feliciter decucurrit, Collegii Pembrochiae Socius cooptatus est, ibique multos per annos Tutoris munus Magistrique Vicemgerentis explevit.

Tot verbis licet ejus vitam describere. Non ille in pulverem strepitumque fori insani descendebat: eruditorum potius in umbraculis per vitam prope totam seclusus, disciplinis et artibus quas optimas a majoribus accepimus totum se dedit. Praestantissima ingenii vi et acumine praeditus, assidua usus sedulitate, cum scriptores Graecos Latinosque luculenter illustrandos sibi potissimum proposuisset, si quid obscurius scripsit Thucydides, si quid subtilius Sophocles pari sagacitate indagabat, nec prius ab improbissimo cessabat labore quam eorum ad ipsa usque penetralia pervenisset. Is autem erat qui, nullius magistri rationi addictus minimeque ceterorum oleo operaque adjutus, lumen sui ipsius ingenii ad locorum obscuritates dissipandas adhiberet. Inter Latinos imprimis Vergilius mel ac deliciae ei erat, cujus e veneribus dicendi miram quandam oblectationem percepit: haud scio an nunquam Aeneida illam quispiam fidelius quam Barton noster solutam in orationem Anglice reddiderit. Ille enim cum verborum dulcedine mirifica tum sono ipso sermonis numerose et apte cadentis ut versuum exquisitam suavitatem imitaretur toto pectore enixus est. Nec mirum, quippe qui et ipse Hippocrenen adiisset: quam lepide enim et eleganter carmina vernacula Latinis versibus interpretatus

7

sit, quantam laudem e dulci Camenarum commercio sibi comparaverit, testatur hicce liber aliaque multa quae pangendo otium fallere solebat. Pedestris etiam sermonis rationem apud scriptores Latinos repertam cum penitus perscrutatus esset, calamistrorum et lenociniorum ut qui maxime contemptor, cuncta quae scribebat ad normam elegantiae exactam accommodabat, neque tamen ita ut oratio elumbis aut enervata esse videretur: nam dictionis tam lacertorum studiosus quam concinnitatis, et verba omnia tanquam aurificis statera examinabat, et lima tam accurate utebatur ut ne Momus quidem menda notare posset.

Idem utpote cui nunquam defervesceret litterarum amor veterisque disciplinae saepenumero earum propugnatorem se praebebat acerrimum: quod patrocinium cum libentissime suscepisset, ferro non rudibus solebat dimicare. Itaque quasi fons is erat perennis unde nonnihil sui ipsius impetus ac diligentiae discipulis redundaret. Non illius in palaestra assuescebant desidiae mollitiaeque adulescentes: tetrica potius ac severa majorum disciplina mentes eorum is exercebat informabatque: nihil incompti nihil impexi in eis tolerabat quae exercitationis causa tractanda exegerat: conversiones Latine minus feliciter compositas tam acriter castigabat ut cerulam ejus miniatam vix minus quam flagellum ipsum discipuli reformidarent. Sic vitam moresque eorum pariter atque indolem ad virtutem corroborabat: sic instituti, sic imbuti sunt ut ea reverentia quam adulescentes conceperant ne aetate qui dem provectioribus usu familiari exolesceret.

Vir erat ille priscae gravitatis benevolentia conditae: nimirum in ingenio tantulum subamari inerat veluti in melle illo Hymettio, quod si quis degustaverit, nihil praestabilius esse asseverabit. Sed cum graviter et severe plerumque se gereret, salibus tamen in loco ac festivitate ita gaudebat ut in circulis conviviisque tanquam rex spectaretur. Ferias quoque sollemnes in memoriam fundatorum et benefactorum institutas quotienscunque celebrabat Collegium Pembrochiae hospitio jucundissimo amicissimoque alumnos suos excipiebat, quorum concursu admirantium plenum semper et frequens erat illius conclave.

Quod ad res divinas pertinet, ecclesiam colebat Anglicanam, nec parcus ille cultor nec infrequens: quod ad res civiles, antiquitatis laudator partibus Optimatum summo studio favebat: immo cum plebis libidinem magis in dies gliscere videret, de imperii fortunis propemodum desperabat.

Beneficus ac liberalis Collegium, cui tamdiu inserviit, donis multis et eximiis augebat; erga amicos spectatae fidei fidum se praestabat et benignum: sorori suae dilectissimae, quacum reliquiae ejus jam requiescunt, frater amantissimus vivae consulebat, mortuae doloris sui immortalis praeclarum dedit monumentum.

Accedit quod, molliorum miris modis haud expers affectuum, Vergilianum illud ‚sunt lacrimae rerum‘ penitus secum sentiebat: adeo quidem ut vel Cassandrae illi moriturae et tristia halucinanti, vel tristissimae illi cladi Cullodenensi, vel rerum mortalium tristitiae ac brevitati nonnunquam, veluti re ipsa et veritate tum primum punctus, soleret illacrimari.

Illum tu quidem intuens, priscae illius severitatis exemplar et imaginem, doctrina adeo praecellentem, in colloquiis tam sapientem et disertum, narrationum tanta varietate, tanto lepore audientes consuetum delectare, sales et argutias sermoni serio tam peritum immiscere, paene dixeris Samuelem Johnson, magnam illam Pembrochiae gloriam, a beatorum insulis tandem regressum in Collegio suo notissimo inter suos sibi locum vindicasse.

Jam in votis fuerat nobis discipulis, ne magistri tam insignis memoria silentio atque oblivione obrueretur, providere ut forma ejus faciesque pictoris penicillo exprimeretur: quam spem cum subita morte abreptus is fefellisset hunc librum quem per annos ferme quadraginta elucubrabat atque expoliebat in lucem edere voluimus quo mentis saltem figura et effigies posteris traderetur.

Restat ut Collegii Pembrochiae Magistro ac Sociis gratias agamus maximas quod nobis pro solita sua humanitate haec poemata rescribendi dederunt occasionem atque hoc opus summo studio prosecuti sunt.

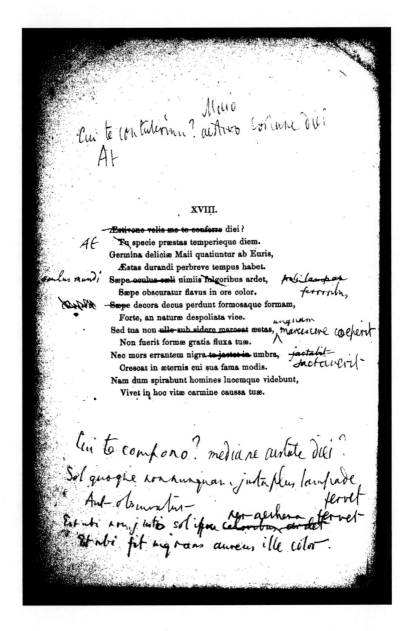

Sonett/Elegie 18. Manuskriptseite von Alfred Thomas Barton.

PREFACE

[second edition, Chiswick Press, London 1923]

THIS translation of Shakespeare's Sonnets into Latin Elegiac verse is the work of Mr. Alfred Thomas Barton, late Fellow, Tutor, and Vice-gerent of Pembroke College, Oxford. Begun as a *parergon* to fill the spare hours of a busy life, it ended by being the most considerable piece of work left behind him by its author, and as such was first published, after his death, in 1913, at the instance of his grateful pupils to be a remembrance of his full and ripe scholarship.

The Memorial volume[3], of which this is a reprint, represents the labour and study of some forty years. Perhaps no more difficult task in its kind was ever attempted. The thought in the Sonnets is profound, elaborate, and complicated, and might well appear alien to the genius of the Latin Elegiac couplet, which as a vehicle suits better epigrammatic sentiment or condensed narrative. But the book found immediate favour with scholars, who admired the ingenuity of thought, the felicity of diction and the apparent inevitableness of the Latin counterpart, which disdained the facile and superficial equivalent, and faced with unflagging courage the hard problem of representing in melodious Latin the truth, the whole truth and nothing but the truth of the original.

But if the version were a mere triumph of expression, a feat of verbal ingenuity, it would have small claim to seek a wider public in this year of the Shakespeare Tercentenary celebrations. What gives it permanent value for all *homines venustiores* is that it asserts in monumental form the bedrock identity of thought and feeling in the old world and the new. The closer it is studied the more apparent will be the penetrating insight of the scholar which detected the essential likeness under the semblance of diversity between the English and the Roman *humanitas*. No one who reads

---

[3] Gulielmi Shakespeare Carmina quae Sonnets nuncupantur Latine reddita ab Alvredo Thoma Barton edenda curavit Joannes Harrower. *Riccardi Press edition limited to 150 copies.* 9 ½ by 6 ½ inches. London 1913.

and ponders over the book with this in his mind will ever sneer at Latin verse-composition as mere knack at the best or dilettante trifling.

It remains to thank the Rev. Douglas Macleane, Canon of Salisbury, and Mr. H. L. Drake, Fellow and Tutor of Pembroke College, Oxford, for the correction of errata which were not expunged in the first edition.

JOHN HARROWER
UNIVERSITY OF ABERDEEN
15 July 1923

Alfred Thomas Barton

GULIELMI SHAKESPEARE CARMINA QUAE SONNETS NUNCUPANTUR LATINE REDDITA AB ALVREDO THOMA BARTON

*

William Shakespeare

THE SONNETS

Vorbemerkung zur Orthographie:

Die zur Zeit Bartons üblichen Abweichungen von der Schreibweise des klassischen Lateins sind in unserem Text nur teilweise beibehalten. So wurde auf die Unterscheidung zwischen vokalischem und konsonantischem *i* (=*j*) gänzlich verzichtet; dagegen wurde im Interesse der Verständlichkeit die Unterscheidung zwischen vokalischem und konsonantischem *u* (=*v*) konsequent durchgeführt (abgesehen vom Wort *tenuis,* dazu Anmerkungen im Text). Das im klassischen Latein unbekannte Längungszeichen ^ wurde nur für die einen Genitiv Plural bezeichnende Endung *-ûm* (statt *-orum*) verwendet. Im englischen Text wurde von Akzenten, wie sie manche Herausgeber der Shakespeare-Sonette verwenden, kein Gebrauch gemacht. Die Endung *-ed* ohne Apostroph ist jedoch innerhalb eines Verses stets als ungekürzte Silbe zu lesen; nur am Versende kann eine auf die 5. Hebung folgende Wortendung *-ed* nach heutigem Gebrauch gekürzt, d.h. mit stummem *e* gesprochen werden.

13

I

Stirpibus a pulchris pulchra est optanda propago,
Ut roseum possit stare perenne decus;
Et, quotiens acto pereat maturior aevo,
In tenerum heredem forma paterna cadat.
Tu vis ipse tuo tantum devotus amori
Vivere, tu flammis ureris ipse tuis.
Quantis ex opibus penuria quanta paratur,
O te qui laceras, o inimice tibi!
Tu, nova totius iam lux et gloria terrae,
Veris venturi nuntia[1] purpurei,
Visne tuam in sterili spem fructus condere gemma?
Prodige, dum parcis; parce, profuse tamen!
Aut patriae miserere, aut, dum male condis avarus
Quod patriae debes, fac Libitina voret.

II

Bruma tibi obsidet cum bis vigesima frontem
Actaque per pulchras ruga profunda genas,
Tum iuvenile decus, quo iam spectaris amictu,
Et lacerum et pretii nullius istud erit.
Deinde requirenti quo forma recesserit oris,
Quo vigor et vegetus fugerit ille dies,
Reddere 'cuncta tuis oculorum ea mersa cavernis'
Et scelus et damnum flebile laudis erat.
Tu potius reddas, formae bene dotibus usus,
'Filius, en, heres, pulcher et ipse, meus.
Ille meum exsolvat nomen, veniamque senectae
Conciliet nato tradita forma patris.'
Sic iterum renovare senex; et sanguinis in te
Quod gelidum sentis, inde calere vides.

---

[1] Die weibliche Form von *nuntius (herald)* ist hier Adjektiv zu *lux et gloria*.

1

From fairest creatures we desire increase,
That thereby beauty's rose might never die,
And[2] as the riper should by time decease,
His tender heir might bear his memory.
But thou, contracted to thine own bright eyes,
Feed'st thy light's flame with self-substantial fuel,
Making a famine where abundance lies -
Thyself thy foe, to thy sweet self too cruel.
Thou that art now the world's fresh ornament
And only herald to the gaudy spring,
Within thine own bud buriest thy content
And, tender churl, mak'st waste in niggarding.
     Pity the world, or else this glutton be,
     To eat the world's due, by the grave and thee.

2

When forty winters shall besiege thy brow,
And dig deep trenches in thy beauty's field,
Thy youth's proud livery, so gaz'd-on now,
Will be a totter'd weed, of small worth held:
Then being ask'd where all thy beauty lies,
Where all the treasure of thy lusty days,
To say 'Within thine own deep-sunken eyes'
Were an all-eating shame and thriftless praise.
How much more praise deserv'd thy beauty's use,
If thou couldst answer 'This fair child of mine
Shall sum my count and make my old excuse,'
Proving his beauty by succession thine!
     This were to be new-made when thou art old
     And see thy blood warm when thou feel'st it cold.

---

[2] Th.: *But* (siehe Anmerkungen).

III

In speculum spectans dic oris imagine visa
'Tempus adest facies ut creet ista novam.'
Eius enim integram ni vis reparare iuventam,
Fraus erit, ac cuidam matris ademptus honos.
Quaenam[3] ita pulchra vides telluris virginis arva
Ut dedignentur vomere culta tuo?
Quisve suum in sese sepelit vesanus amorem
Contentus clausa posteritate mori?
Te tua mater habet speculo, qua reddita cernit
Pulchra iuventutis tempora verque suae;
Perque senes oculos olim rugasque videbis
Ipse tibi hanc auream[4] rursus adesse diem.
Sive agis ut nequid post te vel imaginis exstet,
Fac pereas caelebs, ac simul illa perit.

IV

Consumas in tene, nepos[5] pulcherrime, formam
Quae tibi ab antiquis tradita venit avis?
Mancipio nil dat rerum natura, sed usum
Commodat in largos[6] liberiore manu.
Quodque ea largitur quo largirere vicissim,
Hoc es abusurus, pulcher, avare tamen?
Usurasne facis sine faenore? ponis in usu
Summarum has summas, vivere deinde nequis?
Nam tua si tecum solo commercia fient,
Surripies furtim te tibi, dulce caput.
Quas igitur tabulas aut testamenta relinques
Iusta tuis, hinc te cum tua fata ferent?
Forma, nisi uteris, tecum tumulabitur ista;
Utere, tunc heres vixerit ista tuus.

---

[3] Harrower schreibt *quaene*.
[4] *auream* ist hier als zweisilbiges Wort mit den Diphthongen *au* und *ea* zu lesen.
[5] *Nepos* (Neffe, Enkel) hier in der Nebenbedeutung „liederlicher Verschwender".
[6] *Commodat in largos* („sie leiht den Freigebigen") entspricht den Worten des Thorpe-Texts *she lends to those are free* (richtig wohl *to those who 're free*).

3

Look in thy glass, and tell the face thou viewest
'Now is the time that face should form another';
Whose fresh repair if now thou not renewest,
Thou dost beguile the world, unbless some mother.
For where is she so fair whose unear'd womb
Disdains the tillage of thy husbandry?
Or who is he who fond will be the doom[7]
Of his self-love to stop, posterity?
Thou art thy mother's glass, and she in thee
Calls back the lovely April of her prime:
So thou through windows of thine age shalt see
Despite of wrinkles this thy golden time.
    But if thou live, remember'd not to be,
      Die single, and thine image dies with thee.

4

Unthrifty loveliness, why dost thou spend
Upon thyself thy beauty's legacy?
Nature's bequest gives nothing, but doth lend,
And being frank, she lends to those who 're[8] free.
Then, beauteous niggard, why dost thou abuse
The bounteous largess given thee to give?
Profitless usurer, why dost thou use
So great a sum of sums, yet canst not live?
For having traffic with thyself alone,
Thou of thyself thy sweet self dost deceive;
Then how, when Nature calls thee to be gone,
What acceptable audit canst thou leave?
    Thy unus'd beauty must be tomb'd with thee,
      Which, used, lives the executor to be.

---

[7] Th. : *or who is he so fond will be, the tombe.*
[8] Th.: *to those are* (siehe Fussnote 6).

V

Horae[9] quae tacita geniales arte creabant
Delicias oculi, ruris agreste decus,
Imperiis in eo saevis utentur eaedem,
Dedecoraturae si qua decora nitent.
It sine fine dies; aestas in squalida brumae
Ducitur, inde omnis despoliata iacet.
Deriguere gelu suci, caret arbor honore,
Forma latet multa sub nive, cuncta vacant.
Inde nisi umorem stillasset nectaris aestas
Et lacrima in vitreo carcere capta foret,
Gratiaque aestatis pereunte aestate periret,
Nec species pulchri, nec foret umbra memor.
Sed captis florum lacrimis, ubi bruma recurret
Si deerit species, at remanebit odor.

VI

I, puer, aestatisque tuae breve collige nectar
Ante manu rigida quam spoliarit hiems;
Imple vas aliquod dulcedine, tuque reconde
Ante cupidineas quam moriantur opes.
Haud vetita usura est usus felicior ille
Solvit ubi faenus dulce libenter amor.
'Esto pater' canit hic[10], 'tuaque altera fiat imago,
O deciens felix, tot renovate vices.'
Sis deciens, inquam, felix, si dena per ora
Te suboles referat laetificetque patrem.
Quid faciendum ipsi Libitinae deinde relinquis,
Si moriens vivis posteritate tamen?
Cede, puer, monitis; ista omnia tradere leto
Vermibus in praedam te tua forma vetat.

---

[9] Horae, die wörtliche Übersetzung von *those hours*, bedeutet im Lateini-schen auch „die Jahreszeiten", von denen Sh. erst im 2. Quartett spricht.
[10] Harrower schreibt *hoc*, aber *hic (amor)* dürfte eher gemeint sein als *hoc (faenus)*. In einer früheren Fassung lautet Vers 7 ohne Anführungszeichen: *Hoc valet, esto pater, tuaque altera fiat imago.*

5

Those hours, that with gentle work did frame
The lovely gaze where every eye doth dwell,
Will play the tyrants to the very same
And that unfair which fairly doth excel;
For never-resting Time leads summer on
To hideous winter and confounds him there;
Sap check'd with frost and lusty leaves quite gone,
Beauty o'ersnow'd and bareness everywhere;
Then, were not summer's distillation left,
A liquid prisoner pent in walls of glass,
Beauty's effect with beauty were bereft,
Nor it nor no remembrance what it was:
     But flowers distill'd, though they with winter meet,
     Leese but their show; their substance still lives sweet.

6

Then let not winter's ragged hand deface
In thee thy summer, ere thou be distill'd:
Make swift[11] some vial; treasure thee[12] some place
With beauty's treasure, ere it be self-kill'd.
That use is not forbidden usury
Which happies those that pay the willing loan;
It's[13] for thyself to breed another thee,
Or ten times happier, be it ten for one;
Ten times thyself were happier than thou art,
If ten of thine ten times refigur'd thee:
Then what could Death do, if thou shouldst depart,
Leaving thee living in posterity?
     Be not self-will'd, for thou art much too fair
     To be Death's conquest and make worms thine heir.

---

[11] Th.: *sweet* (siehe Anmerkungen).
[12] Th.: *thou* (siehe Anmerkungen).
[13] Th.: *That's.*

VII

En, ubi sol primum, lucis gratissimus auctor,
Sustulit effulgens ex oriente caput,
Mortales oculi speciem apparentis adorant
Ore observantes inferiore deum.
Cumque poli acclivis victor super ardua constat
Aetatis mediae viribus ille suis,
At mortale genus speciem veneratur eandem,[14]
Omne sequens aureum[15] voltibus eius iter.
Verum ubi lassatus currum declinat ab axe,
Defugiens senio iam titubante diem,
Haec oculi pietas, tractum aversata cadentem
Solis, ad exortus vertitur inde novos.
Te quoque destituent tua robora; curaque nulli,
Ni subolem generas, emoriere, puer.

VIII

Vox liquida, o, cur iam[16] tales tristissimus audis?
Laeta iuvant laetos, dulcia dulcis amat.
Tu quod amas, illud tamen auscultare gravaris,
Anne libens audis quod fit in aure dolor?
Si tibi displiceat liquida haec concordia vocum
Mixtaque coniugiis fila canora suis,
Te dulce increpitant, qui consocianda iugali
Foedere perverse dissociata tenes.
Nectit eas, audisne, inter se mutuus ordo,
Ac sonat in chordae chorda marita sono;
Sic patris et nati matrisque ex ore beatae
It quasi communis dulcisonusque canor.
Verba silent, sed vox a ternis editur una
Talis: 'io, vita caelibe nullus eris.'

---

[14] Harrower interpungiert erst nach *omne* im folgenden Vers.
Dieses *omne* dürfte aber zu *iter*, nicht zu *genus* zu ziehen sein.
[15] *Aureum* ist wie *auream* in 3,12 als Disyllabum zu lesen.
[16] Harrower schreibt *nam*.

7

Lo, in the orient when the gracious light
Lifts up his burning head, each under eye
Doth homage to his new-appearing sight,
Serving with looks his sacred majesty;
And having climb'd the steep-up heavenly hill,
Resembling strong youth in his middle age,
Yet mortal looks adore his beauty still,
Attending on his golden pilgrimage.
But when from highmost pitch, with weary car,
Like feeble age, he reeleth from the day,
The eyes, 'fore duteous, now converted are
From his low tract, and look another way.
   So thou, thyself out-going in thy noon,
    Unlook'd-on diest, unless thou get a son.

8

Music to hear, why hear'st thou music sadly?
Sweets with sweets war not, joy delights in joy.
Why lov'st thou that which thou receiv'st not gladly,
Or else receiv'st with pleasure thine annoy?
If the true concord of well-tuned sounds,
By unions married, do offend thine ear,
They do but sweetly chide thee, who confounds
In singleness the parts that thou shouldst bear.
Mark how one string, sweet husband to another,
Strikes each in each by mutual ordering,
Resembling sire and child and happy mother,
Who, all in one, one pleasing note do sing;
   Whose speechless song, being many, seeming one,
    Sings this to thee: 'thou single wilt prove none.'

IX

An viduae metuens ne cui tingatur ocellus
Caelibe constituis condicione[17] teri?
Si sine prole ereptus eris, te maxima terra
Fleverit, ut coniux coniugis orba viri.
Ut vidua aeterno te fleverit illa dolore
Nulla sibi quod sit forma relicta tui;
Cum viduae liceat privatis aedibus omni
In natorum oculis commeminisse patrem.
Aspice, in orbe[18] nepos rem perdit siquis, easdem
Translatas alio possidet orbis opes;
Formae quod periit per totum perditur orbem,
Quique habet utendi nescius, ille necat.
Nil alios erga sedet huic in corde benignum
Qui struit in sese tam furiale nefas.

X

Proh pudor! esse nega cordi mortalia cuncta
Iam tibi, negligitur cui tua summa salus.
A multis fateor te, si placet illud, amari,
Nil at amari a te iam manifesta fides.
Sic odium crudele in te dominatur, ut ultro
In caput irasci non vereare tuum!
Tuque venusta paras ea vertere tecta ruina
Quae reparandi in te iustior ardor erat!
O animum mutes ut probrum desit; an ira
Dignior hospitio est quam generosus amor?
Sis animo quod es ore tuis, humanus amansque,
Vel minimum in tete consule iusta, puer.
Alterum – amans oro – te gigne, nec aurea forma
Intereat nobis, seu tua, sive tui.

---

[17] *Caelibe condicione* knüpft ebenso *an vita caelibe* (Junggesellenleben) im vorangehenden Gedicht an wie *single life* in 9,2 an single in 8,14.
[18] Harrower schreibt *in urbe*. Das in den drei Versen 9, 10, 11 wiederholte Wort *orbis (orbe, orbem)* entspricht der Wiederholung von *world* bei Shakespeare.

9

Is it for fear to wet a widow's eye
That thou consum'st thyself in single life?
Ah! if thou issueless shalt hap to die,
The world will wail thee, like a makeless wife;
The world will be thy widow and still weep
That thou no form of thee hast left behind,
When every private widow well may keep
By children's eyes her husband's shape in mind.
Look, what an unthrift in the world doth spend
Shifts but its[19] place, for still the world enjoys it;
But beauty's waste hath in the world an end,
And, kept unus'd, the user so destroys it.
   No love toward others in that bosom sits
   That on himself such murderous shame commits.

10

For shame, deny that thou bear'st love to any,
Who for thyself art so unprovident;
Grant, if thou wilt, thou art belov'd of many,
But that thou none lov'st is most evident.
For thou art so possess'd with murderous hate
That 'gainst thyself thou stick'st not to conspire,
Seeking that beauteous roof to ruinate
Which to repair should be thy chief desire.
O, change thy thought, that I may change my mind!
Shall hate be fairer lodg'd than gentle love?
Be, as thy presence is, gracious and kind,
Or to thyself at least kind-hearted prove:
   Make thee another self, for love of me,
   That beauty still may live in thine or thee.

---

[19] Th.: *his.*

XI

Quam cito per senium marces, in prole vicissim
Crescis, ubi partem severis ipse tui;
Quodque in flore tuo vegeti das sanguinis, illud
Crede tuum, iuvenis cum tibi rapta dies.
Providet hoc formae generique; hoc deme, relicta est
Stultitia, et senii marcor, inersque gelu.
Mens tua si cunctis, hic rerum desinat ordo,
Binaque post hominum saecula desit homo.
Is sine prole cadat quem non natura creando
Destinat, informem corpore, mente rudem.
Quaere quibus donet largissima, largius omne
Dat tibi[20], tu dando dona tuere deae.
Te sibi in exemplar sculpsit, pluresque volebat
Sculpere te, posset ne bona forma mori.

XII

Si numero pulsus horae momenta notantes
Seu video in nigra nocte perire diem;
Purpura me violae marcescens sicubi movit
Nigrave caesaries sparsa colore nivis;
Si mihi celsa arbor foliis spoliata videtur
Quae modo contra aestus texerat una gregem,
Seu vehitur plaustro spicis in mergite vinctis
Cana rigens, viruit quae modo verna seges;
Tum mihi cura tua de forma multa recursat,
Tu quod, ubi tempus cetera vastat, eas.
Omnia namque solent formosa ac dulcia sese
Linquere, dumque vident altera nata mori.
Temporis at[21] falcem fugiet res una, propago,
Sospes, ubi victum te quoque tempus habet.

---

[20] *largius dat tibi* entspricht der Emendation *she gave thee more* (Th.: *the more*).
[21] Harrower schreibt *et*. Im Unterschied zu Shakespeares entsprechendem Text, wo die Aufzählung vergänglicher Dinge mit *and nothing* fortgesetzt wird, dürfte hier eher das adversative *at* (doch, hingegen) gemeint sein.

11

As fast as thou shalt wane, so fast thou grow'st
In one of thine, from that which thou departest;
And that fresh blood which youngly thou bestow'st
Thou mayst call thine when thou from youth convertest.
Herein lives wisdom, beauty, and increase;
Without this, folly, age, and cold decay:
If all were minded so, the times should cease,
And threescore year would make the world away.
Let those whom Nature hath not made for store,
Harsh, featureless, and rude, barrenly perish;
Look, whom she best endow'd: she gave thee more;
Which bounteous gift thou shouldst in bounty cherish.
 She carv'd thee for her seal, and meant thereby
 Thou shouldst print more, not let that copy die.

12

When I do count the clock that tells the time,
And see the brave day sunk in hideous night;
When I behold the violet past prime,
And sable curls all silver'd o'er with white;
When lofty trees I see barren of leaves
Which erst from heat did canopy the herd,
And summer's green, all girded up in sheaves,
Borne on the bier with white and bristly beard;
Then of thy beauty do I question make,
That thou among the wastes of Time must go,
Since sweets and beauties do themselves forsake
And die as fast as they see others grow.
 And nothing 'gainst Time's scythe can make defence
 Save breed, to brave him when he takes thee hence.

XIII

O utinam posses tuus esse! at posse negatur
Id tibi post spatium perbreve, care, morae.
Consule in hunc igitur venturum, consule, finem,
Ac speciem nato trade, venuste, tuam.
Sic tibi finitum in tempus iam credita forma
Fit tua, nec iuris terminus ulla dies.
Progenies formam referet si pulchra paternam,
Tu tua post etiam funera vivus eris.
Et quis homo patitur formosa putrescere tecta
Queis[22] modica a cura perpetuetur honos?
Quisve ea non firmat brumas ac flamina contra
Mortisque in rabiem perpetuumque gelu?
O, nisi socordes, nemo; tu, care, creatus
Es patre; fac suboles ut tua dicat idem.

XIV

Si non aetheriis prudentia fluxit ab astris
Ulla mihi, astrologum me tamen esse reor.
Non equidem novi sit sors bona, necne, futura,
An sitis, an febris, candida, necne, dies.
Non ego momentis sua fata volantibus edo,
Quid tonitru aut ventus, quidve minetur hiems.
Non ego vaticinor quo vertat regibus annus,
Saepe requirendo praescia signa poli.
Ex oculis mea cuncta tuis prudentia fluxit;
Ars mea sunt oculi, sidera certa, tui.
Inde lego fidei et formae quae destinet aetas,
Haud tibi, sed generi, si studuisse velis.
Nolueris, de teque hoc auguror: ipse peribis,
Et periere illo forma fidesque die.

---

[22] *Queis* archaisierend für *quibus* (welchen, bezogen auf *tecta*, Häuser).

13

O, that you were yourself! but, love, you are
No longer yours than you yourself here live;
Against this coming end you should prepare,
And your sweet semblance to some other give.
So should that beauty which you hold in lease
Find no determination; then you were
Yourself again after your self's decease,
When your sweet issue your sweet form should bear.
Who lets so fair a house fall to decay,
Which husbandry in honour might uphold
Against the stormy gusts of winter's day
And barren rage of Death's eternal cold?
   O, none but unthrifts! Dear my love, you know:
   You had a father; let your son say so.

14

Not from the stars do I my judgement pluck,
And yet methinks I have astronomy;
But not to tell of good or evil luck,
Of plagues, of dearths, or seasons' quality;
Nor can I fortune to brief minutes tell,
Pointing to each his thunder, rain and wind,
Or say with princes if it shall go well,
By aught[23] predict that I in heaven find.
But from thine eyes my knowledge I derive,
And, constant stars, in them I read such art,
As truth and beauty shall together thrive,
If from thyself to store thou wouldst convert.
   Or else of thee *this* I prognosticate:
   Thy end is truth's and beauty's doom and date.

---

[23] Th.: *oft* (siehe Anmerkungen).

XV

Cum memini innatum cunctis gignentibus esse
Ut breve per tempus stet suus ille vigor;
Undique per mundum spectacula fluxa videri,
Quae super arcanis viribus astra notent;
Cum scio mortales herbarum crescere ritu,
Laetificante uno vel reprimente Iove[24],
Suco luxuriare novo, decrescere adultos,
Mox vegeti floris nil retinere memor;
Talia miranti sortis spectacula fluxae
Ante oculos tu stas, aurea forma, puer;
Stas[25], ubi damnosum tempus seniumque videntur
Consulere, an mutent iam tibi nocte diem.
Noster amor vero capit arma, et quas tibi tempus
Surripiet vires inseret ille novas.

XVI

Cur vero in tristem tempus crudele tyrannum,
Bella magis valido non geris ipse modo?
O si decrepitos iacias munimina in annos
Hac sterili nostra prosperiora lyra!
Stas nunc in summum vectus felicibus horis,
Castaque virgineo despicis arva solo;
Casta, sed et vivos praebere volentia flores,
Plusque relaturos quam simulacra tui.
Viva figura tuam reparat sic denique vitam,
Quod calamo aut tabulis ars hodierna[26] nequit,
Non decus externum, non intus acumina mentis,
Non te demum aliis ponere docta viris.
At dando tu te servas, dulcique necesse est
Tu vivas opera sculptus ab ipse tua.

---

[24] *Jupiter* (Ablativ *Iove*) ist eine gebräuchliche Metonymie für „Himmel".
[25] Harrower schreibt *has*. Eine frühere Version der Verse 10/11 lautet bei Barton: *Tu stas ante oculos aurea forma meos. / Stas, ubi tempus agit...*
[26] Entgegen dem Thorpe-Text und neueren Ausgaben mit Interpunktion nach *this* fasst Barton this *Time's pencil* als Begriffseinheit *(ars hodierna)* auf.

15

When I consider every thing that grows
Holds in perfection but a little moment,
That this huge stage presenteth nought but shows
Whereon the stars in secret influence comment;
When I perceive that men as plants increase,
Cheered and check'd even by the self-same sky,
Vaunt in their youthful sap, at height decrease,
And wear their brave state out of memory;
Then the conceit of this inconstant stay
Sets you most rich in youth before my sight,
Where wasteful Time debateth with Decay,
To change your day of youth to sullied night;
    And all in war with Time for love of you,
    As he takes from you, I engraft you new.

16

But wherefore do not *you* a mightier way
Make war upon this bloody tyrant, Time,
And fortify yourself in your decay
With means more blessed than my barren rhyme?
Now stand you on the top of happy hours,
And many maiden gardens, yet unset,
With virtuous wish would bear your living flowers,
Much liker than your painted counterfeit.
So should the lines of life that life repair,
Which this time's pencil, or my pupil pen,[27]
Neither in inward worth nor outward fair,
Can make you live yourself in the eyes[28] of men.
    To give away yourself keeps your self still,
    And you must live, drawn by your own sweet skill.

---

[27] Th.: *Which this (Times pensel or my pupill pen).* (Siehe Fussnote 26.)
[28] Th.: *in eies of men.*

XVII

Si meus efferret merita in te maxima versus,
Quae fuit in sera posteritate fides?
Scitque deus, multo deceat magis ille sepulcrum,
Sic tua vita in eo, famaque multa, latet.
Scribere si possim quae gratia luminis ista,
Ac vegeto in versu quodque referre decus,
Dicat posteritas, 'o vatem falsa locutum!
Aetheria humanas haud tetigere genas.'
Sic faciat risum mea saeclis lutea charta,
Ut superans verum garrulitate senex;
Iusta etiam tua laus habeatur vana poetae
Fabula, vel prisci carminis ille tumor.
Sed tua si suboles illo sit tempore quaedam,
Bis vivas: in ea carminibusque meis.

XVIII

An similem aestivae pingam te, care, diei?
Haud ita fit constans, haud ita pulchra dies.
Flabra novas agitant, Maio sua gaudia, frondes,
Ac brevis aestivam continet hora moram.
Sol, oculus caeli, nimiis fervoribus ardet
Interdum, aut hebes est aureus ille color;
Pulchraque declinant a pulchro, forte caduca,
Aut quia naturae lex ita flectit iter.
At tibi perpetua est, indeclinabilis, aestas,
Deciderit nulla flos tuus iste die;
Mors nihil ipsa suis de te iactabit in umbris,
Carmine in aeterno dum sine fine vires.
Donec homo spirabit enim poteritque videre,
Vivit in hoc vitae carmine causa tuae.

17

Who will believe my verse in time to come,
If it were fill'd with your most high deserts?
Though yet, Heaven knows, it is but as a tomb
Which hides your life and shows not half your parts.
If I could write the beauty of your eyes
And in fresh numbers number all your graces,
The age to come would say "This poet lies;
Such heavenly touches ne'er touch'd earthly faces."
So should my papers, yellow'd with their age,
Be scorn'd like old men of less truth than tongue,
And your true rights be term'd a poet's rage
And stretched metre of an antique song.
    But were some child of yours alive that time,
    You should live twice: in it, and in my rhyme.

18

Shall I compare thee to a summer's day?
Thou art more lovely and more temperate;
Rough winds do shake the darling buds of May,
And summer's lease hath all too short a date.
Sometimes too hot the eye of heaven shines,
And often is his gold complexion dimm'd;
And every fair from fair sometime declines
By chance, or Nature's changing course untrimm'd.
But thy eternal summer shall not fade
Nor lose possession of that fair thou ow'st;
Nor shall Death brag thou wander'st in his shade,
When in eternal lines to Time thou grow'st:
    So long as men can breathe or eyes can see,
    So long lives this, and this gives life to thee.

XIX

Tempus, tempus edax, ungues obtunde leonum,
Fac subolem tellus hauriat ipsa parens;
Tigridis e malis aciem rape dentis, et ure
Phoenica annosum sanguinis igne sui;
Fac miseros hilaresve annos utcunque libebit,
O rapidum tempus, fac mihi quidquid aves;
Mundo ac deliciis marcentis abutere mundi
Omnibus – hoc unum tu vereare nefas:
Est puer, o ne sculpe horas in fronte venusta
Eius, ibi senii ducere parce notas;
Praetereas unum sine labe, ut^{29} noscere possint
Hoc specimen formae saecla futura virûm.
I tamen, o tempus, quodvis conere maligni,
Hic puer in versu vixerit usque meo.

XX

Virginea ora geris nativo picta colore,
O puer, o animae mascula flamma meae!
Virginis et placidum pectus, quod mobile quidquam
Nesciat, ut fallax scit muliebre genus.
Luce tui excellunt oculi sensuque fideli,
Tangentes auro qualiacunque vident.
Vir specie decus omne tenes, nam percutis idem
Corda puellarum, ducis et ora virûm.
Te facere instituit primo natura puellam,
Ni studio sese falleret inter opus;
Sed nimium addendo spe me deiecit ab omni:
Id dederat quod non ad mea vota facit.
Virginibus te gratum ea fecerat; usus amoris
Detur eis igitur, dum mihi detur amor.

---

[29] Harrower schreibt *et*; eher dürfte hier *ut* (damit) gemeint sein.

19

Devouring Time, blunt thou the lion's paws,
And make the earth devour her own sweet brood;
Pluck the keen teeth from the fierce tiger's jaws,
And burn the long-liv'd Phœnix in her blood;
Make glad and sorry seasons as thou fleet'st,
And do whate'er thou wilt, swift-footed Time,
To all the world[30] and all her fading sweets;
But I forbid thee one most heinous crime:
O, carve not with thy hours my love's fair brow,
Nor draw no lines there with thine antique pen;
Him in thy course untainted do allow
For beauty's pattern to succeeding men.
    Yet do thy worst, old Time: despite thy wrong,
    My love shall in my verse ever live young.

20

A woman's face with Nature's own hand painted
Hast thou, the master-mistress of my passion;
A woman's gentle heart, but not acquainted
With shifting change, as is false women's fashion;
An eye more bright than theirs, less false in rolling,
Gilding the object whereupon it gazeth;
A man in hue, all hues in his controlling,
Which steals men's eyes and women's souls amazeth.
And for a woman wert thou first created;
Till Nature, as she wrought thee, fell a-doting,
And by addition me of thee defeated,
By adding one thing to my purpose nothing.
    But since she prick'd thee out for women's pleasure,
    Mine be thy love and thy love's use their treasure.

---

[30] Th.: *to the wide world.*

XXI

Dissimile ingenium nobis illique poetae
Cui canitur pictis femina nota genis.
Delicias quaerens ipsum scrutatur Olympum,
Cumque venusto omni nominat ille suam.
Comparat huic solem lunamque superbius ille,
Quasve parit gemmas terra vadumque maris;
Comparat Aprilem, et violas, et siquid ubique
Rarius aetheriae continet aura plagae.
Ast ego, verus amans, optarim scribere vera,
Atque ita, sic credas, est mihi pulcher amor:
Nil facie superat, quanquam superare nitore
Aurea per caelum lumina mille puto.
Plura quidem effundent sua qui praeconia curant;
Laus, nihil optanti vendere, quid sit opus?

XXII

Noluerim speculo de canis credere nostris
Ipse iuventutis dum, puer, instar eris;
At senii rugas in te quo tempore cernam,
Et mihi clausam iri tum scio morte diem[31].
Omnis enim forma haec quae te vestire videtur,
Verius insigni cor mihi veste tegit;
Utraque in alterno vivunt nam pectore corda,
Nec sine te possim nomen habere senis.
O tueare ergo mihi te, velut ipse tuebor
Me tibi, custodem cordis, amice, tui;
Haud minus hoc timide gesto quam sedula nutrix
Praetimet infanti quem gerit omne malum.
Nec repetendum hoc ipse, meum si perdis, habeto;
Te mihi non dederas rursus ut ipse darem.

---

[31] Harrower schreibt *clausum iri ... dies*. Der Nominativ *clausa* (nicht *clausus*)
dies findet sich in einer früheren Fassung Bartons, wo Vers 4 lautet: *Nostra
dies etiam clausa, verebor, erit.* Bartons *verebor* oder *tum scio* („dann weiss ich")
dürfte Shakespeares Gedanken richtiger ausdrücken als *then look I* im
Thorpe-Text.

21

So is it not with me as with that Muse
Stirr'd by a painted beauty to his verse,
Who heaven itself for ornament doth use
And every fair with his fair doth rehearse;
Making a couplement of proud compare
With sun and moon, with earth's[32] and sea's rich gems,
With April's first-born flowers, and all things rare
That heaven's air in this huge rondure hems.
O let me, true in love, but truly write,
And then believe me, my love is as fair
As any mother's child, though not so bright
As those gold candles fix'd in heaven's air:
    Let them say more that like of hearsay well;
    I will not praise that purpose not to sell.

22

My glass shall not persuade me I am old,
So long as youth and thou are of one date;
But when in thee Time's furrows I behold,
It looks like[33] Death my days should expiate.
For all that beauty that doth cover thee
Is but the seemly raiment of my heart,
Which in thy breast doth live as thine in me:
How can I then be elder than thou art?
O therefore, love, be of thyself so wary
As I, not for myself but for thee, will;
Bearing thy heart, which I will keep so chary
As tender nurse her babe from faring ill.
    Presume not on thy heart when mine is slain;
    Thou gav'st me thine, not to give back again.

---

[32] Th.: *earth and sea's* (siehe Anmerkungen).
[33] Th.: *Then look I* (siehe Fussnote 31).

XXIII

Ut stupet in scena quis non assuetus agendo
Impositas partes excutiente metu;
Utque ferae vires effervescentis in iram
Immodicus laedit debilitatque furor;
Sic ego nonnunquam linguae diffisus[34] omitto
Plurima quae plane dicere vellet amans,
Et videor languens in amore ac lentior esse,
Quod ruit his in me viribus ille deus.
O igitur sine me voltu mea sensa profari;
Pectoris is fiat vox sine voce mei.
Causam is amoris agat melius, mercedis et optet
Plus sibi quam felix omnia lingua loqui.[35]
O legere addiscas pietatis verba silentis;
Auscultare oculis ingeniosus amor.

XXIV

En oculus pictorem egit mihi, picta per illum
In tabula cordis forma venusta tua est;
Corporis in compage mei pictura tenetur
Pulchra, novoque artis perspicienda modo.
Namque per artificem spectando videris artem
Eius, et effigies quo tua picta situ:
Pectoris in cella est suspensa, vicemque fenestrae
En oculi supplent, irradiantque, tui.
Nunc oculis oculi reddunt quae mutua, quaeso,
Nosce: mei vera te posuere fide;
Perque tuos, nostro claras in corde fenestras,
Sol penetrare, ut te contueatur, amat.
Non oculis tamen omnis inest sollertia: pingunt
Visa sibi, nequeunt corda videre virûm.

---

[34] Während bei Shakespeare nicht ganz klar ist, was mit *for fear of trust* gemeint ist, heisst *linguae diffisus* eindeutig „der eigenen Zunge misstrauend“.
[35] Im Unterschied zu den Worten *more than that tongue that more hath more express'd* im Thorpe-Text ist *plus quam lingua felix omnia loqui* („mehr als eine Zunge, der es gegeben ist alles zu sagen“) klar verständlich.

23

As an imperfect actor on the stage
Who with his fear is put beside his part,
Or some fierce thing replete with too much rage,
Whose strength's abundance weakens his own heart,
So I, for fear of trust, forget to say
The perfect ceremony of love's rite,
And in mine own love's strength seem to decay,
O'ercharg'd with burden of mine own love's might.
O, let my looks be then the eloquence
And dumb presagers of my speaking breast,
Who plead for love and look for recompense
More than that tongue that not hath aught[36] express'd.
  O, learn to read what silent love hath writ:
  To hear with eyes belongs to love's fine wit.

24

Mine eye hath play'd the painter and hath stell'd
Thy beauty's form in table upon[37] my heart;
My body is the frame wherein 't is held,
In perspective, as[38] is best painter's art.
For through the painter must you see his skill,
To find where thy[39] true image pictur'd lies;
Which in my bosom's shop is hanging still,
That hath its windows glazed with mine eyes.
Now see what good turns eyes for eyes have done:
Mine eyes have drawn thy shape, and thine for me
Are windows to thy breast, where-through the sun
Delights to peep, to gaze therein on thee.
  Yet eyes this cunning want to grace their art:
  They draw but what they see, know not the heart.

---

[36] Th.: *more hath more* (siehe Fussnote 35).

[37] Th.: *of.*

[38] Th.: *And perspective it.*

[39] Th.: *your* (siehe Anmerkungen, ebenso zu den Zeilen 8 und 11).

XXV

Ingentis iactet titulos atque urbis honores,
Cui natalicium sidus et hora favet.
Me potius, fastus istos cui fata negarunt,
Id quod praecipuo dignor honore iuvat.
Deliciae qui sunt regum, ceu caltha, colores
Oppandunt domini solis ad ora sui;
Nubila sit facies, illorum gloria fluxit,
Aureaque in sese forma sepulta iacet.[40]
Strenuus et miles felicia notus ob arma,
Si totiens victor vincitur ipse semel,
Raditur e fastis omnino nomen honestis,
Omniaque assiduo gesta labore cadunt.
O ego quam videor felix, immobile pectus
Pectoris immoti semper amantis amans!

XXVI

O cui me fateor iunctum vinctumque teneri
Officio ac meritis, dulcis amice, tuis,
Scripta sinas ad te legem mea, nullius artis
Indicia, at magnam testificata fidem.
Dictaque tanta fides tenui sic arte videri
Nuda potest, desint cum sua verba rei,
Ni tibi quid sensus sperem felicius esse,
Quod capiat corde haec omnia, nuda tamen.
Dum mihi siqua meos discursus stella gubernat
Desuper aspectu me meliore notet,
Ac superinducat quid honestum his sordibus ipsis,
Dignior ut cultu sit tibi[41] noster amor.
Fas animi affectus erga te deinde fateri;
Nunc mea qua noscas ora venire pudet.

---

[40] Gegenüber Shakespeares Text ist hier die Reihenfolge der Verse 7/8 vertauscht: anders als bei Shakespeare verliert der Günstling erst nach dem Stirnrunzeln seines Gönners sein Selbstwertgefühl.

[41] *tibi* entspricht der Emendation *thy sweet respect* (Th.: *their sweet respect*).

25

Let those who are in favour with their stars
Of public honour and proud titles boast,
Whilst I, whom Fortune of such triumph bars,
Unlook'd-for joy in what[42] I honour most.
Great princes' favourites their fair leaves spread
But as the marigold at the sun's eye,
And in themselves their pride lies buried,
For at a frown they in their glory die.
The painful warrior famoused for worth,
Who[43] after a thousand victories once foil'd,
Is from the book of honour razed forth,
And all the rest forgot for which he toil'd:
    Then happy I, that love and am belov'd
    Where I may not remove nor be remov'd.

26

Lord of my love, to whom in vassalage
Thy merit hath my duty strongly knit,
To thee I send this written ambassage,
To witness duty, not to show my wit.
Duty so great, which wit so poor as mine
May make seem bare, in wanting words to show it,
But that I hope some good conceit of thine
On my soul's thought, all naked, will bestow wit[44];
Till whatsoever star that guides my moving
Points on me graciously with fair aspect
And puts apparel on my tatter'd loving,
To show me worthy of thy sweet respect:
    Then may I dare to boast how I do love thee;
    Till then not show my head where thou mayst prove me.

---

[42] Th.: *that.*
[43] Th.: Zeile 10 beginnt ohne *Who* mit *After...*
[44] Th.: *In thy soules thought (all naked) will bestow it.*

XXVII

Lassus ubi repeto mea lecti strata, levamen
Dulce fatigatis membra labore viae,
Continuo sub pectore iter mihi longius iri
Incipit, exhausto corpore mentis opus.
Nam procul a membris dilabitur illa quietis
Teque petens cupide tendere pergit iter;
Pansaque lumina habet lasso, spectantia semper
In tenebras, quales lumina caeca vident.
Ni mihi ad obscuros orbes se mentis imago
Offerat, effigiem visa referre tuam[45];
Illa relucet enim velut umbris pendula nigris
Gemma, novum antiquo noctis in ore decus.
Luce mihi membris, animo mihi nocte negatur
– Sive ego seu tu sis causa – fruenda quies.

XXVIII

Quaene domum reditus igitur feliciter acti
Spes mihi, si nulla sit requiete frui?[46]
Lucis ubi aerumnis nescit nox ipsa mederi,
Noxque die gravior fit mihi, nocte dies;
Alteraque alterius licet adversaria regnis,
Unanimas iungunt in mea damna manus.
Huic iter urgendum curae est, agit illa querelas
Quone locorum a te longius ire velim.
Voce diem solor tristem te lumina terris
Reddere, per totum si nigret umbra polum;
Blandior et furvae nocti, si nulla nitescant
Sidera, te seri vesperis esse decus.
Interea mihi cura die producitur omni,
Omni nocte agitur vi graviore dolor.

---

[45] *Effigiem tuam* entspricht der Emendation *thy shadow* (Th.: *their shadow*).
[46] Mit *requiete frui* knüpft Barton deutlicher als Shakespeare ans Ende des
vorangehenden Gedichts *(fruenda quies)* an.

27

Weary with toil, I haste me to my bed,
The dear repose for limbs with travail tired;
But then begins a journey in my head,
To work my mind, when body's work 's expired.
For then my thoughts, from far where I abide,
Intend a zealous pilgrimage to thee,
And keep my drooping eyelids open wide,
Looking on darkness which the blind do see;
Save that my soul's imaginary sight
Presents thy shadow to my sightless view,
Which, like a jewel hung in ghastly night,
Makes black night beauteous and her old face new.
   Lo! thus by day my limbs, by night my mind,
    For thee and for myself no quiet find.

28

How can I then return in happy plight,
That am debarr'd the benefit of rest,
When day's oppression is not eas'd by night,
But day by night and night by day oppress'd,
And each, though enemies to either's reign,
Do in consent shake hands to torture me,
The one by toil, the other to complain
How far I dwell[47], still farther off from thee?
I tell the day to please him: 'Thou art bright,
And dost him grace' - when clouds do blot the heaven;
So flatter I the swart-complexion'd night,
When sparkling stars twire not: 'Thou gild'st the even.'
   But day doth daily draw my sorrows longer,
    And night doth nightly make grief's strength seem stronger.

---

[47] Th.: *toil* (siehe Anmerkungen).

XXIX

Fortunae fugiens iras oculosque virorum
Sicubi desertum me miserumque fleo;
Sive deûm irrito frustra clamoribus aures,
Meque tuens fatis imprecor omne malum;
Vellem ubi me natum spe cum meliore fuisse,
Huius amicitiis, illius ore parem,
Artemve alterius vel idonea tempora nactum,
Quoque meum magis est hoc minus omne placet;
Tum, per eas idem curas me paene perosus,
Forte tui memini, laetaque cuncta reor;
Ac feror in cantus, ut inerte a caespite surgens
Mane novo ad caeli cantat alauda fores.
Ditat enim sic ipse tui me sensus amoris
Ut mihi tum regum despiciantur opes.

XXX

Cum sedeo meditans, et corda silentia dulce
Acta repraesentant praeteritosque dies,
Deesse gemo permulta olim quaesita, dolorque
Tempus ob effusum fit novus ille mihi.
Tum lacrimis desueta opplentur lumina caros
Propter eos, longa qui mihi nocte silent;
Flere queo exstinctos et amores, flere parata
Gaudia non parvo, sed fugitiva tamen.
Tum renovare libet distantis temporis iras,
Nominaque accepti dinumerare mali;
Omnia quae lacrimis rursum solvenda videntur,
Tanquam eadem nullis ante soluta forent.
Sed meminisse tui per tot, carissime, curas
Omnia compensat damna, fugitque dolor.

29

When, in disgrace with Fortune and men's eyes,
I all alone beweep my outcast state,
And trouble deaf Heaven with my bootless cries,
And look upon myself and curse my fate,
Wishing me like to one more rich in hope,
Featur'd like him, like him with friends possess'd,
Desiring this man's art and that man's scope,
With what I most enjoy contented least;
Yet in these thoughts myself almost despising,
Haply I think on thee, and then elate[48],
Like to the lark at break of day arising
From sullen earth, sing[49] hymns at Heaven's gate;
   For thy sweet love remember'd such wealth brings
   That then I scorn to change my state with kings.

30

When to the sessions of sweet silent thought
I summon up remembrance of things past,
I sigh the lack of many a thing I sought,
And with old woes new wail my dear time's waste.
Then can I drown an eye, unus'd to flow,
For precious friends hid in Death's dateless night,
And weep afresh love's long-since cancell'd woe,
And moan the expense of many a vanish'd sight;
Then can I grieve at grievances foregone,
And heavily from woe to woe tell o'er
The sad account of fore-bemoaned moan,
Which I pay new[50] as if not paid before.
   But if the while I think on thee, dear friend,
   All losses are restor'd, and sorrows end.

---

[48] Th.: *and then my state* (siehe Anmerkungen).
[49] Th.: *sings*.
[50] Th.: *new pay*.

XXXI

Quos desiderium finxit periisse meorum
Morte, tuum pectus, carius inde, tenent;
Omnis ibi pietas et munus amabile regnat,
Cordaque amicorum quae data rebar humo.
Quot lacrimas autem veras ad triste sepulcrum
Ex oculo elicuit relligiosus amor
His velut exstinctis! quae[51] tantum novimus esse
Mota situ, in te[52] nam viva latere tamen.
Pectus, amicitiae custos ac vita sepultae,
Tu mihi carorum pignora quanta capis!
Hi tibi legavere in me sua debita;[53] multis
Quae fuit, ad te nunc ius redit omne rei.
Tot facies caras in te contemplor, habesque
Has ubi tecum omnes, sum tuus omnis ego.

XXXII

Me bene contentis superes si, care, diebus,
Haec ubi mors atrox texerit ossa solo,
Ac relegas iterum fortasse hoc carminis ipsum
Quod rude panxisset, iam tibi raptus, amans,
Cum meliore die lectum conferre memento,
Victumque a calamo quoque tuere tamen.
Tactus amore mei facias, non carminis arte;
Magnorum ingeniis cesserit illa virûm.
Comiter o tum fare, 'mei si versus amici
Robore crevisset cum meliore die,
Ediderat pietas aliquid felicius ista,
Aptius et iunctos fecerat ire pedes.
Quando obiit, meliusque novi scripsere poetae,
Hos arte egregios, hunc pietate, legam.'

---

[51] Der relative Anschluss *quae* (Neutr. Pl.) bezieht sich auf *velut exstinctis*, entsprechend der Formulierung *the dead which now appear but things*.

[52] *in te* entspricht der Emendation *in thee* (Th.: *in there*).

[53] Harrower interpungiert schon nach *sua*. *Sua debita in me* („ihre Verpflichtungen mir gegenüber") ist aber wohl als Begriffseinheit aufzufassen.

31

Thy bosom is endeared with all hearts
Which I by lacking have supposed dead;
And there reigns Love and all Love's loving parts
Of[54] all those friends which I thought buried.
How many a holy and obsequious tear
Hath dear religious Love stol'n from mine eye,
As interest of the dead, which now appear
But things remov'd that hidden in thee lie!
Thou art the grave where buried Love doth live,
Hung with the trophies of my lovers gone,
Who all their parts of me to thee did give:
That due of many now is thine alone.
   Their images I lov'd I view in thee,
   And thou, all they, hast all the all of me.

32

If thou survive my well-contented day,
When that churl Death my bones with dust shall cover,
And shalt by fortune once more re-survey
These poor rude lines of thy deceased lover,
Compare them with the bettering of the time,
And though they be outstripp'd by every pen,
Reserve them for my love, not for their rhyme,
Exceeded by the height of happier men.
O, then vouchsafe me but this loving thought:
'Had my friend's Muse grown with this growing age,
A dearer birth than this his love had brought,
To march in ranks of better equipage:
   But since he died and poets better prove,
   Theirs for their style I'll read, his for his love.'

---

[54] Th.: *And.*

XXXIII

Saepe diem vidi, splendens ut mane niteret
Blanditus summis regius ore iugis;
Pascua caelesti viridantia tangeret auro,
Auro caeruleas pingeret amnis aquas.
Qui breve post tempus nimborum obscaena sinebat
Agmina in aetherio turpiter ore vehi[55];
Mox faciem miseris abdens mortalibus ibat
Occiduum furtim sic maculatus iter.
Haud aliter quodam in frontem mihi mane refulsit
Qui veluti vitae sol erat ipse meae;
Sed miserum, meus esse unam modo perstitit horam,
Abditur in nubis iam regione diu.
Necdum ideo contemnit amor; solemque nigrare
Fas puto mortalem, si nigret ille deus.

XXXIV

Cur faceres tu me, placidae dans omina lucis,
Tam male munitum vestibus ire foras,
Opprimeret nubes ut euntem obscaena, tuusque
Turpibus in fumis occuleretur honos?
Nec quod ea velles interdum erumpere nube
Purgavit madidas id satis imbre genas;
Non ita, nemo hominum laudat fomenta, receptum
Dedecus intactum quae remanere sinant.
At pudet admissi; sed quae medicamina quaeso
Sunt ea? non explet damna recepta pudor.
Quod pudeat sontes illi fit tenue levamen
Grande iniustitiae qui toleravit[56] onus.
At flesti; ah, lacrimae pietas est aurea, flesti;
Omniaque his opibus furta piavit amor.

---

[55] Der Anklang zwischen den Versen 2 und 6 *regius ore iugis* – *turpiter ore vehi* hebt den Kontrast zwischen den Naturschilderungen des ersten und des zweiten Quartetts hervor.

[56] Harrower schreibt *tolerabit*; möglich wäre auch *tolerarit* (= *toleraverit*), am ehesten düfte aber wohl *toleravit* (Indikativ Perfekt) gemeint sein.

33

Full many a glorious morning have I seen
Flatter the mountain-tops with sovereign eye,
Kissing with golden face the meadows green,
Gilding pale streams with heavenly alchemy;
Anon permit the basest clouds to ride
With ugly wrack on his celestial face,
And from the forlorn world his visage hide,
Stealing unseen to west with this disgrace.
Even so my sun one early morn did shine
With all triumphant splendour on my brow;
But, o[57] alack! he was but one hour mine,
The region cloud hath mask'd him from me now.
    Yet him for this my love no whit disdaineth;
    Suns of the world may stain when heaven's sun staineth.

34

Why didst thou promise such a beauteous day,
And make me travel forth without my cloak,
To let base clouds o'ertake me in my way,
Hiding thy bravery in their rotten smoke?
'T is not enough that through the cloud thou break,
To dry the rain on my storm-beaten face,
For no man well of such a salve can speak
That heals the wound and cures not the disgrace;
Nor can thy shame give physic to my grief:
Though thou repent, yet I have still the loss;
The offender's sorrow lends but weak relief
To him that bears the strong offence's cross.
    Ah! but those tears are pearls[58] which thy love sheds,
    And they are rich and ransom all ill deeds.

---

[57] Th.: *out.*
[58] Th.: *pearl* (siehe Anmerkungen).

XXXV

Nolis ulterius, nolis, admissa dolere;
Fert rosa nam spinas, claraque lympha lutum.
Defectu et nebulis maculant sol lunaque sese,
Tetraque sub tenero germine pestis erit.
Sic homines peccant, ego certe, exempla legendo
Auctor nequitiae factus et ipse tuae.
Dedecus inque meum tua purgo sequius acta
Ac veniae supra quem meruere modum.
Siquid amore in me peccas, ibi causor amorem,
Oppositae parti[59] gratificatus opem.
Lis mihi fit quaedam mecum, nam pectoris irae
Cum pietate in me talia bella gerunt,
Ut nequeam non et tua demum furta tueri,
Furta in me domini dulcis amara mei.

XXXVI

Dividuis, fateor, iam nobis vita terenda est,
Quos individuos attinet unus amor;
Sic probra nota meae, mecum restantia, sortis
Te sine, te nullum participante, feram.
Unus amor nobis eadem petit, una duobus
Dissociat vitas ira maligna deûm;
Illaque, ut effectus nunquam mutarit amoris,
Tempora deliciis eius habenda negat.
Illicitum posthac te voltu agnoscere ducam,
Ne sceleris triste hoc sit tibi, care, probro;
Neve palam alloquii tu me digneris honore,
Ni tibi vis demptum qui mihi detur honos.
Quod fieri nolis; te sic amplector, ut ipse
Si meus es, curae sit tua fama meae.

---

[59] Harrower schreibt *partis* (siehe Anmerkungen).

35

No more be griev'd at that which thou hast done:
Roses have thorns, and silver fountains mud;
Clouds and eclipses stain both moon and sun,
And loathsome canker lives in sweetest bud.
All men make faults, and even I in this,
Thy trespass authorizing[60] with compare,
Myself corrupting, salving thy amiss,
Thy sins excusing[61] more than thy sins are;
For to thy senseless[62] fault I bring in sense –
Thy adverse party is thy advocate –
And 'gainst myself a lawful plea commence:
Such civil war is in my love and hate,
   That I an accessary needs must be
   To that sweet thief which sourly robs from me.

36

Let me confess that we two must be twain,
Although our undivided loves are one:
So shall those blots that do with me remain
Without thy help by me be borne alone.
In our two loves there is but one respect,
Though in our lives a separable spite,
Which though it alter not love's sole effect,
Yet doth it steal sweet hours from love's delight.
I may not evermore acknowledge thee,
Lest my bewailed guilt should do thee shame,
Nor thou with public kindness honour me,
Unless thou take that honour from thy name.
   But do not so: I love thee in such sort
   As, thou being mine, mine is thy good report.

---

[60] Th.: *Authorizing thy trespass.*
[61] Th.: *Excusing thy sins.*
[62] Th.: *sensual* (siehe Anmerkungen).

XXXVII

Ut iuvene in nato fortissima cernere gaudet
Invalidus senio decrepitusve pater,
Sic ego, fortunae laesus per tela, levamen
Invenio in meritis ac pietate tuis.
Si bona possideas nonnulla vel omnia demum
Ingenii, formae, nobilitatis, opum,
Sive alio te sub titulo laus ulla coronat,
His etiam cunctis noster adhaeret amor.
Nec fuerit pauper claudusve aut nomine nullo,
Cui solidae tantum sufficit umbra rei;
Laudis namque mihi tua copia praebet abunde,
Ac tua, parsve tuae, gloria vita mihi est.
Cuncta tibi rerum precor optima, compos et eius
Optati deciens inde beatus ego.

XXXVIII

Qui sua materies musam defecerit, auras
Tu mihi vitales donec, amice, trahis,
Tu qui dulce mei sis carminis argumentum[63],
Quod nequeat vilis quisque tenere liber?
O referas ad te, siqua in me digna legendo
Obvenient oculis, si modo digna, tuis;
Mutus ita est quisquamne ut te non dicere possit,
Vatibus o doctis luminis ipse dator?
Tu decima esto Musa, potentior una novenis
Quas rogat antiquus versificator opem;
Invocat et qui te numeros effundere possit
Exsuperaturos saecula multa virûm.
Si tenuis doctae placeat mea musa diei,
Cura mea, at laudis sit tuus omnis honos.

---

[63] Die Stellung des dem Shakespeare'schen *argument* entsprechenden Worts
argumentum am Versende ergibt einen spondeischen fünften Fuss des Hexa-
meters, wie er bei Barton sonst nicht vorkommt.

37

As a decrepit father takes delight
To see his active child do deeds of youth,
So I, made lame by Fortune's meanest[64] spite,
Take all my comfort of thy worth and truth.
For whether beauty, birth, or wealth, or wit,
Or any of these all, or all, or more,
Entitled in thy parts do crowned sit,
I make my love engrafted to this store.
So then I am not lame, poor, nor despis'd,
Whilst that thy[65] shadow doth such substance give
That I in thy abundance am suffic'd
And by a part of all thy glory live.
  Look what is best, that best I wish in thee;
  This wish I have - then ten times happy me!

38

How can my Muse want subject to invent,
While thou dost breathe, that pour'st into my verse
Thine own sweet argument, too excellent
For every vulgar paper to rehearse?
O, give thyself the thanks, if aught in me
Worthy perusal stand against thy sight;
For who 's so dumb that cannot write of[66] thee,
When thou thyself dost give invention light?
Be thou the tenth Muse, ten times more in worth
Than those old nine which rhymers invocate,
And he that calls on thee, let him bring forth
Eternal numbers to outlive long date.
  If my slight Muse do please these curious days,
  The pain be mine, but thine shall be the praise.

---

[64] Th.: *dearest* (siehe Anmerkungen).
[65] Th.: *this*.
[66] Th.: *to*.

XXXIX

Quone verecundo te possim attollere versu,
Altera cum pars sis nobiliorque mei?
Quidne valet mea laus a memet dicta, tuumque
Dum celebro nomen, non ibi laudor ego?
Dividua hinc nobis decurrant stamina vitae,
Cedat ab unius nomine noster amor;
Sic habeam, spatio dum separor, illud, amice,
Reddere quod laudis solus ac[67] ipse meres.
O in suppliciis quid non, absentia, posses,
Ni sinerent tristes dulcia bina morae:
Fallere nempe horam repetendo cordis amores
(Fallitur hoc blande pectus et hora simul)[68];
Tum facere ex uno binos, quo tempore noster
Et praesens laude est et procul inde loco.

XL

Accipe, care, meos et amores, accipe cunctos,
Nam quid in acceptis non fuit ante tuum?
Nil in amore pium quod dicas; illud habendum
Detuleram, et dum non ulteriora petis.
Tum si, me quod amas, oblata receperis, istud
Haud reprobo, utaris quae tibi cedit amor;
Sed reprobo, tua te[69] si decipit ulla libido,
Id sitiens quod ais te renuisse palam.
At, fur blande, tuis ego possum ignoscere furtis,
Vel si pauperiem vis spoliare meam;
Sed gravius, scit quisque, iniuria fertur amici
Omnis ab hostili quam data plaga manu.
O in nequitia pulcher, me confice telis
Invidiae; at nobis hostibus esse nefas.

---

[67] Harrower schreibt *at*. In einer früheren Fassung Bartons lautet Vers 8:
Reddere quod laudis solus, amice, meres.

[68] Mit dieser Version des Verses 12 übernimmt Barton die Emendation *which time and thoughts...doth deceive* (Th.: *dost deceive*).

[69] *Tua te si decipit* entspricht der Emendation *if thou thyself...* (Th.: *this self*).

39

O, how thy worth with manners may I sing,
When thou art all the better part of me?
What can mine own praise to mine own self bring?
And what is 't but mine own when I praise thee?
Even for this let us divided live,
And our dear love lose name of single one,
That by this separation I may give
That due to thee which thou deserv'st alone.
O absence, what a torment wouldst thou prove,
Were it not thy sour leisure gave sweet leave
To entertain the time with thoughts of love,
Which time and thoughts so sweetly doth deceive;
    And that thou teachest how to make one twain,
    By praising him here who doth hence remain!

40

Take all my loves, my love, yea, take them all;
What hast thou then more than thou hadst before?
No love, my love, that thou mayst true love call;
All mine was thine before thou hadst this more.
Then if for my love thou my loves[70] receivest,
I cannot blame thee for my loves[71] thou usest;
But yet be blam'd, if thou thyself deceivest
By wilful taste of what thyself refusest.
I do forgive thy robbery, gentle thief,
Although thou steal thee all my poverty;
And yet love knows it is a greater grief
To bear love's wrong than hate's known injury.
    Lascivious grace, in whom all ill well shows,
    Kill me with spites; yet we must not be foes.

---

[70] Th.: *love.*
[71] Th.: ebenso (siehe Anmerkungen).

XLI

Quod tua libertas in furtis audet amorum
Dum tibi ab immemori pectore labor ego,
Convenit hoc isti bene formae, convenit annis,
Teque feres quoquo sollicitabit amor[72].
Mitis es ingenii facilisque petentibus, ore
Egregio ac cupidis dignior inde peti;
Sique petit virgo, quis eam non rupe creatus
Deseret austere reicietve preces?
Hei mihi, sed velles tu nostrae parcere, velles
Aetati ac formae ponere frena tuae!
Abripiunt studiis nam te ferventibus illo,
Qua duplicem nequeas non violare fidem:
Virginis, illam ad te si traxeris ore, tuamque
Ipsius, idcirco si mihi falsus eris.

XLII

Tu quod habes illam, fuerit carissima quamvis
Et mihi, non omnis fit meus inde dolor:
Flendum habeo potius quod te tenet illa; medullam
Cordis eo tactam volnere sentit amor.
Vos tamen, o cupidi, purgem: tu diligis illam
Et mihi dilectam quatenus esse vides;
Illaque me iuvit, specie crudelis, amico
Ipsa meo ob causam morigerata meam.
Quidquid in illo igitur perdam, tamen invenit illa;
Illaque si falsa est, ille lucratus erit.
At sese inveniunt ambo, careoque duobus,
Et mihi certe illi consuluere bono.
Sed laetum: meus est idem mihi iunctus in unum;
Illaque me solum – credere fas sit – amat.

---

[72] Dem Shakespeare'schen *temptation follows where thou art* würde eigentlich *sollicitabis amorem* („du wirst Liebe erregen") entsprechen. Hier ist dieser Gedanke abgewandelt zu „du wirst dort hingehen, wo immer die Liebe dich hinlockt".

41

Those pretty wrongs that liberty commits,
When I am sometime absent from thy heart,
Thy beauty and thy years full well befits,
For still temptation follows where thou art.
Gentle thou art and therefore to be won,
Beauteous thou art, therefore to be assailed;
And when a woman woos, what woman's son
Will sourly leave her till she have prevailed?
Ay me! but yet thou mightst my suit[73] forbear,
And chide thy beauty and thy straying youth,
Who lead thee in their riot even there
Where thou art forc'd to break a twofold truth:
   Hers, by thy beauty tempting her to thee,
   Thine, by thy beauty being false to me.

42

That thou hast her, it is not all my grief,
And yet it may be said I lov'd her dearly;
That she hath thee, is of my wailing chief,
A loss in love that touches me more nearly.
Loving offenders, thus I will excuse ye:
Thou dost love her, because thou know'st I love her;
And for my sake even so doth she abuse me,
Suffering my friend for my sake to approve her.
If I lose thee, my loss is my love's gain,
And losing her, my friend hath found that loss;
Both find each other, and I lose both twain,
And both for my sake lay on me this cross.
   But here's the joy: my friend and I are one;
   Sweet flattery! then she loves but me alone.

---

[73] Th.: *seate.*

XLIII

Est oculis visus in me vis optima clausis,
Namque die observant respiciuntque nihil;
Verum ubi dormivi, te clare deinde tuentur,
Perque diem caeci perbene nocte vident.
At tua si noctis tenebras illuminat umbra,
Quantum, o, laetifices clarior ipse diem!
Eniteas quanto tu lumine, cuius imago
Tenuis[74] ad occlusas est ita clara genas!
O iucundum oculis, inquam, super omnia nostris
Te luce in viridi cernere posse palam,
Qui super obscuros orbes somnoque gravatos
Forma nites[75] tenuis, forma venusta tamen.
Clara dies, dum te videam, densissima nox est;
Noxque dies, ubi te sistit ob ora sopor.

XLIV

Tarda caro si mens esset, distantia terris
Invida nullum ad te detinuisset iter;
Finibus e longis spatiorum ignarus adessem
Continuo, stares quo mihi cunque loco.
Intererat nihili si pes insisterat oram
Quae foret extremo dissociata situ;
Nam maria et terras ea transsilit, acta volando
Tam rapide ut secum[76] quo velit ire putat.
Sed crucior quod mens non sum, longissima saltu
Millia te versus quae superare queat;
Me grave onus tardat liquidi crassique, coactum
Temporis ignavas, hei mihi, flere moras.
Nam lacrimas tantum mihi rerum sufficit illud
Par grave, fortunae tristis utrimque notam.

---

[74] *Tenuis* ist hier (anders als nachher in Vers 12, aber wie *tenue* in XXXIV, 11) als zweisilbiges Wort mit langer Anfangssilbe und konsonantischem u (=v) zu lesen.
[75] *Qui ... forma nites tenuis* („die du als Schatten strahlst") entspricht der nicht allgemein akzeptierten Emendation *thy* (Th.: *their*) *shade*.
[76] *Secum putare:* überlegen.

43

When most I wink, then do mine eyes best see,
For all the day they view things unrespected;
But when I sleep, in dreams they look on thee,
And darkly bright are bright in dark directed.
Then thou, whose shadow shadows doth make bright,
How would thy shadow's form form happy show
To the clear day with thy much clearer light,
When to unseeing eyes thy shade shines so?
How would, I say, mine eyes be blessed made
By looking on thee in the living day,
When in dead night thy fair imperfect shade
Through heavy sleep on sightless eyes doth stay?
    All days are nights to me[77] till I see thee,
    And nights bright days when dreams do show thee me.

44

If the dull substance of my flesh were thought,
Injurious distance should not stop my way;
For then despite of space I would be brought
From limits far remote, where thou dost stay.
No matter then although my foot did stand
Upon the farthest earth remov'd from thee;
For nimble thought can jump both sea and land
As soon as think the place where he would be.
But, ah! thought kills me that I am not thought,
To leap large lengths of miles where[78] thou art gone,
But that, so much of earth and water wrought,
I must attend Time's leisure with my moan,
    Receiving nought by elements so slow
    But heavy tears, badges of either's woe.

---

[77] Th.: *see.*
[78] Th.: *when.*

XLV

Altera bina in me, levis aura et purior aether,
Te prope sunt, quoquo me rapit hora loci.
Hic animam signat, spes illa, et adesse videntur
Absentes, tanta mobilitate meant.
Nam quotiens ad te par hoc animosius ivit
Significaturum quae pia mandat amor,
Vita mea, ex istis retinens elementa quaternis
Bina modo, ad mortem paene redacta dolet,
Dum cito legatis a te revolantibus illis
Vita recomposita est, ut fuit ante, mihi.
Nam citius dicto revolarunt, deque salute
Certa tua[79] docti me quoque certa docent.
Laetor in auditis, nec longum gratia durat;
Namque remitto ambos, et redit ille dolor.

XLVI

In me lis oculo cum pectore saevit, in utro
Copia picturae debeat esse tuae.
Volt oculus nam pectus ab omni iure videndi
Claudere; volt oculo demere pectus idem.
Te positum in sese pectus docet esse, nec unquam
Lucentes oculos hunc penetrasse locum.
Alter it infitias ea dici vera, tuamque[80]
Effigiem in sese semper inesse docet.
Arbitrium in litis coguntur conscia veri
Sensa, cliens cordis contiguumque genus.
Lite perorata decernunt illa decere
Quas oculum partes, quas mage pectus amans:
Nempe ut in externis oculus regat, intima vero[81]
Qua pietas habitet pectoris esse volunt.

---

[79] *De salute tua* entspricht der Emendation *of thy* (Th.: *their*) *fair health.*
[80] *Tuam effigiem* entspricht der Emendation *thy* (Th.: *their*) *fair appearance.*
[81] Der Anklang zwischen den letzten drei Hexametern *conscia ver(i) – illa decer(e) – intima ver(o)* ist vielleicht eine Nachahmung der auffallenden Reim- und Wortwiederholungen *(heart – part – part – heart)* in Sonett 46.

45

The other two, slight air and purging fire,
Are both with thee, wherever I abide;
The first my thought, the other my desire,
These present-absent with swift motion slide.
For when these quicker elements are gone
In tender embassy of love to thee,
My life, being made of four, with two alone
Sinks down to death, oppress'd with melancholy;
Until life's composition be recured
By those swift messengers return'd from thee,
Who even but now come back again, assured
Of thy fair health, recounting it to me.
  This told, I joy; but then no longer glad,
  I send them back again and straight grow sad.

46

Mine eye and heart are at a mortal war
How to divide the conquest of thy sight;
Mine eye my heart thy picture's sight would bar,
My heart mine eye the freedom of that right.
My heart doth plead that thou in him dost lie,
A closet never pierc'd with crystal eyes,
But the defendant doth that plea deny,
And says in him thy fair appearance lies.
To 'cide this title is impanneled
A quest of thoughts, all tenants to the heart;
And by their verdict is determined
The clear eye's moiety and the dear heart's part
  As thus: mine eye's due is thy outward part,
  And my heart's right thy inward love of heart.

LVII

Sic oculus panxit cum pectore foedus, et ambo
Obsequia alternant officiique vices.
Sic quotiens oculus desiderat ora videre
Vera tua, et lacrima pectus inundat amor,
Protinus ille famem restinguit imagine picta,
Ac iubet ad falsas pectus adesse dapes.
Utitur hospitio tum pectoris; eius amori
Eius imaginibus se sociare libet.
Sic, sive a tabula seu cordis imagine factum
Credimus, hinc absens tu mihi semper ades[82].
Nam mea sensa extra nullus tibi, care, recessus
Linquitur; adsum illis semper et illa tibi.
Sensaque paullisper si languent, pectus in omnes
Delicias oculo visa tabella ciet.

XLVIII

Quo studio excedens abdebam frivola rerum
Omnia post firmas quantulacunque seras,
Integra ut illa meos asservarentur in usus,
Fidaque rimantem falleret arca manum!
Tu mihi, gemma omnis prae quo sordere videtur,
Solamen solitum tu mihi, iamque dolor,
Unus amicorum carissimus, unaque cura,
Desereris, cuivis praeda relicta malo.
Te loculis condo in nullis, nisi septa tenere
Mollia te possint pectoris ipsa mei;
Qua quotiens non es, fingo te credulus esse,
Ac venias liber, liber et inde migres.
Ac tamen ex illo ne tu rapiare verendum est;
Talibus in spoliis non bene firma fides.

---

[82] *Ades* (du bist anwesend) entspricht der Emendation *art present*
(Th.: *are present*).

47

Betwixt mine eye and heart a league is took,
And each doth good turns now unto the other:
When that mine eye is famish'd for a look,
Or heart in love with sighs himself doth smother,
With my love's picture then my eye doth feast
And to the painted banquet bids my heart;
Another time mine eye is my heart's guest
And in his thoughts of love doth share a part.
So, either by thy picture or my love,
Thyself away art present still with me
For thou not farther than my thoughts canst move,
And I am still with them and they with thee;
   Or, if they sleep, thy picture in my sight
   Awakes my heart to heart's and eye's delight.

48

How careful was I, when I took my way,
Each trifle under truest bars to thrust,
That to my use it might unused stay
From hands of falsehood, in sure wards of trust!
But thou, to whom my jewels trifles are,
Most worthy comfort, now my greatest grief,
Thou, best of dearest and mine only care,
Art left the prey of every vulgar thief.
Thee have I not lock'd up in any chest,
Save where thou art not, though I feel thou art,
Within the gentle closure of my breast,
From whence at pleasure thou mayst come and part;
   And even thence thou wilt be stol'n, I fear,
   For truth proves thievish for a prize so dear.

XLIX

Illud ego in tempus, si quando venerit illud,
Durior in vitiis cum videare meis,
Ac tibi amicitiae ratio sit ducta severe
Admonitis uso consiliisque senum;
Cum me praetereas ore ignorantis, eosque[83]
Vix oculos tollens, sidera bina, tuos;
Atque amor, affectu quantum mutatus ab illo,
Incipiat multum de gravitate loqui;
Illud ego in tempus[84] iam munimenta paravi
Tuta, nihil fassus me meruisse boni[85].
Attollensque manum me contra, dicta tuebor
Omnia quae possint ius stabilire tuum.
Iure quidem multo miserum me linquere possis,
Quem nequeo causam dicere cur quis amet.

L

Quam gravis ire viam pergo, cum finis eundi
Tantopere optatus tristius illud habet,
Ut requies nocturna mihi decantet in aure
'A caro tot habes millia mensa tuo.'
Vector equus mecum hac oppressus mole dolorum
Repit iners, in me tale gravatus onus;
Ceu sciat instinctu naturae, nil mihi velox
Esse volenti, a te dum properamus iter.
Sanguineum calcar porro non urget euntem
Quo subita interdum confodit ira cutem.
Ille gravi gemitu respondet; acerbius istud
Auribus his lateri quam mea plaga fuit,
Cum gemitu pecudis quoniam cura illa recursat:
Porro tristitiam, laeta iacere retro.

---

[83] Harrower schreibt *easque*.
[84] Wiederholung des Gedichtanfangs wie bei Shakespeare in Zeilen 5 und 9.
[85] Entgegen der Auffassung von *mine own desert* als „mein Wert", „meine Tugend" stellt Barton klar, dass *desert* (Th.: *desart*) hier „Unwert" oder „verdiente Strafe" *(nihil meruisse boni)* bedeutet.

49

Against that time, if ever that time come,
When I shall see thee frown on my defects,
When as thy love hath cast his utmost sum,
Call'd to that audit by advis'd respects;
Against that time when thou shalt strangely pass,
And scarcely greet me with that sun, thine eye,
When love, converted from the thing it was,
Shall reasons find of settled gravity;
Against that time do I ensconce me here
Within the knowledge of mine own desert,
And this my hand against myself uprear,
To guard the lawful reasons on thy part.
   To leave poor me thou hast the strength of laws,
   Since why to love I can allege no cause.

50

How heavy do I journey on the way,
When what I seek, my weary travel's end,
Doth teach that ease and that repose to say
"Thus far the miles are measur'd from thy friend!"
The beast that bears me, tired with my woe,
Plods dully on, to bear that weight in me,
As if by some instinct the wretch did know
His rider lov'd not speed being made from thee.
The bloody spur cannot provoke him on
That sometimes anger thrusts into his hide;
Which heavily he answers with a groan,
More sharp to me than spurring to his side;
   For that same groan doth put this in my mind:
   My grief lies onward and my joy behind.

LI

Sed pietate mea sic excusata caballi
Segnitia est, a te cum mihi tardat iter:
Hinc, ubi tu restas, quo praeceps auferor? inquam;
Dum redeam, alatis non eget usus equis.
Quid tamen, o, veniae tandem miser ille merebit,
Cum rapidi nihilum non videatur iners?
Utar enim calcare procellis vectus in ipsis,
Vixque habeat motum praepetis ala mihi.
His desideriis nil respondebit equinum,
Ardor at ipse unus quem pius excit amor.
Hinniet hic, non lenta pecus, certaminis igne;
Illa sed hoc veniae pro pietate feret:
Libera eat, quoniam sic a te segnis abibat,
Et pedibus versum te mihi cursus erit.

LII

En ego sum diti similis, qui possit adire
Clavis ope abstrusas, si videatur, opes;
Quas tamen ille hora non contemplabitur omni,
Ne perdant aciem gaudia rara suam.
Relligio est festis longi sollemnibus anni
Maxima, quod redeunt rarius illa tamen;
Stant intervallis, ut magni quaeque iubaris[86]
Gemma, vel egregius torquis in orbe lapis.
Te retinens tempus quasi cista est arcave, dicam,
Talis ubi possit vestis honesta tegi,
Omnium ut horarum fit felicissima demum
Una, diu inclusus cui reseretur honos.
Tu potius felix, virtutem propter amicis
Absens seu praesens spesve decusve tuis.

---

[86] Das von Harrower überlieferte Wort *ruboris* am Versende dürfte auf einem
Lesefehler beruhen; statt *magni ruboris* („von grosser Röte") ist wohl eher
magni iubaris („von grossem Glanz") gemeint (bei Shakespeare *stones of worth,
captain jewels*). Als *gemma* werden insbesondere durchsichtige Juwelen oder
Perlen bezeichnet.

51

Thus can my love excuse the slow offence
Of my dull bearer when from thee I speed:
From where thou art why should I haste me thence?
Till I return, of posting is no need.
O, what excuse will my poor beast then find,
When swift extremity can seem but slow?
Then should I spur, though mounted on the wind;
In winged speed no motion shall I know.
Then can no horse with my desire keep pace;
Therefore desire, of perfect'st love being made,
Shall weigh[87] no dull flesh in his fiery race;
But love, for love, thus shall excuse my jade:
 Since from thee going he went wilful-slow,
 Towards thee I'll run, and give him leave to go.

52

So am I as the rich, whose blessed key
Can bring him to his sweet up-locked treasure,
The which he will not every hour survey,
For blunting the fine point of seldom pleasure.
Therefore are feasts so solemn and so rare,
Since, seldom coming in the long year set,
Like stones of worth they thinly placed are,
Or captain jewels in the carcanet.
So is the time that keeps you as my chest,
Or as the wardrobe which the robe doth hide,
To make some special instant special blest,
By new unfolding his imprison'd pride.
 Blessed are you, whose worthiness gives scope,
 Being had, to triumph; being lack'd, to hope.

---

[87] Th.: *naigh* (siehe Anmerkungen).

LIII

Qua tu materie, quo demum corpore constas
Unus, at innumeris cinctus imaginibus?[88]
Dum species aliis una est sua cuique, figuras[89]
Reddere tu cunctas, una figura, potes.
Enumera veneres in Adonide, pictaque prave
Quamlibet effigies os habet illa tuum.
Pinge Helenen, eiusque genis offunde venustum
Omne: sub Argivo tu novus ore venis.
Si loquimur de vere aut ubere divitis anni,
Purpureus veris fit tuus iste color;
Illa tui nobis generosi cordis imago est,
Teque refert species optima quaeque rei.
Sed tua dum pars fit quacunque est gratia formae,
Te penes est unum pectoris ista fides.

LIV

O quam forma solet formosior illa videri
Cui decus accessit quod dabit una fides!
Forma rosae pulchra est, at pulchrior esse putatur
Aura quod in medio vivit odora sinu.
Flosculus in pratis tanto splendore rubescit
Quantus odoriferis est color ille rosis;
Pensilis in spina simili lascivit ut illae,
Cum Zephyri timidas elicit aura comas.
Sed, species tantum, spretus floretque caditque;
Labitur, at nemo tollere curat humo.
Non ea fit natura rosis: dulcissimus unus
Nascitur ex illis cum moriuntur odor.
Sic tibi, dulce caput, dum formae gloria marcet,
Stat fidei testis pagina nostra[90] tuae.

---

[88] Während sonst die Pentameter-Endwörter bei Barton fast immer zwei-silbig sind, verstärkt hier das fünfsilbige *imaginibus* den Eindruck der Vielheit (*innumeris imaginibus*, bei Shakespeare *millions of shadows*).

[89] Harrower schreibt *figurae* und interpungiert erst am Versende.

[90] *Pagina nostra* entspricht der Emendation *my verse* (Th.: *by verse*).

53

What is your substance, whereof are you made,
That millions of strange shadows on you tend?
Since every one hath, every one, one shade,
And you, but one, can every shadow lend.
Describe Adonis, and the counterfeit
Is poorly imitated after you;
On Helen's cheek all art of beauty set,
And you in Grecian 'tires are painted new.
Speak of the spring and foison of the year:
The one doth shadow of your beauty show,
The other as your bounty doth appear,
And you in every blessed shape we know.
    In all external grace you have some part,
    But you like none, none you, for constant heart.

54

O, how much more doth beauty beauteous seem
By that sweet ornament which truth doth give!
The rose looks fair, but fairer we it deem
For that sweet odour which doth in it live.
The canker-blooms have full as deep a dye
As the perfumed tincture of the roses,
Hang on such thorns and play as wantonly
When summer's breath their masked buds discloses:
But, for their only virtue[91] is their show,
They live unwoo'd and unrespected fade,
Die to themselves. Sweet roses do not so:
Of their sweet deaths are sweetest odours made.
    And so of you, beauteous and lovely youth,
    When you shall fade, my verse[92] distills your truth.

---

[91] Th.: *their virtue only.*
[92] Th.: *When that shall vade, by verse* (siehe Fussnote 90).

LV

Marmora non poterunt regumve aurata sepulcra[93]
Durando numeros exsuperasse meos;
Clarior et multo tu praefulgebis in illis
Quam lapide in putri pulvereoque situ.
Cum statuas fera bella ruent, interque tumultus
Marmoribus structum discutietur opus,
Nec Martis gladius nec belli concita flamma
Hoc monumentum uret discutietve tui.
Prodieris superans oblivia mortis iniqua
Ipse, tuis fuerit laudibus usque locus;
Ultima posteritas oculos nam figet in illis
Hunc habitura orbem donec in igne cadet.
Iudicii sic ad tempus quando ipse resurges,
Vivis in hoc, et te perlegit omnis amans.

LVI

Collige, dulcis amor, renovatum collige robur,
Nec minus esse acer tu videare gula.
Nam gula quantumvis hodie satietur edendo,
Institerit certe cras renovata fames.
Tu quoque idem facias: hodie si clausa tenebis
Lumina deliciis exsatiata suis,
Lumina cras aperi, nec amoris spiritus ille
Langueat aeterno victus inersque situ.
Sit tibi discidium hoc ut binos inter amantes
Pontus, ubi immissis litora findit aquis:
Quoque die adveniunt oras, visuque beantur
Si modo longinquus dispiciatur amor.
Vel sit hiems oppleta gelu: ter amabilis aestas
Cum fuerit Zephyris terque morata suis.[94]

---

[93] *sepulcra* (Pl.) entspricht der Emendation *monuments* (Th: *monument*).
[94] „Dreifach erwünscht ist der Sommer, wenn sich sein Beginn durch Ausbleiben der Zephyrwinde dreifach verzögert hat." Der Zephyr (Westwind) war bei den antiken Autoren sprichwörtlich als Bote des Sommers. (Siehe auch *Zephyri aura* für *summer's breath* in LIV, 8.)

55

Not marble, nor the gilded monuments
Of princes, shall outlive this powerful rhyme;
But you shall shine more bright in these contents
Than unswept stone besmear'd with sluttish Time.
When wasteful war shall statues overturn,
And broils root out the work of masonry,
Nor Mars's[95] sword nor war's quick fire shall burn
The living record of your memory.
'Gainst Death and all-oblivious enmity
Shall you pace forth: your praise shall still find room
Even in the eyes of all posterity
That wear this world out to the ending doom.
   So, till the judgement that yourself arise,
   You live in this, and dwell in lovers'eyes.

56

Sweet love, renew thy force; be it not said
Thy edge should blunter be than appetite,
Which but today by feeding is allay'd,
Tomorrow sharpen'd in his former might.
So, love, be thou: although today thou fill
Thy hungry eyes even till they wink with fullness,
Tomorrow see again, and do not kill
The spirit of love with a perpetual dullness.
Let this sad interim like the ocean be
Which parts the shore, where two contracted new
Come daily to the banks, that, when they see
Return of love, more blest may be the view;
   Or call it winter, which being full of care
   Makes summer's welcome thrice more wish'd, more rare.

---

[95] Th.: *Mars his.*

LVII

Me tibi subiectum quidni delectet adesse
Horis arbitrii temporibusque tui?
Donec enim tu me posces, nullum utile tempus
Est mihi, nulla meum cura requirit opus.
Taedia vix ausim longa increpitare diei,
Respiciens horas dum mihi, care, redis;
Noluerim valde sit visa absentia tristis,
Cum mihi digrediens dixeris ore 'vale'.
Noluerim et curis illud dubitare malignis
Quone loco degas, quid meditere rei;
Me teneam, ut servus, sensu defixus in uno,
Quam facias hilares quos apud esse velis.
Credula res amor est, et quae tua cunque fuere
Acta, voluntatem consulit ille boni.

LVIII

Me tibi qui domuit deus hoc avertat, ut ausim
Ulla voluptatis tempora nosse tuae,
Utve petat servus causas rescire morandi,
Otia cui[96] iustum est opperiatur heri.
O potius patiar quodcunque absentia mandat,
Quae tibi libertas, si mihi carcer erit;
Sim patiens mitisque animi toleransque morarum,
Coniciens in te crimina nulla mali.
Sis ubi vis, id iuris habes ut tempora rebus
Partiri possis, quae quibus ipse velis.
Arbitrio blandire tuo; fas esse fatemur
Ut tibi condones dum facis omne nefas.
Exspectare meum est, o perquam triste, nec ullis
Irasci imperiis, sint pia necne, tuis.

---

[96] Harrower schreibt *qui*.

57

Being your slave, what should I do but tend
Upon the hours and times of your desire?
I have no precious time at all to spend,
Nor services to do, till you require.
Nor dare I chide the world-without-end hour
Whilst I, my sovereign, watch the clock for you,
Nor think the bitterness of absence sour
When you have bid your servant once adieu;
Nor dare I question with my jealous thought
Where you may be, or your affairs suppose,
But, like a sad slave, stay and think of nought
Save, where you are how happy you make those.
  So true a fool is Love that in your will,
  Though you do anything, he thinks no ill.

58

That god forbid that made me first your slave,
I should in thought control your times of pleasure,
Or at your hand the account of hours crave[97],
Being your vassal, bound to stay your leisure!
O, let me suffer, being at your beck,
The imprison'd absence of my[98] liberty;
And patience, tame to sufferance, bide each check,
Without accusing you of injury.
Be where you list, your charter is so strong
That you yourself may privilege your time;
Do[99] what you will: to you it doth belong
Yourself to pardon of self-doing crime.
  I am to wait, though waiting so be hell;
  Not blame your pleasure, be it ill or well.

---

[97] Th.: *of hours to crave.*
[98] Th.: *your* (siehe Anmerkungen).
[99] Th.: *to* (siehe Anmerkungen).

LIX

Si novitas nulla est, hodiernaque cuncta fuere,
Ut misere vatum fallitur omne genus,
Qui studio ingenti certant nova gignere versu
Atque, nefas! aliis ante creata creant!
O utinam solis quingentos ante meatus
Historiae penetret dispiciatque fides,
Teque mihi antiquo monstret sub imagine libro
Qua fuerit primis mens imitata notis!
Rescierim quid sit de te mirata vetustas
Tot decora in formam consociante tuam;
An melior sit nostra dies an vicerit illa[100],
An referant rerum cursus et orbis idem.
O certe a priscis immensam saepe poetis
Materies laudem non ita digna tulit.

LX

Ut pelagi fluctus lapidosa ad litora currunt
Ad finem properant tempora nostra suum;
Excipit hora horas, undam premit unda priorem,
Contendunt omnes ulteriora sequi.
Natus in immensas sol ingens luminis oras
Inde suum repit, dum sit adultus, iter;
Verum ibi defectus oppugnant eius honorem,
In donoque suo temporis ira furit.
Scit vegetum iuvenis[101] florem corrumpere tempus,
Fronte in virginea tempus arare notas;
Tempus edit rari quidquid natura creavit,
Statque nihil quod non denique falce metat.
Sed versu hoc tua laus venturum stabit in aevum,
In te saevierit quamlibet illa manus.

---

[100] *an vicerit illa* entspricht der Emendation *or whe'er* bzw. or *whether*
(Th.: *or where*). Möglich wäre auch *or were*.
[101] Harrower schreibt *iuveni*.

59

If there be nothing new, but that which is
Hath been before, how are our brains beguil'd,
Which, labouring for invention, bear amiss
The second burthen of a former child!
O, that record could with a backward look,
Even of five hundred courses of the sun,
Show me your image in some antique book,
Since mind at first in character was done!
That I might see what could the old world[102] say
To this composed wonder of your frame;
Whether we are mended, or whe'er better they,
Or whether revolution be the same.
 O, sure I am, the wits of former days
 To subjects worse have given admiring praise.

60

Like as the waves make towards the pebbled shore,
So do our minutes hasten to their end;
Each changing place with that which goes before,
In sequent toil all forwards do contend.
Nativity, once in the main of light,
Crawls to maturity, wherewith being crown'd,
Crooked eclipses 'gainst this[103] glory fight,
And Time that gave doth now his gift confound.
Time doth transfix the flourish set on youth
And delves the parallels in beauty's brow,
Feeds on the rarities of Nature's truth,
And nothing stands but for his scythe to mow.
 And yet to Time in hope my verse shall stand,
 Praising thy worth, despite his cruel hand.

---

[102] Th.: *the old world could.*
[103] Th.: *his* (siehe Anmerkungen).

LXI

Anne tuo iussu tua visa ipsius imago
Me prohibet lassas claudere nocte genas?
Quo vaga forma meos ita visus ludere possit
Siccine somnorum est discutienda quies?
An tuus est animus, quem tu, mea facta notatum,
Tam procul a membris huc volitare velis?
Nequitias lentasve in me, reor, inspicit horas;
Is tibi curarum nam solet ire tenor.
Haud ita; quidquid amor magnus valet, omne valere
Non datur: ut vigilem, me meus urget amor.
Qui mihi sic noctu somnos interficit, ille est,
Ut pro te partis excubitoris agam.
Excubiis nec desum; alibi vigil ipse teneris
Me sine, dans aliis te propiore frui.

LXII

Me mea mirari noxa est dominata perinde
Menti, oculo, membris omnibus una meis.
Et dubito capiat numquid medicaminis illa,
Sic mihi radices cordis in ima tulit.
Nulla alibi voltus par gratia, nulla figura
Iustior, affirmo, nullaque tanta fides.
Quae merita in me sunt ita metior, omnibus omnes
Ut meritis unum me superare putem.
Verum ubi me speculum mihi detegit, ora perusta
Solibus, antiquis dedecorata notis,
Haud ea miratus[104], sed eis contraria cunctis,
Me video; iste sui turpe fuisset amor.
Te – sumus unus – ea signabam laude, meumque
Pingebam senium flore, venuste, tuo.

---

[104] Harrower schreibt *miratum*, gemeint ist aber wohl das Partizip von *mirari*
im Nominativ (*haud ea miratus me video, sed eis contraria:* „ich sehe nicht, mich
selber bewundernd, diese Dinge, sondern deren Gegenteil").

61

Is it thy will thy image should keep open
My heavy eyelids to the weary night?
Dost thou desire my slumbers should be broken,
While shadows like to thee do mock my sight?
Is it thy spirit that thou send'st from thee
So far from home into my deeds to pry,
To find out shames and idle hours in me,
The scope and tenor of thy jealousy?
O, no! thy love, though much, is not so great:
It is *my* love that keeps mine eyes[105] awake;
Mine own true love that doth my rest defeat,
To play the watchman ever for thy sake.
　　For thee watch I whilst thou dost wake elsewhere,
　　From me far off, with others all too near.

62

Sin of self-love possesseth all mine eye
And all my soul and all my every part;
And for this sin there is no remedy,
It is so grounded inward in my heart.
Methinks no face so gracious is as mine,
No shape so true, no truth of such account;
And for myself mine own worth I[106] define,
As I all others[107] in all worths surmount.
But when my glass shows me myself indeed,
Beated and chopp'd with tann'd antiquity,
Mine own self-love quite contrary I read:
Self so self-loving were iniquity.
　　'T is thee, my self, that for myself I praise,
　　Painting my age with beauty of thy days.

---

[105] Th.: *eye.*
[106] Th.: *do.*
[107] Th.: *other.*

LXIII

Ante, mei similis, iaceat quam noster amicus,
Fractus ab iniusta temporis ipse manu,
Aut vegetus sit sanguis ab insidiantibus horis
Haustus, et insculptis frons ea plena notis;
Hoc ubi nondum illo progressum mane iuventae
Noctis in abruptum protinus unde cadat,
Regiave haec species vanescere coeperit omnis,
Aut evanuerit, veris et eius opes;
Illud ego in tempus iam munimenta cruentas
Falciferi ad furias firma futura paro,
Ne faciem humanis hanc cordibus exsecet unquam,
E vita fuerit cum mihi raptus amor.
Nigris forma notis ea iam mandetur, ibique
Vivat in aeternis versibus ille virens.

LXIV

Cum video antiqui quondam decora aurea saecli
Omnia damnosis eruta temporibus,[108]
Eversasque solo turris, aeternaque ferri
Robora mortali subdita saevitiae;
Cum video fluctus partem violenter avaros
Demere harenoso litoris imperio
Et terram liquidas invadere rursus in undas,
Partaque pro demptis, proque ope pauperiem;
Cum sic ire vices video per mutua rerum,
Factumque e solidis molibus exitium,
Me quoque tanta ruina monet quandoque futurum
Ut dirimat nostram tempus amicitiam.
O dolor exanimans, o et deflendus, habere
Id cui praemetuas tu tamen interitum!

---

[108] Während Barton sonst seine Distichen meist mit einem zweisilbigen Wort abschliesst, klingen hier wie in den Gedichten 122 und 146 sämtliche Distichen mit einem vier- oder fünfsilbigen Wort aus. Ein bestimmter Grund für diese formale Besonderheit ist hier nicht erkennbar.

63

Against my love shall be, as I am now,
With Time's injurious hand crush'd and o'erworn;
When hours have drain'd his blood and fill'd his brow
With lines and wrinkles; when his youthful morn
Hath travell'd on to age's steepy night,
And all those beauties whereof now he's king
Are vanishing or vanish'd out of sight,
Stealing away the treasure of his spring;
For such a time do I now fortify
Against confounding age's cruel knife,
That he shall never cut from memory
My sweet love's beauty, though his[109] lover's life:
   His beauty shall in these black lines be seen,
   And they shall live, and he in them still green.

64

When I have seen by Time's fell hand defaced
The rich proud cost of outworn buried age;
When sometime lofty towers I see down-razed
And brass eternal slave to mortal rage;
When I have seen the hungry ocean gain
Advantage on the kingdom of the shore,
And the firm soil win of the watery main,
Increasing store with loss and loss with store;
When I have seen such interchange of state,
Or state itself confounded to decay,
Ruin hath taught me thus to ruminate:
That Time will come and take my love away.
   This thought is as a death, which cannot choose
   But weep to have that which it fears to lose.

---

[109] Th.: *my* (siehe Anmerkungen)

LXV

Sique aeris, lapidis, terrae, vastique profundi
Robora sic letum lugubre cuncta domet,
Gratia quid formae ad tantas contenderit iras,
Vix superans propriis viribus illa rosam?
Mellifer aestatis num spiritus arma dierum
Expugnatorum perniciosa feret,
Si non indomitae rupes, non ferrea claustra
Stent valida, at longus subruat omne dies?
O meditanti atrox! ubi tempus tuta malignum
Optima naturae gemma latere queat?
Quisve manu rapidam conatur sistere pestem,
Ac formae spoliis abstinuisse iubet?
Nemo, nisi hoc mirum valeat: meus ille videndus
Perpetuo in nigris aurea forma notis.

LXVI

Mortem aveo fessus multis ego; nempe videndo
Virtutem genitam pauperiore loco,
Quidquid egens et inops nitido spectabile cultu,
Pollutamque pii pectoris esse fidem,
Omnibus indignos auri fulgore nitentes,
Tum sua virginibus nomina laesa probris,
Improba vel sanctis obiecta, valentiaque arma
Claudorum auspiciis debilitata ducum,
Imperio siluisse artes, notumque[110] medentes
Inter, ab inscitis scita solere regi,
Simplicibus verisque affigi nomen ineptis,
Postque malum victrix[111] optima capta trahi;
His ego defessus cunctis abscedere vellem,
Ni mihi sic esset destituendus amor.

---

[110] *Notumque* ist unverständlich; statt von einem *notus* müsste von einem
ignotus (in aktiver Bedeutung, also einem Unkundigen oder Ignoranten) die Rede
sein. Gemeint ist wohl: *imperio siluisse art(em), ignotumque medentes / inter..*
[111] Statt des hier sinnlosen Worts *victrix* (Siegerin) dürfte *virtus* (Tugend)
optima capta als Übersetzung von *captive Good* gemeint sein.

65

Since brass, nor stone, nor earth, nor boundless sea,
But sad mortality o'er-sways their power,
How with this rage shall beauty hold a plea,
Whose action is no stronger than a flower?
O, how shall summer's honey breath hold out
Against the wreckful siege of battering days,
When rocks impregnable are not so stout,
Nor gates of steel so strong, but Time decays?
O fearful meditation! where, alack,
Shall Time's best jewel from Time's chest lie hid?
Or what strong hand can hold his swift foot back?
Or who his spoil of beauty can forbid?
    O, none, unless this miracle have might,
    That in black ink my love may still shine bright.

66

Tir'd with all these, for restful death I cry,
As, to behold desert a beggar born,
And needy nothing trimm'd in jollity,
And purest faith unhappily forsworn,
And gilded honour shamefully misplac'd,
And maiden virtue rudely strumpeted,
And right perfection wrongfully disgrac'd,
And strength by limping sway disabled,
And art made tongue-tied by authority,
And folly, doctor-like, controlling skill,
And simple truth miscall'd simplicity,
And captive Good attending captain Ill:
    Tir'd with all these, from these would I be gone,
    Save that, to die, I leave my love alone.

LXVII

Et scelerum haec inter contagia vivat, habendus
In lenociniis, proh pudor, ille mali?
Impietas lucretur enim sibi commoda multa,
Eniteatque, eius scilicet ipsa comes.
Illius et faciem fucusne fefellerit arte,
Exanime a vivo surpueritque decus?[112]
Cur adeo quaeratur enim minus ore venustis
Falsa rosa, est illi dum rosa vera genis?
Quid tenet in vivis illum? quasi viribus haustis
Natura, ad venas orba rubore, iacet.
Illius auxiliis ea pendet tota, trahensque
Gloriam ab innumeris vivit ab eius ope.
Hinc ea servat eum, quam dives talibus esset
Ante malos hodie testificata dies.

LXVIII

Ille diem voltu revocat cum vixit obitque
Mortali species, ut sua cuique rosae;
Gessit ubi nemo fictae simulamina formae,
Falsa super vivas ausa sedere genas;
Aurea caesaries necdum, ius triste sepulcri,
Erasa exanimis frontibus ulla fuit,
In capite alterius traheretur ut altera vita,
Vivaque defunctae vellere compta foret.
En pictura viris antiquae sancta diei,
Pura sine ornatu, candida, tota sui;
Non aliunde virens effloruit illius aestas,
Non veterum exuviis enitet ille novus;
Quem natura tuens falsae docet artis amantes
Quid fuerit priscis forma decora viris.

---

[112] *Exanime decus* (lebloser Schmuck) entspricht offenbar der Emendation
dead seeming (Th.: *dead seeing*).

67

Ah, wherefore with infection should he live,
And with his presence grace impiety,
That sin by him advantage should achieve
And lace itself with his society?
Why should false painting imitate his cheek,
And steal dead seeming of his living hue?
Why should poor beauty indirectly seek
Roses of shadow, since his rose is true?
Why should he live, now Nature bankrupt is,
Beggar'd of blood to blush through lively veins?
For she hath no exchequer now but his,
And, proud of many, lives upon his gains.
    O, him she stores, to show what wealth she had
    In days long since, before these last so bad.

68

Thus is his cheek the map of days outworn,
When beauty liv'd and died as flowers do now,
Before these bastard signs of fair were born,
Or durst inhabit on a living brow;
Before the golden tresses of the dead,
The right of sepulchres, were shorn away,
To live a second life on second head;
Ere beauty's dead fleece made another gay.
In him those holy antique hours are seen,
Without all ornament, itself and true,
Making no summer of another's green,
Robbing no old to dress his beauty new.
    And him as for a map doth Nature store,
    To show false Art what beauty was of yore.

LXIX

Quae videt in te volgus egent nullius, eisque
Fingere mens nihilum pulchrius ulla potest.
Haec tibi per cunctas concessa est gloria linguas,
Dictaque verum intra, laudat ut hostis homo.
Externam speciem sic laus externa coronat;
Haec tamen ora ipsis dissona multa crepant,
Quodque dabant laudis conturbant omne, videndo
Ulterius quam se fert oculata fides.
Sitne tibi inquirunt animi par candor, et illud
Noscitur ex actis coniciturve tuis;
Blandaque dum facies illis, mens invida secum
'Foetorem lolii flos', ait, 'iste refert.'
At lolium si flos oleat, causam esse putarim
Hanc ego: communi creverat ille loco[113].

LXX

Non quia culparis meruisse videbere: livor
Egregium telo destinat omne suo.
Gloria pulchrorum est suspectos esse malignis;
In liquido cornix aethere multa volat.
Sis bonus[114], eniteat tua quoque in crimine virtus
Clarior, ex ipso tempore nacta fidem.
Primitiae florum mordaci a peste petuntur,
At tua dedecoris pura iuventa nitet.
Insidias iuveni structas aut effugis omnis
Integer, aut victor[115], si peterere malo.
Laus datur, at linguas frenat non illa malignas,
Haec tibi in aeternum libera pestis aget.
Si speciem obtegeret nullam[116] tibi livida fama,
Tu regeres unus pectora cuncta virûm.

---

[113] *Locus communis* bedeutet u.a. Bordell. Die Blume *(flos)* stinkt, weil sie an einem anrüchigen Ort wächst.

[114] *Sis bonus* entspricht der Emendation *thy worth* (Th.: *their worth*).

[115] Die *aut-aut*-Konstruktion in den Versen 9/10 dürfte einer *or-or*-Konstruktion bei Shakespeare entsprechen (Th.: *either-or*).

[116] Statt *speciem nullam* muss *nulla fama* gemeint sein (siehe Anmerkungen).

69

Those parts of thee that doth the world's eye[117] view
Want nothing that the thought of hearts can mend;
All tongues, voices of souls[118], give thee that due,
Uttering bare truth, even so as foes commend.
Thy outward thus with outward praise is crown'd;
But those same tongues that give thee so thine own
In other accents do this praise confound
By seeing farther than the eye hath shown.
They look into the beauty of thy mind,
And that, in guess, they measure by thy deeds:
Then, churl, thy thoughts, although thine eyes are kind[119],
To thy fair flower add the smell[120] of weeds:
    But why thy odour matcheth not thy show,
    The soil is this: that thou dost common grow.

70

That thou art blam'd shall not be thy defect,
For slander's mark was ever yet the fair;
The ornament of beauty is suspect,
A crow that flies in heaven's sweetest air.
So thou be good, slander doth but approve
Thy worth the greater, being woo'd of time;
For canker vice the sweetest buds doth love,
And thou present'st a pure unstained prime.
Thou hast pass'd by the ambush of young days,
Or[121] not assail'd, or victor being charg'd;
Yet this thy praise cannot be so thy praise,
To tie up envy evermore enlarg'd.
    If some suspect of ill mask'd not thy show,
    Then thou alone kingdoms of hearts shouldst owe.

---

[117] Th.: *that the world's eye doth.*
[118] Th.: *All toungs (the voice of soules).*
[119] Th.: *Then churls their thoughts (although their eies were kind).*
[120] Th.: *the rancke smell.*
[121] Th.: *Either* (siehe Fussnote 115).

LXXI

Flere mihi nolis quando, dilecte, supremum
Raucus campanae planxerit ille sonus;
Nuntius ille sonus fugisse haec tristia vitae
Me semel ac vermes inter habere locum.
Quin etiam releges si forte haec verba, recuses
Quaenam ea panxisset vel meminisse manus;
Tantus amor meus est ut labi malit ab isto
Pectore, quam memorem te doluisse mei.
O, inquam, versum hunc si tum fortasse videbis
Quando ego communi pulvere mixtus ero,
Nomen rite meum labris committere noli;
Fac potius mecum sit tumulatus amor.
Ne sapiens possit, causam scrutatus, habere
Ludibrio lacrimas ob mea fata tuas.

LXXII

O grave ne quondam ducas recitasse petenti
Quid meritum in me sit post mea fata coli;
Post mea fata meum, care, obliviscere nomen,
Nil habeas in me namque docere boni.
Ni pietas ausit mendacia fingere quaedam
Plus mihi promeritis auxiliata meis,
Possit ut id laudis cumulari in morte peremptum
Quod nequeat vivo reddere vera fides.
O tua ne[122] pietas fallax habeatur in isto,
Optima quod de me, ficta sed illa, canas,
Fac tumulatum una mihi sit cum corpore nomen,
Neve superfuerit tantus utrique rubor.
Nam rubor est mihimet nihilo dignanda creanti,
Ac pariter tibi sit, si leviora colas.

---

[122] *O tua ne* klingt an *o grave ne* am Gedichtanfang an, entsprechend dem
wiederholten *o lest* am Beginn der Verse 1 und 9 des Sonetts 72.

71

No longer mourn for me when I am dead
Than you shall hear the surly sullen bell
Give warning to the world that I am fled
From this vile world, with vilest worms to dwell.
Nay, if you read this line, remember not
The hand that writ it; for I love you so
That I in your sweet thoughts would be forgot,
If thinking on me then should make you woe.
O, if, I say, you look upon this verse,
When I perhaps compounded am with clay,
Do not so much as my poor name rehearse,
But let your love even with my life decay -
   Lest the wise world should look into your moan
   And mock you with me after I am gone.

72

O, lest the world should task you to recite
What merit lived in me that you should love,
After my death, dear love, forget me quite,
For you in me can nothing worthy prove;
Unless you would devise some virtuous lie,
To do for me more[123] than mine own desert,
And hang more praise upon deceased I
Than niggard truth would willingly impart.
O, lest your true love may seem false in this,
That you for love speak well of me untrue,
My name be buried where my body is,
And live no more to shame nor me nor you.
   For I am sham'd by that which I bring forth,
   And so were[124] you, to love things nothing worth.

---

[123] Th.: *To doe more for me.*
[124] Th.: *should.*

LXXIII

In me, care, potes velut anni noscere tempus,
Lutea cum pendens arbore rara coma est,
Vel potius cum nulla[125], at frigore nuda tremiscunt
Bracchia, nuper avis templa canora sono.
Tale meae videas lumen pallere diei,
Pallet ad occiduas vespere quale plagas;
Quod nox furva brevi totum, mors altera, tollit,
Omniaque obsignans inde secuta quies.
Dispicias in me tantum vitale caloris,
In cinere est quantum relliquiisque foci,
Qua rubet exiguo languescens igne favilla
Ab nutrimentis interitura suis.
Illa vides, et amas auctis affectibus omne
Unde recedendum post breve tempus erit.

LXXIV

At sis contentus, cum vis horrenda, vadari
Nescia, me saeva prenderit illa manu:
Nonnihil in versu hoc linquam vitale, quod una
Cum numeris habeas usque meique memor.
Tuque recensebis simul his unum illud, amice,
Quod tibi devovi seposuique sacrum[126];
Fas cinis ad cinerem redeat, sed spiritus ipse
Est tuus, interior pars meliorque mei.
Inde puta ereptum vitae modo vile putamen,
Cum mihi mortale hoc, vermibus esca, cadit:
Id cadit ignavus potuit quod vincere culter;
Tam miserae nolis tu meminisse rei.
Eius enim valuit modo quod vitale latebat
Intus, in his autem versibus illud habes.

---

[125] Die Reihenfolge *rara (coma)* – *nulla* („wenige oder gar keine Blätter")
scheint logischer zu sein als die umgekehrte Folge *or none, or few*.
[126] Barton gibt Shakespeares Zeile 6 wieder, wie wenn sie *the very part I
consecrate to thee* gelautet hätte. Dies wäre in der Tat verständlicher als die
Version des Thorpe-Texts *the very part was consecrate to thee*.

73

That time of year thou mayst in me behold
When yellow leaves, or none, or few, do hang
Upon those boughs which shake against the cold,
Bare ruin'd choirs where late the sweet birds sang.
In me thou see'st the twilight of such day
As after sunset fadeth in the west;
Which by and by black night doth take away,
Death's second self, that seals up all in rest.
In me thou see'st the glowing of such fire
That on the ashes of his youth doth lie,
As on the death-bed where[127] it must expire,
Consum'd with that which it was nourish'd by.
  This thou perceiv'st, which makes thy love more strong,
  To love that well which thou must leave ere long.

74

But be contented: when that fell arrest
Without all bail shall carry me away,
My life hath in these lines[128] some interest,
Which for memorial still with thee shall stay.
When thou reviewest this, thou dost review
The very part I[129] consecrate to thee:
The earth can have but earth, which is her[130] due;
My spirit is thine, the better part of me.
So then thou hast but lost the dregs of life,
The prey of worms, my body, being dead,
The coward conquest of a wretch's knife,
Too base of thee to be remembered.
  The worth of that is that which it contains,
  And that is this, and this with thee remains.

---

[127] Th.: *As the death bed, whereon.*
[128] Th.: *this line.*
[129] Th.: *was* (siehe Fussnote 126).
[130] Th.: *his.*

LXXV

Sensibus omne meis illud, carissime, praestas
Pabula quod pecori, gratus et imber humo;
Teque super mecum certamina tanta peregi
Quanta habet aggestas inter avarus opes,
Qui modo laetus eis inhiat, modo respicit,[131]aevum
Mente rapax an se despoliare paret.
Sic mihi iam praestat solo tecum esse, measque
Deinde voluptates quemque videre virum;
Nunc oculos implere tua dulcedine possum,
Tum faciem avertis, discruciorque fame.
Nil scio, nil aveo iucundum ea praeter, amice,
Quae mihi das, vel quae tu dare solus habes.
Sic ego quoque die nullis atque omnibus utor
Deliciis, versa plenus inopsque vice.

LXXVI

Cur adeo est[132] venerum sterilis mea musa novarum,
Tam procul a varia flexibilique vice?
Cur ego non saecli de more recentia dignor
Respicere, inque novos verba reflexa modos?
Cur genus est scriptis unum mihi semper idemque
Vestis et inventis inditur una meis,
Paene meum ut nomen prodat vox altera quaeque
Et faciat certam, fluxerit unde, fidem?
O quia te solum cepi, dilecte, canendum,
Materia super hac, teque et amore, moror.
Ars mea sic una est, notis nova gratia verbis
Danda[133], vel eiusdem forma novanda rei.
Ut renovatur enim sol cursu semper eodem,
Sic eadem narrans et renovatur amor.

---

[131] Harrower interpungiert erst nach *rapax* nach Vers 6. *Mente rapax* ist aber wohl eine adverbiale Ergänzung zu *despoliare paret*, nicht zu *respicit*.

[132] *Est* fehlt in Harrowers Text wohl aus *Versehen (cur adeo est = why is...so).*

[133] *notis nova gratia verbis danda* erinnert an Horazens Wort *dixeris egregie, notum si callida verbum reddiderit iunctura novum* (ars 47 f.)

75

So are you to my thoughts as food to life,
Or as sweet-season'd showers are to the ground;
And for the peace of you I hold such strife
As 'twixt a miser and his wealth is found:
Now proud as an enjoyer and anon
Doubting the filching age will steal his treasure;
Now counting best to be with you alone,
Then better'd that the world may see my pleasure;
Sometime all full with feasting on your sight,
And by and by clean starved for a look;
Possessing or pursuing no delight,
Save what is had or must from you be took.
   Thus do I pine and surfeit day by day,
    Or gluttoning on all, or all away.

76

Why is my verse so barren of new pride,
So far from variation or quick change?
Why with the time do I not glance aside
To new-found methods and to compounds strange?
Why write I still all one, ever the same,
And keep invention in a noted weed,
That every word doth almost sell[134] my name,
Showing their birth and whence[135] they did proceed?
O know, sweet love, I always write of you,
And you and Love are still my argument;
So all my best is dressing old words new,
Spending again what is already spent.
   For as the sun is daily new and old,
    So is my love still telling what is told.

---

[134] Th.: *fel* (siehe Anmerkungen).
[135] Th.: *where.*

LXXVII

Admonitus speculo tua quam indurabile[136] forma,
Ac labente umbra quam fugitiva dies,
I, puer, his vacuis tua sensa inscribe tabellis,
Eque tuo possis discere multa libro.
Quae speculum verax rugosa ostenderit ora,
Ora sepulcrorum te meminisse volent;
Lapsaque furtive te gnomonis umbra monebit
Furtive ad mortem tendere cuique viam.
En, age, siqua minus retinebit talia pectus,
Chartarum in vacuas illa tuenda refer;
Sensa tua invenies illic nutrita fuisse,
Cumque nova facie pectus inire tuum.
Officia haec rerum prosunt, si respicis, ipsi,
Factus et exemplis ditior inde liber.

LXXVIII

Nomine sub musae quoniam te saepe vocavi,
Ac numeris totiens auxiliare meis,
Scriptorum[137] se quisque meo corroborat usu
Subque tuo affatu spargit ubique libros.
Lumina quae mutum cantus docuere canoros
Ista tua, ac stolidum corde superna sequi,
En, aliquid pennarum et doctis vatibus addunt,
Ac maiestati fit geminatus honos.
Tu tamen in nostra potius laetere Camena,
Eius enim tua vis, aut oriunda tua est.
Corrigis in reliquis quod durius incidit auri,
Artibus et magnis additur ista venus;
At mihi tu constas ars ipsa, rudisque loquendi
Aequiparo per te pectora docta virûm.

---

[136] Harrower schreibt *quam durabile*, gemeint ist aber wohl *qu(am) indurabile forma* („wie unbeständig die Schönheit ist").
[137] Harrower schreibt *scriptorem*.

77

This[138] glass will show thee how thy beauties wear,
This dial how thy precious minutes waste;
The vacant leaves thy mind's imprint will bear,
And of this book thy[139] learning mayst thou taste.
The wrinkles which the[140] glass will truly show
Of mouthed graves will give thee memory;
Thou by the dial's shady stealth mayst know
Time's thievish progress to eternity.
Look, what thy memory cannot contain,
Commit to these waste blanks, and thou shalt find
Those children nurs'd, deliver'd from thy brain,
To take a new acquaintance of thy mind.
    These offices, so oft as thou wilt look,
    Shall profit thee, and much enrich thy book.

78

So oft have I invok'd thee for my Muse
And found such fair assistance in my verse,
As every alien pen hath got my use
And under thee their poesy disperse.
Thine eyes that taught the dumb one[141] high to sing,
And heavy ignorance aloft to fly,
Have added feathers to the learned's wing
And given grace a double majesty.
Yet be most proud of that which I compile,
Whose influence is thine and born of thee:
In others' works thou dost but mend the style,
And arts with thy sweet graces graced be;
    But thou art all my art and dost advance
    As high as learning my rude ignorance.

---

[138] Th.: *Thy,* ebenso *thy dial* in Zeile 2 (siehe Anmerkungen).
[139] Th.: *this.*
[140] Th.: *thy,* ebenso *thy dial's* in Zeile 7 (siehe Anmerkungen).
[141] Th.: *the dumbe on.*

LXXIX

Auxilium mea musa tuum dum sola rogavit,
Illa tuam ad numeros sola recepit opem;
Sed mihi iampridem versus ea gratia marcet,
Datque alii musae saucia nostra locum.
Et tua, confiteor, formae pingenda venustas
Officio calami nobilioris eget;
Sed tuus hic vates, de te quantum invenit, omne
A te furatur, restituitque tibi.
Si dat honestatem, a gestu furatur honesto,
Si decus, hoc istis vidit inesse genis;
Dotes praeter eas in te quas vivere notum est,
Hic tibi nil unquam reddere laudis habet.
Non referas igitur grates mera verba loquenti;
Quod tibi nam debet solvis id ipse rei.

LXXX

Te canere, o, quantum metuo, sub nomine vero
Quem scio cantari nobiliore lyra!
Vires ille suas in laudem nominis effert,
Quo mea de meritis vinciat ora metu.
Sed quoniam tua laus ingens ut pontus aquarum est,
Qua pariter classes naviculaeque natant,
Et mea cymba procax in eis appareat undis,
Inferior valde viribus ipsa tamen.
Me tua sustineant etiam breviora natantem,
Ille per immensas naviget actus aquas.[142]
Naufraga sit, nostrae nulla est iactura carinae,
Grandia sunt illi robora, grande decus.
Sic florente illo peream si naufragus, unum
Sit grave: naufragii causa fidelis amor.

---

[142] Zweifellos zutreffend fasst Barton die Verse 9/10 als Gegenüber-stellung von seichtem Ufergewässer *(your shallows, tua breviora)* und Meerestiefe *(your soundless deep, immensae aquae)* auf. *Shallows* und *deep* sind offenbar substantivierte Adjektive; in Zeile 9 dürfte demnach your *shallows' help* zu lesen sein.

79

Whilst I alone did call upon thy aid,
My verse alone had all thy gentle grace;
But now my gracious numbers are decay'd
And my sick Muse doth give another place.
I grant, sweet love, thy lovely argument
Deserves the travail of a worthier pen;
Yet what of thee thy poet doth invent
He robs of thee[143], and pays it thee again.
He lends thee virtue and he stole that word
From thy behaviour; beauty doth he give
And found it in thy cheek: he can afford
No praise to thee but what in thee doth live.
   Then thank him not for that which he doth say,
   Since what he owes thee thou thyself dost pay.

80

O, how I faint when I of you do write,
Knowing a better spirit use[144] your name,
And in the praise thereof spend[145] all his might,
To make me tongue-tied, speaking of your fame!
But since your worth, wide as the ocean is,
The humble as the proudest sail doth bear,
My saucy bark inferior far to his
On your broad main doth wilfully appear.
Your shallows' help[146] will hold me up afloat,
Whilst he upon your soundless deep doth ride;
Or, being wreck'd, I am a worthless boat,
He of tall building and of goodly pride.
   Then if he thrive and I be cast away,
   The worst was this: my *love* was my decay.

---

[143] Th.: *He robs thee of.*
[144] Th.: *a better spirit doth use.*
[145] Th.: *spends.*
[146] Th.: *Your shallowest helpe* (siehe Fussnote 142).

LXXXI

Seu numeris flero te raptum, sive superstes
Tu fueris, tabet cum mihi funus humo,
Nil metuas; hinc te mors nulla evellere possit,
Exstinctum fuerit cum memor omne mei.
Nomen vita tuum sic immortalis habebit[147],
Mortua si mecum sit mea fama simul;
Meque ubi communis celarit terra, sepulcrum
In populorum oculis stabit, amice, tuum.
Ac tua erunt monumenta pio mea condita versu
Carmina, quae nondum lumina nata legent;
Et poterunt linguae de te narrare futurae
Presserit has linguas cum diuturna quies.
Semper eris, versus est illa potentia nostri,
Vivus, ubi vera est vita, per ora virûm.

LXXXII

Te fateor nostrae sponsum non esse Camenae,
Fictaque cuiusvis tu sine fraude legas
Omnia quae scriptor de forma excogitat eius
Cui, lucra prospectans[148], dedicat ille librum.
Tum studiis idem florens atque ore, meaeque
Inveniens laudis te superasse modum,
Cogeris, ut vatum fulsit iam doctior aetas,
Inde recens aliquid conciliare notae.
Et facias, dilecte; at cum laus inde tumebit
Maxima rhetorica quam quis ab arte trahat,
Tu, facie egregius, fueras ita simplice versu
Dictus ab hac musa cui placet una fides.
Quos adhibent alii fucos decuere genarum
Exsangues; in te talia nulla cadunt.

---

[147] Shakespeares *Your name ... immortal life shall have* wäre eigentlich zu übersetzen mit *nomen tuum vitam immortalem habebit.* Bartons Version bedeutet umgekehrt „Das unsterbliche Leben wird deinen Namen haben".
[148] *lucra prospectans* sagt deutlicher als der Originaltext, was mit *blessing every book* gemeint sein dürfte: die Dichter erhoffen sich Gewinn in klingender Münze.

81

Or I shall live your epitaph to make,
Or you survive when I in earth am rotten;
From hence your memory Death cannot take,
Although in me each part will be forgotten.
Your name from hence immortal life shall have,
Though I, once gone, to all the world must die;
The earth can yield me but a common grave,
When you entombed in men's eyes shall lie.
Your monument shall be my gentle verse,
Which eyes not yet created shall o'er-read;
And tongues to be your being shall rehearse,
When all the breathers of this world are dead.
   You still shall live – such virtue hath my pen –
   Where breath most breathes: in the mouths[149] of men.

82

I grant thou wert not married to my Muse,
And therefore mayst without attaint o'erlook
The dedicated words which writers use
Of their fair subject, blessing every book.
Thou art as fair in knowledge as in hue,
Finding thy worth a limit past my praise;
And therefore art enforc'd to seek anew
Some fresher stamp of this time's[150] bettering days.
And do so, love; yet when they have devis'd
What strained touches rhetoric can lend,
Thou truly fair wert truly sympathiz'd
In true plain words by thy true-telling friend;
   And their gross painting might be better us'd
   Where cheeks need blood; in thee it is abus'd.

---

[149] Th.: *breaths, even in the mouths.*
[150] Th.: *the time.*

LXXXIII

Nec mihi visus eras fucis eguisse, nec ullis
Propterea per me tangitur iste decor;
Reppereram, aut rebar, caneret quodcunque poeta,
Illius exiguum te superasse modum.
Inque tua idcirco dormivi laude, quod illud
Ipse palam nobis testificatus ades,
Quantopere infelix os sit mediocre locutum
De meritis, in te quanta sit ista seges.
Tu mihi vertebas haec ipsa silentia culpae,
Maxima qua laus est obticuisse mihi;
Nam tua dum per me forma est illaesa silendo,
Cantantum in numeris illa sepulta fuit.
Ex oculis istis vitae plus vivit in uno
Quam tibi par vatum reddere laude potest.

LXXXIV

Utrane vox potior? quisve illud laudis opimae
Vicerit, esse unum te tibi laude parem?
Quod spatio breviore amplectitur omnia demum
Quorum ope noscatur par aliunde satus.
In calamo scriptoris egestas nuda videtur
Qui decoris nil dat gloriolaeve rei ;
Scribere qui te volt, si callet qualis es ipse
Pingere, materie nobilitavit opus.
Si modo describat naturae scripta, velitque
Illius argutam non hebetasse manum,
Ingenium artificis pictura simillima volgat,[151]
Undique et hoc artis crescit honore genus.
Sed bona corrumpis tua maxima, laudis amator,
Qualis et egregiis dotibus ipsa nocet.

---

[151] Harrower interpungiert erst nach *undique* im folgenden Vers.

83

I never saw that you did painting need,
And therefore to your fair no painting set;
I found, or thought I found, you did exceed
The barren tender of a poet's debt.
And therefore have I slept in your report,
That you yourself, being extant, well might show
How far a modern quill doth come too short,
Speaking of worth, what worth in you doth grow.
This silence for my sin you did impute,
Which shall be most my glory, being dumb:
For I impair not beauty being mute,
When others would give life and bring a tomb.
   There lives more life in one of your fair eyes
   Than both your poets can in praise devise.

84

Who is it that says most which can say more
Than this rich praise, that you alone are you?
In those confines[152] immured is the store
Which should example where your equal grew.
Lean penury within that pen doth dwell
That to his subject lends not some small glory;
But he that writes of you, if he can tell
That you are you, so dignifies his story.
Let him but copy what in you is writ,
Not making worse what Nature made so clear,
And such a counterpart shall fame his wit,
Making his style admired everywhere.
   You to your beauteous blessings add a curse,
   Being fond on praise, which makes your praises worse.

---

[152] Th.: *whose confine* (siehe Anmerkungen).

LXXXV

Lingua verecunde dum se mea continet, alter
Commenta in laudes pangit opima tuas;
Par sibi[153], si quando, stilus aureus ille superbit,
Aureaque a Musis verba polita novem.
Ast ego, vera putans, aliis sublimia linquo
Fanda, sed indocti more profata probo,
Ceteraque et versu si spiritus ille subacto
Condere volt de te quae propiora deis.
Laus ea cum sonuit, 'nihil istis verius' inquam,
Nec nihil ad summam laudis et ipse fero;
Id tamen est mecum, veri nam fervor amoris,
Verba retro ut veniant, anteit illa gradu.
Verba sonumque colas aliorum, sensaque cordis
Tu mea, in effectu sensa diserta suo.

LXXXVI

Num quia velivoli versus splendore superbus
In teque et nimias navigat alter opes,
Nostrane clauduntur stupefacto pectore sensa,
Sub natalicio viva sepulta loco?
An, lemurum auxiliis ultra mortalia doctus
Scribere, me maior spiritus ille necat?
Non ita; non nostram stupefecerat ille Camenam,
Nec socium siquid nocte ministrat opem.
Ille nihil de me, nihil ulla affabilis umbra
Ingenia instillans omnia noctis, ovet[154];
Non fuerint illis iactanda silentia nostra,
Qui fueram haud ullo saucius inde metu.
Sed favor ut numeros fulsit tuus eius, ibidem
Materies ac vis destituere meos.

---

[153] *Par sibi* („sich selber gleich") scheint dem Wortlaut *Reserve their character* zu entsprechen. *Their* dürfte hier aber – wie oft bei Thorpe – mit einem anderen Pronomen (hier *your*) verwechselt sein.

[154] Harrower schreibt *ovat*. Die Aussage im Konjunktiv *nihil ... ovet* („er soll nicht auftrumpfen") entspricht besser dem Shakespeare'schen *he ... cannot boast*.

85

My tongue-tied Muse in manners holds her still,
While comments of your praise, richly compil'd,
Reserve your[155] character with golden quill,
And precious phrase by all the Muses fil'd.
I think good thoughts, whilst others[156] write good words
And like unletter'd clerks still cry 'Amen'
To every hymn an[157] able spirit affords
In polish'd form of well-refined pen.
Hearing you prais'd, I say 'Tis so, 'tis true',
And to the most of praise add something more;
But that is in my thought, whose love to you,
Though words come hindmost, holds his rank before.
   Then others for the breath of words respect,
   Me for my dumb thoughts, speaking in affect[158].

86

Was it the proud full sail of his great verse,
Bound for the praise[159] of all-too-precious you,
That did my ripe thoughts in my brain inhearse,
Making their tomb the womb wherein they grew?
Was it his spirit, by spirits taught to write
Above a mortal pitch, that struck me dead?
No, neither he, nor his compeers by night
Giving him aid, my verse astonished;
Nor he, nor that affable family ghost[160]
Which nightly gulls him with intelligence,
As victors of my silence cannot boast:
I was not sick of any fear from thence -
   But when your countenance fill'd up his line,
   Then lack'd I matter; that enfeebled mine.

---

[155] Th.: *their* (siehe Fussnote 153).
[156] Th.: *other,* ebenso im folgenden Vers Singular *clerk.*
[157] Th.: *that.*
[158] Th.: *effect* (siehe Anmerkungen).
[159] Th: *prize.*
[160] Th.: *He nor that affable familiar ghost.*

LXXXVII

Care, mihi valeas, nec te sum dignus habere,
Et pretii tandem gnarus es ipse tui.
Omne caput meriti te liberat, omnia iura
Cassa mea in te sunt, syngrapha siqua dedit.
Quo sis iure meus nisi te donante, meaque
A parte o tantas quid mereatur opes?
Muneris egregii causa in me defuit omnis,
Iamque revertatur muneris ille favor.
Te dederas ignarum a te maiora mereri,
Cuive dabas tete non ego notus eram.
Gratia sic ingens, ipsis erroribus aucta,
Recidit in dantis, res ubi nota, manum.
Teque habui, tanquam somno quis lusus inani:
Nocte quidem rex est, luce dieque nihil.

LXXXVIII

In numero cum me nullo censurus habendum
Incipies meritis indubitare meis,
Mecum ego pugnabo tua proelia; falsus et omnis
Cum fueris, vincam te tenuisse fidem.
Conscius et mihimet vitiorum, ea cuncta libellis
Scripta dabo, causae subveniamque tuae;
Probra quibus teneor multis recludere possum,
Meque relinquenti gloria maior erit.
Nec nihilum interea fuero lucratus ibidem,
Figitur in te nam pectoris omnis amor;
Sique meis oritur fortasse iniuria rebus,
Nil mihi non prosit, si tibi prosit idem.
Totus amans totusque tuus, nil ferre malorum
Noluerim, ut capias nonnihil ipse boni.

87

Farewell! thou art too dear for my possessing,
And like enough thou know'st thy estimate:
The charter of thy worth gives thee releasing;
My bonds in thee are all determinate.
For how do I hold thee but by thy granting?
And for that richess[161] where is my deserving?
The cause of this fair gift in me is wanting,
And so my patent back again is swerving.
Thyself thou gav'st, thy own worth then not knowing
Or me, to whom thou gav'st it, else mistaking;
So thy great gift, upon misprision growing,
Comes home again on better judgement making.
   Thus have I had thee, as a dream doth flatter:
   In sleep a king, but waking no such matter.

88

When thou shalt be dispos'd to set me light
And place my merit in the eye of scorn,
Upon thy side against myself I'll fight,
And prove thee virtuous, though thou art forsworn.
With mine own weakness being best acquainted,
Upon thy part I can set down a story
Of faults conceal'd, wherein I am attainted;
That thou in losing me shalt win much glory.
And I by this will be a gainer too:
For bending all my loving thoughts on thee,
The injuries that to myself I do,
Doing thee vantage, double-vantage me.
   Such is my love, to thee I so belong,
   That for thy right my self will bear all wrong.

---

[161] Th.: *ritches* (*richess* bzw. *richesse* als Singular ist in der Shakespeare-Zeit belegt).

LXXXIX

Ede in flagitio te me liquisse repertum,
Protinus id vincam turpe fuisse nefas.
Ede vacillantes ob gressus, debilis ibo;
Reiciet causam vox mea nulla tuam.
Dedecoris nequeas mihi, care, imponere tantum,
Quo vicis optatae sit tamen ille color,
Quantum ego non duplicem; demum si malle fateris,
Notitiam voltu dissimulare queo.
Non adero quocunque loci spatiabere, nomen
Dulce tuum in lingua non habitare sinam;
Impietas oris quaedam ne peccet in illo,
Prodere amicitiae forsitan ausa notas.
Omnia me contra pro te facienda vovebo;
Osus eris quem tu, non meus is sit amor.

XC

Me ferias cum vis, si quando, hoc tempore malim,
Omnia cum votis stant inimica meis;
Adde tuos fortunae ictus, incumbe cadenti,
Nec venias subito tu novus ipse dolor.
Ah minime, hos fuerit si fas evadere luctus,
Tu mihi crudelis post mala victa veni;
Flamina ne noctis duplicaveris imbre diei,
Sitve per accitas tracta ruina moras!
Linquere me si vis, parcas ipse ultimus ire
Cum desaevierit tenuibus[162] ira malis;
Aggredere in primis tu me, mihi prima ferenda
Fortunae veniat pessima plaga velim.
Cetera deinde meae sortis iam tristia visa
Sint ad discidium non ita visa tuum.

---

[162] *Tenuibus* ist als dreisilbiges daktylisches Wort (lang-kurz-kurz) mit konsonantischem u (= v) zu lesen.

89

Say that thou didst forsake me for some fault,
And I will comment upon that offence;
Speak of my lameness, and I straight will halt,
Against thy reasons making no defence.
Thou canst not, love, disgrace me half so ill,
To set a form upon desired change,
As I'll myself disgrace, knowing thy will:
I will acquaintance strangle and look strange,
Be absent from thy walks, and in my tongue
Thy sweet beloved name no more shall dwell,
Lest I, too much profane, should do it wrong
And haply of our old acquaintance tell.
  For thee against myself I'll vow debate,
  For I must ne'er love him whom thou dost hate.

90

Then hate me when thou wilt, if ever, now;
Now, while the world is bent my deeds to cross;
Join with the spite of Fortune, make me bow,
And do not drop in for an after-loss.
Ah, do not, when my heart hath 'scap'd this sorrow,
Come in the rearward of a conquer'd woe;
Give not a windy night a rainy morrow,
To linger out a purpos'd overthrow.
If thou wilt leave me, do not leave me last,
When other petty griefs have done their spite,
But in the onset come: so shall I taste
At first the very worst of Fortune's might,
  And other strains of woe, which now seem woe,
  Compar'd with loss of thee will not seem so.

XCI

Est atavis, est qui subtili mente superbit,
Corpore firmo unus, vi magis alter opum;
Sunt quibus arridet vestis nova pravaque forma,
Hunc canis, hunc currus accipiterve iuvant.
Ingeniis aliis alia est adiuncta libido,
Causa voluptatis maxima cuique suae.
His ego particulis me nullus metior, uno
Praeditus has omnes exsuperante bono:
Pluris amor tuus est genere alto stirpis habendus,
Pluris opes quam sunt vel pretiosa chlamys;
Dulcior est avibus vel equis mihi, compos et eius
Possideo quidquid gloria cuique sua est[163];
Anxius hoc uno, quod habes ea cuncta vicissim
Auferre, ac summae me dare tristitiae.[164]

XCII

I, facias quodvis te furaturus amanti:
Per vitam meus es, sic mihi certa fides;
Vitaque amore tuo nescit diuturnior esse,
Ex illo quoniam pendet ut esse queat.
Propterea mihi nulla gravis sit noxa timenda,
Cui minima extemplo clauserit ipsa diem;
Sortis iter video mihi fortunatius ire
Arbitrio quam si pendeat illa tuo.
Perfidia haud possis tu me vexare rebelli,
Rupit ubi vitae stamina ruptus amor;
O ego bis felix, cui sors est utraque dulcis,
Dulce in amore tuo vivere, dulce mori!
Sed quid ita excellit nihil ut metuatur iniqui?
Falsus, ubi nildum suspicor, esse potes.

---

[163] Der Anklang an Vers 6 *maxima cuique suae – gloria cuique sua (e)st* verdeutlicht die Gliederung des Haupttexts Vv. 1-12 in zwei Hälften.
[164] Der Schlusseffekt mit dem viersilbigen Endwort *tristitiae* erinnert an Properz, in dessen Elegie 3.11 von insgesamt 36 Distichen das letzte mit einem Tetrasyllabum schliesst, während alle übrigen Endwörter zweisilbig sind.

91

Some glory in their birth, some in their skill,
Some in their wealth, some in their bodies' force;
Some in their garments, though new-fangl'd ill,
Some in their hawks and hounds, some in their horse.
And every humour hath his adjunct pleasure,
Wherein it finds a joy above the rest;
But these particulars are not my measure:
All these I better in one general best.
Thy love is better than high birth to me,
Richer than wealth, prouder than garments' cost,
Of more delight than hawks or horses be;
And having thee, of all men's pride I boast -
   Wretched in this alone, that thou mayst take
   All this away and me most wretched make.

92

But do thy worst to steal thyself away,
For term of life thou art assured mine;
And life no longer than thy love will stay,
For it depends upon that love of thine.
Then need I not to fear the worst of wrongs,
When in the least of them life hath an end[165]:
I see a better state to me belongs
Than that which on thy humour doth depend.
Thou canst not vex me with inconstant mind,
Since that my life on thy revolt doth lie -
O, what a happy title do I find,
Happy to have thy love, happy to die!
   But what's so blessed fair that fears no blot?
   Thou mayst be false, and yet I know it not.

---

[165] Th.: *my life hath end.*

XCIII

Vivere sic pergam decepti coniugis instar
Te ratus integra pectoris esse fide;
Nam speciem ostendes, penitus mutatus, eandem:
Ore meus vel dum pectus aberrat amans.
Nec, quia nil oculis odiosum vivit in istis,
Scire tuas animi fas erit inde vices.
In vario voltu rugisve aut fronte coacta
Plurimum apud numerum perfida corda leges;
Te bonitas divina creans decrevit in ista
Ut facie nunquam non habitaret amor;
Quidquid consuleres, quidquid sub corde moveres,
In facie voluit nil nisi dulce legi.
O genita in pestem mortalibus aurea forma,
Intima ni virtus aequet in ore decus.

XCIV

Laedere qui potis est nec volt, fecisse recusans
Quae genitum imprimis ad facienda putes[166];
Corda movens aliis, friget dum marmoris instar
Ipse cupidinibus succubuisse piger;
Dona deûm in sese merito trahit ille, suaeque
Indolis ingenitas ille tuetur opes.
Ille sui est voltus dominus, sua possidet ora;
In multis aliis[167] servit id omne decus.
Flosculus aestati est aestivo gratus odore,
Floreat ac pereat cum tamen ipse sibi;
Siquid at incessit tetrae robiginis illum,
Gramine ab agresti vincitur eius honos.
Optima corrumpas in pessima; sique putrescunt
Lilia, non loliis[168] est ita foedus odor.

---

[166] Zu ergänzen ist hier *eum (ad quae facienda eum genitum putes)*.
[167] Harrower schreibt *alii*.
[168] Shakespeares *weeds* gibt Barton in Vers 12 mit *gramen agreste* (Ackergras), in
Vers 14 wie im Gedicht LXIX mit *lolia* wieder, was hier eine reizvolle
Gegenüberstellung zu *lilia* und zugleich einen Anklang an Vers 8 *(aliis – loliis)*
ergibt.

93

So shall I live supposing thou art true,
Like a deceived husband; so love's face
May still seem love to me, though alter'd new:
Thy looks with me, thy heart in other place.
For there can live no hatred in thine eye,
Therefore in that I cannot know thy change;
In many's looks the false heart's history
Is writ in moods and frowns and wrinkles strange.
But Heaven in thy creation did decree
That in thy face sweet love should ever dwell;
Whate'er thy thoughts or thy heart's workings be,
Thy looks should nothing thence but sweetness tell.
  How like Eve's apple doth thy beauty grow,
  If thy sweet virtue answer not thy show!

94

They that have power to hurt and will do none,
That do not do the thing they most do show,
Who, moving others, are themselves as stone,
Unmoved, cold, and to temptation slow;
They rightly do inherit Heaven's graces
And husband Nature's richess[169] from expense;
They are the lords and owners of their faces,
Others but stewards of their excellence.
The summer's flower is to the summer sweet,
Though to itself it only live and die,
But if that flower with base infection meet,
The basest weed outbraves his dignity.
  For sweetest things turn sourest by their deeds:
  Lilies that fester smell far worse than weeds.

---

[169] Th.: *ritches* (siehe Fussnote 161).

XCV

Est tibi quod nomen maculat floremque iuventae,
Qualis odoriferam pestis operta rosam;
Est tamen, o, in te quam dulce et amabile visu,
Deliciis celans omnibus omne malum!
Istaque lingua tuae quae volgat facta diei,
Libera de lusu nequiter[170] ausa loqui,
Cuncta tamen laudat carpendo, ac fama piatur
Pessima, si nomen nuncupat illa tuum.
Et quibus es vitiis tu iam lectissima sedes,
O quam felicem sunt ea nacta domum!
Qua macula obtentis veletur quaeque venustis,
Quodque vident oculi vestiat omne decor.
Care, cave in noxam ne tanta licentia vertat;
Culter abutendo dente retusus erit.

XCVI

Ille iuventam in te culpat magis, alter amorem;
Hic tibi non parvum credit utrumque decus.
Sitque decus seu non, adamavit summus et imus;
Mendaque noscuntur si tua, menda placent.
Ut bene laudatur semper vilissima gemma
Reginae in digitis, cum sedet alta throno,
Sic vitiosa in te virtutes esse videntur
Scilicet, inque bonis obtinuisse locum.
Quot lupus ille agnos potuisset fallere, voltus
Callidus agninos imposuisse sibi!
Tuque oculos hominum quos, o, corrumpere possis
Omnibus istarum viribus usus opum!
Quod mihi tu nolis; illo sociamur amore
Ut pariter curae sit tua fama[171] meae.

---

[170] Harrower schreibt *nequitur.*
[171] Wie bei Shakespeare klingt der Schlussvers ans Ende des ersten Quartetts an: *resort – report, si tua menda – sit tua fama.* Ferner stimmt das Schlussdistichon nahezu wörtlich mit demjenigen der Elegie XXXVI überein, während bei Shakespeare die Couplets der Sonette 36 und 96 gleich lauten.

95

How sweet and lovely dost thou make the shame
Which, like a canker in the fragrant rose,
Doth spot the beauty of thy budding name!
O, in what sweets dost thou thy sins enclose!
That tongue that tells the story of thy days,
Making lascivious comments on thy sport,
Cannot dispraise, but in a kind of praise,
Naming thy name, blesses an ill report.
O, what a mansion have those vices got
Which for their habitation chose out thee,
Where beauty's veil doth cover every blot
And all things turn[172] to fair that eyes can see!
   Take heed, dear heart, of this large privilege:
   The hardest knife ill-us'd doth lose its[173] edge.

96

Some say thy fault is youth, some wantonness;
Some say thy grace is youth and gentle sport;
Both grace and faults are lov'd of more and less:
Thou mak'st faults graces that to thee resort.
As on the finger of a throned queen
The basest jewel will be well esteem'd,
So are those errors that in thee are seen
To truths translated and for true things deem'd.
How many lambs might the stern wolf betray,
If like a lamb he could his looks translate!
How many gazers mightst thou lead away,
If thou wouldst use the strength of all thy state!
   But do not so; I love thee in such sort
   As thou being mine, mine is thy good report.

---

[172] Th.: *turnes.*
[173] Th.: *his.*

XCVII

Qualis hiems illud tempus dum separor a te,
Quo sine nil varius quod iuvet annus habet!
Frigus erat quantum, quam raris ulla diebus
Lumina, quae species nuda Decembris agro!
Inter at aestivum fuit illa absentia tempus,
Tempus et autumnum, faenore dives opum,
Spe tumida tandem lascivi veris onustum,
Ut gravida erepti viscera prole viri.
Spe tamen hac fetus tantummodo postuma proles
Ostensa, ac dubiae poma futura notae;
Te quoniam penes est aestas eiusque voluptas
Omnis, avesque ipsae te sine voce silent.
Sive canunt, adeo vox illaetabilis illis
Ut metuens hiemes[174] palleat omne nemus.

XCVIII

Te sine ver solus degi, dum pulcher Aprilis
Vestitus specie multicolore nitet,
Idque iuventae afflat terris, Saturnus ut ipse
Riserit insultans, tam gravis ille deus.
Me nec avis cantu movit, nec gratia multi
Floris, odorve suus cuique, suusve color;
Vernum ego nil versu memini; florumque superbit
Copia, nativo non mihi carpta toro.
Lilia qui pallor cepisset non ego miror,
Non ego puniceas purpura quanta rosas;
Dulcis odor speciesve illis dulcedinis umbra
Capta tuae, o praestans omnibus omne decus;
Sed mihi bruma fuit; cum flore et quoque cavillor
Absentis speciem quod ferat ille tuam.

---

[174] Harrower schreibt *hiemis*. Gemeint ist offenbar der Akkusativ Plural *hiemes* (Winterstürme). Die beiden verwandten Worte in den Randversen des Gedichts *(hiems – hiemes)* entsprechen der Wiederholung von *winter* in den Zeilen 1 und 14 des Sonetts 97.

97

How like a winter hath my absence been
From thee, the pleasure of the fleeting year!
What freezings have I felt, what dark days seen,
What cold[175] December's bareness everywhere!
And yet this time remov'd was summer's time;
The teeming autumn big with rich increase,
Bearing the wanton burthen of the prime,
Like widow'd wombs after their lords' decease.
Yet this abundant issue seem'd to me
But hope of orphans and unfather'd fruit;
For summer and his pleasures wait on thee,
And, thou away, the very birds are mute -
    Or, if they sing, 't is with so dull a cheer
    That leaves look pale, dreading the winter 's near.

98

From you have I been absent in the spring,
When proud-pied April, dress'd in all his trim,
Hath put a spirit of youth in everything,
That heavy Saturn laugh'd and leap'd with him.
Yet nor the lays of birds nor the sweet smell
Of different flowers in odour and in hue
Could make me any summer's story tell,
Or from the[176] proud lap pluck them where they grew:
Nor did I wonder at the lily's white,
Nor praise the deep vermilion in the rose;
They were but sweet, but figures of delight,
Drawn after you, you pattern of all those.
    Yet seem'd it winter still, and, you away,
    As with your shadow I with these did play.

---

[175] Th.: *old.*
[176] Th.: *their.*

XCIX

Increpito veris violam: 'fur dulcis, odorem
Unde nisi ex dominae surripis ore meae?
Haec tibi sublucens tam molli purpura voltu
Heu male virgineo sanguine tincta rubet.'[177]
Lilia de furto damnat tua palma, tuumque
Crinem in amaracina suspicor esse coma.
Stat rosa quaeque tremens in spinis, conscia culpae;
Huic pudor erubuit, palluit illa metu.
Tertia rubra albet binos furata colores,
Ac furtis animam iunxerat illa tuam.
Quod sceleris propter media florente iuventa
Illa rosa ultrici peste subesa perit.
Plus etiam vidi florum, nec in omnibus unum
Cui tua non species aut tuus esset odor.

C

O ubi, musa, diu latitas oblita canendi
Illius unde oritur vis tua, siqua, lyrae?
An furis in vili quo carmine? vilia rerum
Illustrans artem dedecorasne tuam?
Musa, redi, o nimium cantus oblita, piosque
Per numeros vanae damna repende morae.
Aurem adeas eius qui te desiderat, unde
Ingenium calamo materiamque trahis.
Surge, remissa; mei frontem scruteris amantis
Numquid ibi antiquae sculpserit hora notae.
Siquid tale vides, excanta protinus omne,
Ut spolia in risum temporis ista cadant.
Famam da citius quam tempore forma teratur,
Falciferique a te praevenietur opus.

---

[177] Shakespeares Sonett 99 beginnt mit einer fünfzeiligen Strophe statt wie
sonst mit einem Quartett. Diese Abweichung von der Normalform liess
sich in einem aus elegischen Distichen bestehenden Gedicht nicht
wiedergeben.

99
The forward violet thus did I chide:
'Sweet thief, whence didst thou steal thy sweet that smells,
If not from my love's breath? The purple pride
Which on thy soft cheek for complexion dwells
In my love's veins thou hast too grossly dyed.'
The lily I condemned for thy hand,
And buds of marjoram hath stol'n thy hair;
The roses fearfully on thorns did stand,
One blushing shame, another white despair;
A third, nor red nor white, had stol'n of both
And to his robbery had annex'd thy breath;
But for his theft in pride of all his growth
A vengeful canker ate him up to death.
  More flowers I noted, yet I none could see
  But sweet or colour it had stol'n from thee.

100
Where art thou, Muse, that thou forget'st so long
To speak of that which gives thee all thy might?
Spend'st thou thy fury on some worthless song,
Darkening thy power, to lend base subjects light?
Return, forgetful Muse, and straight redeem
In gentle numbers time so idly spent;
Sing to the ear that doth thy lays esteem
And gives thy pen both skill and argument.
Rise, resty Muse, my love's sweet face survey,
If Time have any wrinkle graven there;
If any, be a satire to decay,
And make Time's spoils despised everywhere.
  Give my love fame faster than Time wastes life;
  So thou prevent'st his scythe and crooked knife.

CI

Quod sileas una iunctas formamque fidemque,
Tu mihi poenarum quid, vaga musa, dabis?
Aque[178] meo imprimis puero res utraque pendet,
Unde quidem pendes ipsa, trahisque decus.
Musa, refer: nullo, dices, sunt vera colore
Indiga, quippe illis est suus ipse color;
Nec calamis opus est ut formae gratia detur;
Pura sine immixtis optima cuncta placent.
Laude meus quod non egeat tu, musa, silebis?
Non excusari sic taciturna potes;
Ut multum superans auratis ille sepulcris
Fulgeat in sera posteritate, tuum est.
Musa, tuum praesta; qualem nunc cernimus illum
Te doceo ad longam perpetuare diem.

CII

Rarior indiciis, amor in me robore crevit,
Nec, minor ad speciem, me minus ille regit.
Mercis habes instar quando possessor amoris
Aestimat, ac volgo venditat, eius opes.
Cum novus esset amor vernoque in tempore noster,
Excipiebatur cantibus ille meis;
Sic veniente canit Philomela aestate, diesque
Cum maturuerint voce silebit avis.
Non quod adulta aestas sit eis insuavior horis
Cum noctem fletu mulserat illa suo;
Sed numeris sine lege istis nemus omne gravatum
Sentit, et illecebris dulcia trita carent.
Sic ego nonnunquam, velut illa, silentia servo,
Ne nimius tibi sit noster et ipse canor.

---

[178] Harrower schreibt *atque*.

101

O truant Muse, what shall be thy amends
For thy neglect of truth in beauty dyed?
Both truth and beauty on my love depends;
So dost thou too, and there art[179] dignified.
Make answer, Muse, wilt thou not haply say:
'Truth needs no colour, with his colour fix'd;
Beauty no pencil, beauty's truth no[180] lay;
But best is best, if never intermix'd?'
Because he needs no praise, wilt thou be dumb?
Excuse not silence so, for 't lies in thee
To make him much outlive a gilded tomb,
And to be prais'd of ages yet to be.
   Then do thy office, Muse; I teach thee how
   To make him seem long hence as he shows now.

102

My love is strengthen'd, though more weak in seeming;
I love not less, though less the show appear:
That love is merchandiz'd whose rich esteeming
The owner's tongue doth publish everywhere.
Our love was new, and then but in the spring,
When I was wont to greet it with my lays;
As Philomel in summer's front doth sing,
And stops her pipe in growth of riper days:
Not that the summer is less pleasant now
Than when her mournful hymns did hush the night,
But that wild music burthens every bough,
And sweets grown common lose their dear delight.
   Therefore, like her, I some time hold my tongue,
   Because I would not dull you with my song.

---

[179] Th.: *therein.*
[180] Th.: *to* (siehe Anmerkungen).

CIII

Heu quam musa ferax est paupertatis, ibique
Qua fuit immensum gloria nacta locum;
Pluris, io, visa est communibus edita verbis
Materies, nullis laudibus aucta meis.
O non argueris tu me, quod nulla canendi
Vis mihi sit! speculum consule, voltus inest;
Voltus inest superans hoc nata in pectore sensa,
Ac versus hebetis causa, mihique rubor.
Sitne nefas igitur quod vis augere canendo
Laedere, praesertim quod fuit ante bonum?
Namque alium spectant finem mea carmina nullum
Quam decora et laudes enumerare tuas;
Pluraque, multo plura, meus quam versus habebit
Concipere, in speculi videris ipse vitro.

CIV

Pulcher, ut in prima cum lumina iunximus hora,
Te mihi non unquam rebor, amice, senem.
Ter bruma aestivos nemorum decussit honores,
Veris in autumnum ter rubuere comae,
Aprilem ter odorum exussit Iunius ignis,
Tot varias anni vidimus isse vices,
Cum memini primum te cernere, et ille virentis
Flos tuus aetatis nunc hodieque viret.
Ah, sed inobservata solet sua gratia formam
Linquere, ut occulto labitur umbra gradu;
Isque color fortasse tuus, dum stare videtur,
Motum habuit, visu decipiorque meo.
Quod metuens, o vos moneo, venientia saecla:
Flos hominum vestram fluxerat ante diem.

103

Alack, what poverty my Muse brings forth,
Though[181] having such a scope to show her pride!
The argument, all bare, is of more worth
Than when it hath my added praise beside.
O, blame me not, if I no more can write!
Look in your glass, and there appears a face
That over-goes my blunt invention quite,
Dulling my lines and doing me disgrace.
Were it not sinful, then, striving to mend,
To mar the subject that before was well?
For to no other parts[182] my verses tend
Than of your graces and your gifts to tell;
     And more, much more, than in my verse can sit
     Your glass will show[183] you when you look in it.

104

To me, fair friend, you never can be old,
For as you were when first your eye I ey'd,
Such seems your beauty still. Three winters cold
Have from the forests shook three summers' pride,
Three beauteous springs to yellow autumn turn'd
In process of the seasons have I seen,
Three April perfumes in three hot Junes burn'd,
Since first I saw you fresh, which yet are green.
Ah, yet doth beauty, like a dial-hand,
Steal from his figure and no pace perceiv'd;
So your sweet hue, which methinks still doth stand,
Hath motion and mine eye may be deceiv'd:
     For fear of which, hear this, thou age unbred;
     Ere thou wert born[184] was beauty's summer dead.

---

[181] Th.: *That.*
[182] Th.: *passe.*
[183] Th.: *Your own glasse showes.*
[184] Th.: *Ere you were borne* (siehe Anmerkungen).

CV

Non hominem supra dicar veneratus amicum,
Aut par ille[185] habitus relligione deis,
Assiduis adeam quia cantu ac laudibus unum,
Pectus amans unum, par sibi, semper idem.
Continuo bonus est hodie mihi crasque futurus,
Egregia constans pectoris ille fide;
Ac fidei imprimis celebrandae dedita musa,
Hanc recinens, dispar omne valere iubet.
Assiduum it carmen: pietas, bonitasque, fidesque,
Res eadem, varias nomine passa vices;
Nec[186] vicibus super his exerceor, amplaque cedit
Materia inventis, una triplexque, meis.
Quaeque suas olim sedes habuere seorsum
Denique in hoc uno tres coiere viro.

CVI

Praeteriti in scriptis quotiens annalibus aevi
Corpora pulchrorum carmine picta lego,
Ac veteres mollit numeros laudata venustas
Virginis occasae[187], visque decora viri;
Praecipue quando laudantur ut optima formae
Palma, pedes, labrum, lumina, frontis honos;
Tum video expressum priscos voluisse poetas
Quale venustatis tu genus unus habes.
Sic ea laus habuit vere praesagia nostri
Temporis, hoc in te vaticinata decus.
At nisi vidissent divinitus, illa canendi
Ingenium[188] antiquos vix habuisse putem.
Nos, ea cernentes oculis praesentia nostris,
Attoniti aspicimus, sed tenet ora pudor.

---

[185] Zu ergänzen ist *dicatur* (analog zu *dicar* in Vers 1).
[186] Harrower schreibt *et.*
[187] Harrower schreibt *occisae* (getötet). *Virginis occasae* entspricht dem Shakespeare'schen *ladies dead.*
[188] *Ingenium* entspricht der Emendation *skill* (Th.: *still*).

105

Let not my love be call'd idolatry,
Nor my beloved as an idol show,
Since all alike my songs and praises be
To one, of one, still such, and ever so.
Kind is my love to-day, to-morrow kind,
Still constant in a wondrous excellence;
Therefore my verse to constancy confin'd,
One thing expressing, leaves out difference.
'Fair, kind, and true' is all my argument,
'Fair, kind, and true', varying no[189] other words;
And in this change is my invention spent,
Three themes in one, which wondrous scope affords.
    Fair, kind and true have often liv'd alone,
    Which three till now never kept seat in one.

106

When in the chronicle of wasted time
I see descriptions of the fairest wights,
And beauty making beautiful old rhyme
In praise of ladies dead and lovely knights,
Then, in the blazon of sweet beauty's best,
Of hand, of foot, of lip, of eye, of brow,
I see their antique pen would have express'd
Even such a beauty as you master now.
So all their praises are but prophecies
Of this our time, all you prefiguring;
Yet[190], for they look'd but with divining eyes,
They had not skill enough your worth to sing:
    And[191] we, which now behold these present days,
    Have eyes to wonder, but lack tongues to praise.

---

[189] Th.: *to* (siehe Anmerkung zu 101).
[190] Th.: *And.*
[191] Th.: *For.*

CVII

Non mea, non populi timidae praesagia mentis,
Rerum venturas vaticinata vices,
Tempus amicitiae poterunt iam ponere nostrae,
Quam modo clausuri carcer et uncus[192] erant.
Luna laborando defecit, et irrita vertunt
Omina terrifici quae cecinere senes.
Anxia iam festis, curae cessere coronis,
Pacis inexhaustos ducit oliva dies.
Nunc viret ambrosiae liquidis sub roribus horae
Noster amor, cedit nunc Libitina mihi;
In tenui hoc versu vivam, dum quamlibet illa
Saevit in elinguis ac sine voce tribus;
Aeternumque tui monumentum hoc stabit, amice,
Cum tumidis regum molibus aera cadent.

CVIII

Ecquid inest animo scriptis imitabile signis
Quo mea se nondum est testificata fides?
Ecqua notae novitas aut lectae vocis amorem[193]
Quo movear vel quem tu mereare canet?
Nulla, puer dilecte, at divos more precantum
Sunt eadem nobis quoque canenda die.
Nil sonat antiquum tibi quo coniungar, ut olim
Quando adii primo nomen honore tuum.
Immortalis amor, quod in illo cunque novetur,
Ponderat annorum damna situmque nihil.
Nil senii rugis concedit, at omne vetustum,
Omne sibi antiquum cedere cogit amor,
Gnarus ibi teneros persaepe virescere sensus
Qua periisse anni, voltus et ipse, ferant.

---

[192] *carcer et uncus* symbolisieren die Todesstrafe; *uncus*, der Haken des zum Tode
Verurteilten, ist bei Horaz (c.35.20) ein Attribut der unerbittlichen *Necessitas*.
[193] *Novitas* bezieht sich sowohl auf Geschriebenes *(nota)* wie auf Gelesenes *(lecta
vox)*. Ganz analog dürfte bei Shakespeare *new to speak, new to register* (nicht *now
to register* wie im Thorpe-Text) zu lesen sein.

107

Not mine own fears, nor the prophetic soul
Of all the[194] world, dreaming on things to come,
Can yet the lease of my true love control,
Suppos'd as forfeit to a confin'd doom.
The immortal moon hath her eclipse endur'd,
And those sad augurs mocks[195] their own presage;
Incertainties now crown themselves assur'd
And peace proclaim[196] olives of endless age.
Now with the drops of this most balmy time
My love looks fresh, and Death to me subscribes
Since, spite of him, I'll live in this poor rhyme,
While he insults o'er dull and speechless tribes.
   And thou in this shalt find thy monument,
   When tyrants' crests and tombs of brass are spent.

108

What's in the brain that ink may character
Which hath to thee not figur'd[197] my true spirit?
What's new to speak, what new to register,
That may express my love or thy dear merit?
Nothing, sweet boy; but yet, like prayers divine,
I must each day say o'er the very same,
Counting no old thing old, thou mine, I thine,
Even as when first I hallow'd thy fair name.
So that eternal love in love's fresh case
Weighs not the dust and injury of age,
Nor gives to accessary[198] wrinkles place,
But makes antiquity for aye his page;
   Finding the first conceit of Love there bred
   Where Time and outward form would show it dead.

---

[194] Th.: *the wide.*
[195] Th.: *The mortal moon hath her eclipse endur'd / And the sad augurs mock.*
[196] Th.: *proclaims* (siehe Anmerkungen).
[197] Th.: *not figur'd to thee.*
[198] Th.: *necessary.*

CIX

Dixeris, o, nunquam me falsum, absentia quanquam
Visa sit ardoris vim minuisse mei;
Non animam citius quam memet linquere possum,
Inque tui septo pectoris illa iacet.
Cara mihi domus ista; ut sim fortasse vagatus,
At redeo, qualis qui pede fecit iter,
Adque diem rediens, ac non mutatus ut ille;
Lympha viae sordes quae luat, ipse fero.
Nunquam, o credideris, pectus si prava tenerent
Cuncta quot obsidunt sanguinis omne genus,
Flagitio infectum fuit hoc, ut linquere vellet
Te, nihilum propter, te, mea summa boni.
Totus enim mundus prae te, flos optime rerum,
Fit nihili; e cunctis unus es omne mihi.

CX

Hei mihi, sed verum est, huc illuc isse locorum
Me scio, qua variae vestis et oris eram;
Irrisi mea sensa, habui carissima venum
Cuncta, cupidinibus lusus, ut ante, novis.
Pura fides oculis est a me censa malignis;
Hoc tamen affirmo per quod ubique deûm est:
Dum fluito, pietas antiqua renascitur imo
Corde, tuamque probant cetera falsa fidem.
His posui finem; cape iam sine fine futura:
Non iterum cote hac est acuendus amor.
Eius non iterum renovo tentamina, nostras
Inter amicitias qui Iovis instar habet.
Optime post illum[199], tu me dignare benigne
Accipere, inque tuum condere pectus amans.

---

[199] „Du Bester nach jenem" – d.h. nach dem im vorangehenden Vers ge-
nannten *Jupiter* (Genitiv Iovis), der zugleich höchster Gott und Meto-nymie
des Himmels ist – entspricht den Worten *next to Heaven my best.*

122

109

O, never say that I was false of heart,
Though absence seem'd my flame to qualify;
As easy might I from myself depart
As from the[200] soul which in *thy* breast doth lie.
That is my home of love: if I have rang'd,
Like him that travels I return again,
Just to the time, not with the time exchang'd,
And I myself[201] bring water for my stain.
Never believe, though in my nature reign'd
All frailties that besiege all kinds of blood,
That I[202] could so preposterously be stain'd,
To leave for nothing all thy sum of good -
   For nothing this wide universe I call,
   Save *thou*, my rose: in it thou art my all.

110

Alas, 't is true I have gone here and there
And made myself a motley to the view,
Gor'd mine own thoughts, sold cheap what is most dear,
Made old offences of affections new;
Most true it is that I have look'd on truth
Askance and strangely: but, by all above,
These blenches gave my heart another youth,
And worse essays prov'd thee my best of love.
Now all is done, have what shall have no end:
Mine appetite I never more will grind
On newer proof, to try an older friend,
A god in love, to whom I am confin'd.
   Then give me welcome, next to Heaven my best[203],
   Even to thy pure and most most loving breast.

---

[200] Th.: *my* (siehe Anmerkungen).
[201] Th.: *So that myself.*
[202] Th.: *it.*
[203] Th.: *next my heaven the best* (siehe Fussnote 199).

CXI

O potius pro me Fortunae corripe nomen,
Quae dea delictis praesidet una meis;
Illa mihi ad vitam tantum nonnulla pararat
Publica, par morum nascitur unde genus.
Hinc macula aspersum nomen, naturaque rebus
Victa, velut fuco tingitur usa manus.
Omnia quae volvens tu me miserare, voveque
Hoc mihi, ut incipiam pectus habere novum.
Aeger ero patiens, et aceti pocula quot sunt
Ebibero si sit tanta repressa lues.
Nil ego triste habeam, vel poenam poena priorem
Si geminet, domitum perdomitura malum.
Me miserare igitur; sat enim, carissime, firmo
Esse salutiferum, si miseratus eris.

CXII

Omne mihi explesti, dum me miseraris amasque,
Sculpserat in frontem quod mala fama notae.
Laudet enim culpetve alius: quid noscere curem,
Prava coloraris tu modo, recta probes.
Es mihi tu mundus: quid rectum quidve probrosum,
Me decet a labris quaerere, care, tuis;
Vivit nemo mihi, nullique ego, ferrea sensa
Qui queat haec in fas flectere sive nefas.
Do barathro vocum curas aliunde crepantum
Quodlibet, austero sive favente sono;
His habeo occlusos, frigens ut vipera, sensus.
Quem tuear fastum qua ratione, vide:
Consiliis tu sic nostris cognatus, amice,
Efficis ut reliquos mortua corda putem.[204]

---

[204] Der Schlussvers entspricht der Emendation *that all the world besides methinks are (they're) dead* (Th.: *that all the world besides me thinks y'are dead*).

124

111

O, for my sake do *you* with Fortune chide,
The guilty goddess of my harmful deeds,
That did not better for my life provide
Than public means which public manners breeds.
Thence comes it that my name receives a brand,
And almost thence my nature is subdued
To what it works in, like the dyer's hand:
Pity me then and wish I were renew'd,
Whilst like a willing patient I will drink
Potions of eisel 'gainst my strong infection;
No bitterness that I will bitter think,
Nor double penance too[205] correct correction.
   Pity me then, dear friend, and I assure ye
   Even that your pity is enough to cure me.

112

Your love and pity doth the impression fill
Which vulgar scandal stamp'd upon my brow;
For what care I who calls me well or ill,
So you o'er-green my bad, my good allow?
You are my all-the-world, and I must strive
To know my shames and praises from your tongue;
None else to me, nor I to none alive,
That my steel'd sense or changes right or wrong.
In so profound abysm I throw all care
Of others' voices, that my adder's sense
To critique and to flattery[206] stopped are.
Mark how with my neglect I do dispense:
   You are so strongly in my purpose bred
   That all the world besides methinks are dead.

---

[205] Th.: *to* (siehe Anmerkungen).
[206] Th.: *To critic and to flatterer* (siehe Anmerkungen).

CXIII

En oculus, simulac te liqui, sola tuetur
Praeterita, et regimen deserit omne viae.
Parte puto caecum, nam visus sicubi iusti
Fert speciem, visu conficit inde nihil.
Tradit enim menti formae nihil ille receptae[207],
Sit volucris, sit flos, sitve figura viri;
E rapide oblatis aliquid mens prendere nescit,
Quaeque oculus prendit vix ea firma tenet.
Quodlibet aspiciat, perquam rude, perve decorum,
Distortum membris egregiumve genus;
Mons, mare, lux, nox sit, cornix aut candida penna,
Ille sibi in speciem mitigat omne tuam.
Te plena, accipiunt aliud nil corda, vetatque
Una fides aliam pectus habere fidem.

CXIV

An mihi plena ob te regali pectora fastu
Blanditias sitiunt, regibus acre malum?
Anne oculum dicam de visis vera referre,
Per magicen illi quam tuus addat amor,
Unde reformari monstra indigestaque rerum
Aetheria specie, consimilique tuae;
Sic oculum[208] promptum e pravis formosa creare
Omnia, sub radios eius ut omne cadit?
O reor est illud, visus blandissima fingit,
Blandaque regum instar mens animosa vorat;
Deinde, quod est oculo mentis bene nota voluptas,
Protinus ad mentis miscuit ille sitim.
Falsaque si miscet, minor eius culpa, quod ipse
Est avidus falsi, libat et omne prior.

---

[207] *Formae receptae* entspricht der Emendation *shape which it doth latch* (Th.: *lack*).
[208] Harrower schreibt *oculo*. Es handelt sich aber offenbar um einen immer noch von *anne dicam* in Vers 3 abhängigen a.c.i. mit *oculum promptum* („das bereitwillige Auge") als Subjekt.

113

Since I left you, mine eye is in my mind,
And that which governs me to go about
Doth part its[209] function and is partly blind,
Seems seeing, but effectually is out;
For it no form delivers to the heart
Of bird, of flower, or shape, which it doth latch;
Of its[210] quick objects hath the mind no part,
Nor his own vision holds what it doth catch;
For if it see the rud'st or gentlest sight,
The most sweet-favour'd[211] or deformedst creature,
The mountain or the sea, the day or night,
The crow or dove, it shapes them to your feature.
    Incapable of more, replete with you,
    My most true mind thus makes mine eye untrue[212].

114

Or whether doth my mind, being crown'd with you,
Drink up the monarch's plague, this flattery?
Or whether shall I say, mine eye saith true,
And that my love taught *him*[213] this alchemy,
To make of monsters and things indigest
Such cherubins as your sweet self resemble,
Creating every bad a perfect best,
As fast as objects to his beams assemble?
O, 't is the first, 't is flattery in my seeing,
And my great mind most kingly drinks it up:
Mine eye well knows what with his gust is 'greeing,
And to his palate doth prepare the cup.
    If it be poison'd, 't is the lesser sin
    That mine eye loves it and doth first begin.

---

[209] Th.: *his*.
[210] Ebenso (siehe Anmerkungen zu 114).
[211] Th: *sweet-favor* (siehe Anmerkungen).
[212] Th.: *maketh mine untrue* (siehe Anmerkungen).
[213] Th.: *your love taught it* (siehe Anmerkungen).

CXV

O penitus falsos mihi versus, posse negantes
Hoc fieri ut noster carior esset amor!
Nondum habui notum quare plenissima pridem
Postmodo lucidior flamma futura foret.
Et metui tempus: tot casibus inter amantes
repere, tot regum vertere iussa solet,
Os pulchrum violare, acres obtundere sensus,
Deprimere ad rerum fortia corda vices.
Temporis has metuens iras cur deinde vererer
Scribere 'non possis carior esse mihi'?
Certus in ambiguis rerum, praesentia laude
Dignor ego, incertus cetera quidne vehant.
Sed quod amor puer est errabat versus, adultum
Id memorans, crescit quod mihi quoque die.[214]

CXVI

Noluerim verum cordis cum corde fideli
Coniugia externas impediisse moras;
Non mutatur amor si quid mutabile rerum
Invenit ad fluxam fluxus et ipse fidem.
O amor est constans, amor est immotus ut iras
Despiciens ponti non tremefacta Pharos;
Est homini, quod stella incertis alta carinis,
Vis superans captum, suspicienda tamen.
Nil patitur per tempus amor, iuvenilia labra
Dum metit ac roseas falx ea curva genas.
Mensium et horarum brevitates negligit ille;
Dum pereant fato cuncta, fidelis amor.
Quae fuerint unquam si falsa, in meque probata,
Non ego sum vates, nullus amavit homo.

---

[214] Die beiden Schlussverse weichen in ihrer Aussage leicht ab von denjenigen Shakespeares (siehe Anmerkungen).

115

Those lines that I before have writ do lie,
Even those that said I could not love you dearer:
Yet then my judgement knew no reason why
My most full flame should afterwards burn clearer.
But reckoning Time, whose million'd accidents
Creep in 'twixt vows and change decrees of kings,
Tan sacred beauty, blunt the sharp'st intents,
Divert strong minds to the course of altering things –
Alas, why, fearing of Time's tyranny,
Might I not then say 'Now I love you best',
When I was certain o'er incertainty,
Crowning the present, doubting of the rest?
  Love is a babe; then might I not say so,
    To give full growth to that which still doth grow?

116

Let me not to the marriage of true minds
Admit impediments. Love is not love
Which alters when it alteration finds,
Or bends with the remover to remove:
O, no! it is an ever-fixed mark,
That looks on tempests and is never shaken;
It is the star to every wandering bark,
Whose worth is unknown, though his height be taken[215].
Love 's not Time's fool, though rosy lips and cheeks
Within his bending sickle's compass come;
Love alters not with his brief hours and weeks,
But bears it out even to the edge of doom.
  If this be error and upon me prov'd,
    I never writ, nor no man ever lov'd.

---

[215] Th.: *Whose worths unknowne, although his higth be taken.*

CXVII

Tu mihi des culpae tractatum parcius omne,
Gratia cum meritis esset habenda tuis;
In numeris siluisse tui vel nomen amoris,
Cui nova me iungunt vincula quoque die;
Auribus ignotis indultum, horaeque volanti
Iura tua, et magno iura redempta, dari.
Pandere me dicas vel ad omnes carbasa ventos,
Siqua tuo e visu longius aura ferat;
Nequitiam, peccata, severis scribe tabellis
Omnia, et ex iusta conice plura fide;
Omne supercilium coge in me frontis, amice,
At subitum teli dirigat ira nihil.
Actis testor eis illud me noscere velle,
An tuus et constans et pius esset amor.

CXVIII

Ut, gula si nobis est irritanda, palatum
Praestat amaritie sollicitare cibi;
Pellimus ut tectos purgando pectora morbos,
Effugiumque mali est anticipasse malum;
Sic tua dulcedo, nequeo sat cuius habere,
Me tamen ad victus asperiora movet.
Deliciis impletus eundum ad tristia duxi
Tempore, cum nondum talibus esset opus.
Sic in amore sagax illud, ventura pericla
Praecipere, in praesens sensimus ire nefas.
Ipsa salus cupiit commissa medentibus esse,
Aegra bonis, optans esse refecta malo.
Hinc didici verumque habeo[216]: quem morbus amandi
Te capit, huic omnis sumpta medela nocet.

---

[216] *Didici verumque habeo* („ich habe gelernt und halte für wahr") gibt im
Unterschied zum Thorpe-Text *(I learne and find…true)* den zeitlichen Ablauf
(Folge Perfekt-Praesens) korrekt wieder.

117

Accuse me thus: that I have scanted all
Wherein I should your great deserts repay;
Forgot upon your dearest love to call,
Whereto all bonds do tie me day by day;
That I have frequent been with unknown minds,
And given to Time your dear-purchased[217] right;
That I have hoisted sail to all the winds
Which should transport me farthest from your sight.
Book both my wilfulness and errors down,
And on just proof surmise accumulate;
Bring me within the level of your frown,
But shoot not at me in your waken'd hate;
   Since my appeal says I did strive to prove
   The constancy and virtue of your love.

118

Like as, to make our appetites more keen,
With eager compounds we our palate urge;
As, to prevent our maladies unseen,
We sicken to shun sickness when we purge,
Even so, being full of your ne'er-cloying sweetness,
To bitter sauces did I frame my feeding;
And, sick of welfare, found a kind of meetness
To be diseas'd ere that there was true needing.
Thus policy in love, to anticipate
The ills that were not, grew to faults assured,
And brought to medicine a healthful state
Which, rank of goodness, would by ill be cured.
   But thence I learn'd[218], and find the lesson true:
   Drugs poison him that so fell sick of you.

---

[217] Th.: *your owne deare purchas'd.*
[218] Th.: *learne* (siehe Fussnote 216).

CXIX

Philtra ego virgineis, o, quae stillantia ocellis
Sirenum saturis improbitate bibi!
Quas spes quosve metus inter miserabilis egi,
Victus, io, victor qua mihi visus eram!
Quam misere erravit fatuum mihi pectus, ibique
Se penitus felix, ut nihil ante, ratum;
Interdum mihi paene suis ex orbibus acta
Lumina, dum pectus distrahit ille furor.
O sed in adversis bona sunt, usuque docemur
Optima ab oppositis esse probata malis.
Nobilior surgit, maior, robustior ille
Rursum e relliquiis aedificatus amor.
Commonitus redeo sic ad meliora, lucratus
Per mala pro sumptu faenora terna meo.

CXX

Utile nunc habeo quod eras crudelior olim
Tu mihi, per nostrum qui cruciare nefas;
Illius et luctus memorem me flere necesse est,
Ni teneat sensus aes rigidusve chalybs.
Te mea nam si torsit, ut inclementia quondam
Me tua, degisti tu per amara dies;
Necdum ego crudelis ducta ratione pependi
Quid fuerim offensa passus et ipse tua.
Si modo, si nox illa animo sculpsisset in imo
Quam penitus feriat pectora vera dolor[219];
Quaeque mihi tuleras, eadem fomenta tulissem
Ipse tibi, ut laesum volnere pectus avet!
Iam tua subsidio venit inclementia; delet
Si mea nunc istam, deleat ista meam.

---

[219] Statt *pectora vera* müsste es eher *verus dolor (true sorrow)* heissen, was aber metrisch unmöglich wäre. Auch die Wortwiederholung *pectora – pectus* in den Versen 10 und 12 deutet auf einen an dieser Stelle noch nicht ganz ausgefeilten Text hin.

119

What potions have I drunk of Siren tears,
Distill'd from limbecks foul as hell within,
Applying fears to hopes and hopes to fears,
Still losing when I saw myself to win!
What wretched errors hath my heart committed,
Whilst it hath thought itself so blessed never!
How have mine eyes out of their spheres been fitted
In the distraction of this madding fever!
O benefit of ill! now I find true
That better is by evil still made better;
And ruin'd love, when it is built anew,
Grows fairer than at first, more strong, far greater.
　　So I return rebuk'd to my content,
　　And gain by ills thrice more than I have spent.

120

That you were once unkind befriends me now,
And for that sorrow which I then did feel
Needs must I under my transgression bow,
Unless my nerves were brass or hammer'd steel.
For if you were by my unkindness shaken,
As I by yours, you've pass'd a hell of time;
And I, a tyrant, have no leisure taken
To weigh how once I suffer'd in your crime.
O, that our night of woe might have remember'd
My deepest sense, how hard true sorrow hits,
And soon to you, as you to me then, tender'd
The humble salve which wounded bosoms fits!
　　But that your trespass now becomes a fee:
　　Mine ransoms yours, and yours must ransom me.

CXXI

Turpis ero potius quam falso turpis habebor,
Si sit idem meritis immeritisque probrum;
Iustaque depereat, non quae sentitur in actu
Gratia[220], verum alii quatenus acta vident.
Cur oculis quidam limis ut turpe salutet
Quod meus in iuveni sanguine ludit amor,
Nequitiaeve meae custodia nequior adsit,
In vitium id vertens quod reor esse bonum?
Non ita, me voluit quod sum natura, meosque
Qui petit errores denotat ipse suos.
Quae facimus recte si prave iudicat alter,
Propterea accipient actane nostra notam?
Non, nisi damnemus genus omne, et quisque putetur
Improbus, ac praestans improbitate regat.

CXXII

Intus corde meo tua restant dona, tabellae
Perpetuis scriptae mentis imaginibus;[221]
Quas humile id supra fastigium, et omnia supra
Saecla, vel aeternas, en, fore vaticinor.
Vel minimum dico: donec mortalibus ullis
Mens animusque uno foedere constiterint,
Nec quod habent ambo de te reddetur inani
Exitio, nunquam laus tua defuerit.
Ista tabellarum brevitas male ceperat illa
Omnia, amorque tuus non eget indiciis;
Ausus eas igitur fueram dimittere, teque
Capturis melius credere pectoribus.
Ad reminiscendum velle adiumenta tenere
Talia me potius proderet immemorem.

---

[220] Mit *iustaque depereat...gratia* übernimmt Barton fast wörtlich die Formulierung des Thorpe-Texts *and the just pleasure lost*. Statt des hier als Adjek-tiv eher fragwürdigen *just* könnte allerdings *just that pleasure...* gemeint sein.
[221] Dieses Gedicht ist eine der drei Elegien Bartons mit regelmässig vier- bis fünfsilbigen Pentameter-Endwörtern. *Imaginibus* findet sich schon als Endwort von Vers LIII,2.

121

'T is better to be vile than vile esteem'd,
When not to be receives reproach of being,
And just that pleasure 's lost[222] which is so deem'd
Not by our feeling, but by others' seeing.
For why should others' false adulterate eyes
Give salutation to my sportive blood?
Or on my frailties why are frailer spies,
Which in their wills count bad what I think good?
No, I am that I am, and they that level
At my abuses reckon up their own:
I may be straight though they themselves be bevel;
By their rank thoughts my deeds must not be shown;
   Unless – this general evil they maintain –
   All men are bad, and in their badness reign.

122

Thy gift, thy tables, are within my brain
Full character'd with lasting memory,
Which shall above that idle rank remain
Beyond all date even to eternity;
Or at the least, so long as brain and heart
Have faculty by Nature to subsist;
Till each to raz'd oblivion yield his part
Of thee, thy record never can be miss'd.
Their[223] poor retention could not so much hold,
Nor need I tallies thy dear love to score;
Therefore to give them from me was I bold -
To trust those tables that receive thee more.
   To keep an adjunct to remember thee
   Were to import forgetfulness in me.

---

[222] Th.: *And the just pleasure lost* (siehe Fussnote 220).
[223] Th.: *That* (*their* bezogen auf *thy tables* im Anfangsvers).

CXXIII

Non ita, mutato non me laetabere, tempus;
Quid nova pyramidum tu mihi monstra refers?
At mihi non nova sunt, non admiranda tuenti,
Hac specie antiquum dissimulatur opus.
Nostra dies brevis est, quodcunque vetustius ergo
Promis, id attonitus deveneratur homo;
Mavolt nempe suis illud natum esse cupitis,
Nec meminit fando talia nota diu.
Odi ego te fastosque tuos, praesentia fingant
Actave, mirandum nil mihi tale puto.
Falso scripta soles, falso conspecta referre,
Curta tibi aeterna, vel nimis aucta, fuga.
Hoc voveo steteritque: fidem me fallere nullam;
Tu licet, o tempus, cetera falce ruas.

CXXIV

Si mihi natus amor fulgenti forte fuisset,
Ille videretur turpe nothumque genus,
Temporis obsequio subiectum, temporis irae,
Hic in honore ut flos, hic velut alga nihil.
Non ita; ab his vicibus rerum procul ille creatus
Nil patitur quando pompa renidet opum;
Plebis obaeratae nullos ille excipit ictus,
Quo sceleris nostros tempora prona vocant.
Utilitas, leve nomen, ab illo nulla timetur,
Quae brevium horarum solvere pacta solet;
Solus enim in sese stat prudens, conscius ille
Nullius a nimio sole nec imbre metus.
Testificor miseros quos[224] fallax tempus adegit
Triste nefas ausos pro pietate mori.

---

[224] Harrower schreibt *quot.* In einer früheren Fassung (siehe Manuskript-seite
auf S. 208) lautet das Schlussdistichon:
vos mihi iam testes, lusit quos tempus, adeste /
qui male vixistis, laus quibus una, mori.

123

No, Time, thou shalt not boast that I do change:
Thy pyramids built up with newer might
To me are nothing novel, nothing strange;
They are but dressings of a former sight.
Our dates are brief, and therefore we admire
What thou dost foist upon us that is old,
And rather make them born to our desire
Than think that we before have heard them told.
Thy registers and thee I both defy,
Not wondering at the present nor the past,
For thy records and what we see doth lie,
Made more or less by thy continual haste.
    This I do vow and this shall ever be:
    I will be true, despite thy scythe and thee.

124

If my dear love were but the child of state,
It might for Fortune's bastard be unfather'd,
As subject to Time's love or to Time's hate,
Weeds among weeds, or flowers with flowers gather'd.
No, it was builded far from accident;
It suffers not in smiling pomp, nor falls
Under the blow of thralled discontent,
Whereto the inviting time or[225] fashion calls;
It fears not policy, that heretic,
Which works on leases of short-number'd hours,
But all alone stands ugly[226] politic,
That it nor grows with heat nor drowns with showers.
    To this I witness call the fools of Time,
    Which die for goodness, though[227] have liv'd for crime.

---

[225] Th.: *our.*
[226] Th.: *hugely.*
[227] Th.: *who.*

CXXV

Referretne mea, qualis mihi gratia gestus,
Corporis egregii significatus honos?
Illave in aeternum fundamina iacta putarem,
Quae, citius quam vis eruat, ipsa cadunt?
Non video forma captum sua vota superque
Destruere, obsequii ni sciat esse modum?
Blanda ferens gustu pro simplice fallitur ipse,
Ut cupide spectet nactus inane lucrum.
Non ita, at[228] obsequium tu nostrum corde prehendas:
Paupera, sed pura mente pieque, fero;
Artis in oblato nihil est panisve secundi[229],
Sed paria acceptis reddita, meque tibi.
Hinc mendax delator abi, tua crimina veris
Pectoribus minimum maxima quaeque nocent.

CXXVI

O formose puer, qui dedita temporis arma,
Falcem horasque, tua sub dicione tenes;
Qui, quot eunt anni, florentior ipse, tuorum
Ora pari monstras consenuisse gradu:
Si natura, potens regere aut impellere fata,
Te retrahit, porro ne properere viae,
Hoc agit ut sollers illudat tempus agendo,
Tuque sibi horarum taedia longa neces.
O metuas illam, servate libidinis ergo!
Nec quod habet cari scit retinere diu.
Tandem erit illius ratio reddenda, ratamque
Te quoque dedendo fecerit esse, puer.

---

[228] Harrower schreibt *et* (vgl. auch Manuskriptseite auf S. 228).
[229] *Panis secundus* sagt Horaz von einem Brot geringerer Qualität; *seconds* bei
Shakespeare bedeutet minderwertige Ware. In einer früheren Fassung
Bartons, siehe Manuskript S. 228, lauten die Verse 11/12:
Non vili de pane fero, non arte parata /
me tibi, me donis pro tot, amice, tuis.

125

Were't aught to me I bore the canopy,
With my extern thy[230] outward honouring,
Or laid great bases for eternity,
Which prove more short than waste or ruining?
Have I not seen dwellers on form and savour
Lose all, and more, by paying too much rent,
For compound sweet forgoing simple favour[231],
Pitiful thrivers, in their gazing spent?
No, let me be obsequious to[232] thy heart,
And take thou my oblation, poor but free,
Which is not mix'd with seconds, knows no art,
But mutual render, only me for thee.
    Hence, thou suborn'd informer! a true soul
    When most impeach'd stands least in thy control.

126

O thou, my lovely boy, who in thy power
Dost hold Time's sickle, glass, and fickle hour;[233]
Thou[234] hast by waning grown, and therein show'st
Thy lover's withering as thy sweet self grow'st;
If Nature, sovereign mistress over wrack,
As thou goest onwards, still will pluck thee back,
She keeps thee to this purpose, that her skill
May Time disgrace and wretched minutes kill.
Yet fear her, O thou minion of her pleasure!
She may detain but not still keep her treasure:
    Her audit, though delay'd, answer'd must be,
    And her quietus is to render thee.

---

[230] Th.: *the.*
[231] Th.: *savour,* umgekehrt *favour* in Zeile 5 (siehe Anmerkungen).
[232] Th.: *in.*
[233] Th.: *times fickle glasse, his sickle, hower* (siehe Anmerkungen).
[234] Th.: *Who.*

CXXVII

Si veteres inter nigri fuit ulla coloris
Gratia, pulchrarum non fuit ille color;
Iam niveae nigrum formae supponitur heres,
Illius infame est vile nothumque decus.
Nunc, ubi naturae sibi ius manus arrogat omnis,
Ac speciem obscaenis allinit arte genis,
Candida nomen habent nullum, nil sedis honestae,
Nec nisi fucatis ullus habetur honos.
Ipsa superciliis oculisque est Cynthia[235] nigris,
Utraque sed luctum significare reor:
Luget eas, nulla naturae dote venustas,
Quae genuina audent assimulare dolo.
Isque decet sic luctus eam, fateamur ut omnes
Virginea in specie pulchrius esse nihil.

CXXVIII

Ut numeros pulsas dulces, o dulcior ipsa,
Lignaque sub digitis buxea mota sonant,
Ac regis in liquidum concordia fila canorem
Attonitaeque aures obstupuere meae,
Invidia moveor cernens salientia ligna
Ista tibi in teneras oscula ferre manus,
Dum mihi labra, quibus messis fuit ista metenda,
Ausum ad nequitiae tale pudica rubent.
Delicias ob eas mutare libentius optent
Ipsa suum buxu cum saliente locum,
Quam digiti motu lustrant labente, beantque
Mortua ligna, at non vivida labra viri.

---

[235] *Cynthia* heisst die Geliebte in den Elegien des Properz. Die *supercilia nigra* (schwarze Augenbrauen) entsprechen einer Konjektur von Staunton und Brae; bei Thorpe ist nur von schwarzen Augen die Rede.

Improbitas quoniam sic floret, ad oscula lignis
Cede manum[236], at labris, o, tua labra meis!

127

In the old age black was not counted fair,
Or if it were, it bore not beauty's name;
But now is black beauty's successive heir,
And beauty slander'd with a bastard shame:
For since each hand hath put on Nature's power,
Fairing the foul with art's false borrow'd face,
Sweet beauty hath no name, no holy bower,
But is profan'd, if not lives in disgrace.
Therefore my mistress' eyes are raven black,
Her eyes so suited, and they mourners seem
At such who, not born fair, no beauty lack,
Slandering creation with a false esteem.
  Yet so they mourn, becoming of their woe,
  That every tongue says beauty should look so.

128

How oft, when thou, my music, music play'st,
Upon that blessed wood whose motion sounds
With thy sweet fingers, when thou gently sway'st
The wiry concord that mine ear confounds,
Do I envy those jacks that nimble leap
To kiss the tender inward of thy hand,
Whilst my poor lips, which should that harvest reap,
At the wood's boldness by thee blushing stand!
To be so tickled, they would change their state
And situation with those dancing chips,
O'er whom thy fingers walk with gentle gait,
Making dead wood more blest than living lips.
  Since saucy jacks so happy are in this,
  Give them thy fingers, me thy lips to kiss.

---

[236] Über die typische Verwechslung von *their* und *thy* in den Versen 11 und
14 des Thorpe-Textes geht Barton hinweg, indem er *digiti* und *manum* ohne
Possessivpronomina schreibt.

CXXIX

Corporis ac mentis vires in foeda profusas
Prodit in actu illud quod vocitatur amor,
Volvit adusque actum periuria, crimina, caedes,
Trux, ferus, immanis, saevus, egensque fide;
Contemptum satias affert. Insanius idem
Appetitur, donec copia facta rei;
Insano tunc est odio, velut esca vorata
Cum posita in furias illa vorantis erat.
Nam furit in nactis, furit in venantibus ille,
Olim, hodie, posthac, immoderatus amor;
Cuilibet utenti felix, tristissimus uso[237],
Pollicitus prae se gaudia, postque nihil.
Scitque ea dum quivis, caelum vitare, venitur
Per quod in hunc Erebum, scit bene nullus homo.

CXXX

Non oculis aequat, fateor, mea Cynthia solem,
Curaliis impar eius in ore rubor;
Pectora prae nivibus prope dixi gilva, comaeque
Si sunt fila, eius fert nigra fila caput;
Est rosa diversis lita guttis, alba rubensque,
Quae rosa non nota est eius in ore mihi;
Est quibus unguentis fragrantius effluit aura
Quam mihi dilectae virginis ulla venit;
Eius amo voces audire, idemque sonare
Dulcius agnosco fila canora lyrae;
Divas, confiteor, spectavi nullus euntes,
Cynthia enim plantis ambulat, itque solo;
Atque Iovem testor, virgo non rarior ulla est
Vatis imaginibus ludificata novis.

---

[237] Die Gegenüberstellung *utenti – uso* entspricht derjenigen von *in proof* und *proved* (Th.: *proud*).

129

The expense of spirit in a waste of shame
Is lust in action; and till action, lust
Is perjur'd, murderous, bloody, full of blame,
Savage, extreme, rude, cruel, not to trust;
Enjoy'd no sooner but despised straight;
Past reason hunted, and no sooner had,
Past reason hated, as a swallow'd bait
On purpose laid to make the taker mad:
Mad in pursuit and in possession so;
Had, having, and in quest to have, extreme;
A bliss in proof, and prov'd, a very woe;
Before, a joy propos'd; behind, a dream.
    All this the world well knows; yet none knows well
    To shun the heaven that leads men to this hell.

130

My mistress' eyes are nothing like the sun;
Coral is far more red than her lips' red:
If snow be white, nay[238], then her breasts are dun;
If hairs be wires, black wires grow on her head.
I have seen roses damask'd, red and white,
But no such roses see I in her cheeks;
And in some perfumes there is[239] more delight
Than in the breath that from my mistress reeks.
I love to hear her speak, yet well I know
That music hath a far more pleasing sound;
I grant I never saw a goddess go:
My mistress, when she walks, treads on the ground.
    And yet, by Heaven, I think my love as rare
    As any she belied with false compare.

---

[238] Th.: *why.*
[239] Th.: *is there.*

CXXXI

Talis es, atque in me pariter dominata puellis
Quas facit immites omnis in ore venus;
Nam fatuo huic cordi tamen es pulcherrima rerum,
Unaque per terram, scis bene, gemma mihi.
Atque fide vera spectans non nemo negavit
Esse tibi in voltu quo caperetur amor;
Quos ego deceptos verear si dicere, semper
Id mihi iuratum est interiore sinu.
Sensaque firmantes animi, simul ora recordor
Ista tua, en, gemitus intima cordis agunt,
Post alios alii testantes candida cuncta
Iudice me nigris esse secunda tuis.
Praecipue vero factis es nigra, malusque
De facie rumor nascitur inde, puto.

CXXXII

Cynthia, totus amo tua lumina, meque vicissim
Conscia quam crucies illa dolere reor;
Sunt ideo pullata, suum testantia luctum,
Pulchroque intuitu commiserata meum.
Et fateor, nunquam lux matutina videtur
Eoi in glaucis tam speciosa genis,
Nec vespertinas inducens Hesperus umbras
Enitet, occidui gloria tanta poli,
Quam tua pullatis facies ornatur ocellis;
O animum pariter fac decus ornet idem.
Ex animo miserere, rei si gratia tanta est,
Omnibus ut pietas partibus una regat.
Fuscam ego tum Venerem iurabo, interque venustas
Non recipi, desit cui tuus iste color.

131

Thou art as tyrannous, so as thou art,
As those whose beauties proudly make them cruel;
For well thou know'st to my dear doting heart
Thou art the fairest and most precious jewel.
Yet in good faith some say that thee behold
Thy face hath not the power to make love groan:
To say they err I dare not be so bold,
Although I swear it to myself alone.
And to be sure that is not false I swear,
A thousand groans, but thinking on thy face,
One on another's neck, do witness bear:
Thy black is fairest in my judgement's place.
    In nothing art thou black save in thy deeds,
    And thence this slander, as I think, proceeds.

132

Thine eyes I love, and they, as pitying me,
Knowing thy heart torments me with disdain,
Have put on black and loving mourners be,
Looking with pretty ruth upon my pain.
And truly not the morning sun of heaven
Better becomes the grey cheeks of the east,
Nor that full star that ushers in the even
Doth half that glory to the sombre[240] west,
As those two mourning eyes become thy face:
O, let it then as well beseem thy heart
To mourn for me, since mourning doth thee grace,
And suits[241] thy pity like in every part.
    Then will I swear Beauty herself is black
    And all they foul that thy complexion lack.

---

[240] Th.: *sober* (siehe Anmerkungen).
[241] Th: *sute.*

CXXXIII

Vae tibi, vexanti per eandem, femina, plagam
Volneris infandi meque meumque simul!
Mene habeas lacerare parum, meus unus amicus
Eiusdem subeat servitiine iugum?
Me rapuisti a me pridem crudelis ocellis,
Et geminum iam me vel mage saeva rapis;
Orbus eo, te, meque vagor, perpessus in uno
Tergeminum poenae suppliciique genus.
Ferrea, corde tuo me clausum semper habeto,
Si meus accepto me vade^{242} liber eat;
Me teneat quivis, illum mihi cede tuendum,
Sic minor in me sit carceris iste rigor.
Nec fueris non dura, isto nam pectore clausi
Cogimur imperiis ipse meusque tuis.

CXXXIV

Confiteor demum tuus est; tuus ille, puella, est;
Magna meam firmant pignora namque fidem;
Sed tradar tamen ipse, mihi si cesseris illum,
Me geminum, ac vitae spemque decusque meae.
At renues, nec se vinclis ita liberat ille;
Tu nimis es furax, ac nimis ille bonus:
Scriptum aliquod tulerat sponsor quasi noster, eumque
Continuo quae me firma catena tenet.
Iusque venustarum quodcunque est, uteris omni,
O nimium sollers vertere quidque lucro.
A vade tu nostro ius exigis; orbor et illo,
Hei mihi, sic eius turpiter usus ope.
Nosque tenes ambos, illo namque omne volente
Solvere pro binis, non ego liber eo.

---

^{242} *accepto me vade* („wobei ich Bürgschaft leiste") entspricht der Emendation
let my poor heart bail (Th.: *bale*).
146

133

Beshrew that heart that makes my heart to groan
For that deep wound it gives my friend and me!
Is 't not enough to torture me alone,
But slave to slavery my sweet'st friend must be?
Me from myself thy cruel eye hath taken,
And my next self thou harder hast engross'd;
Of him, myself, and thee, I am forsaken:
A torment thrice threefold thus to be cross'd.
Prison my heart in thy steel bosoms ward,
But then my friend's heart let my poor heart bail;
Whoe'er keeps him[243], let my heart be his guard;
Thou canst not then use rigour in my jail.
   And yet thou wilt; for I, being pent in thee,
   Perforce am thine, and all that is in me.

134

So, now I have confess'd that he is thine
And I myself am mortgag'd to thy will,
Myself I'll forfeit, so that other mine
Thou wilt restore, to be my comfort still:
But thou wilt not, nor he will not be free,
For thou art covetous and he is kind;
He learn'd but surety-like to write for me,
Under that bond that him as fast doth bind.
The statute of thy beauty thou wilt take,
Thou usurer, that put'st forth all to use,
And sue a friend 'come[244] debtor for my sake;
So him I lose through my unkind abuse.
   Him have I lost; thou hast both him and me:
   He pays the whole, and yet am I not free.

---

[243] Th.: *me.*
[244] Th.: *came.* (*'come* für *become.*)

CXXXV

Quod cupiunt aliae, tu felix ipsa potiris,
Quippe duos uno nomine nacta viros![245]
Me sentis superesse, velutque incommodus adsum
Delicias optans amplificare tuas.
Tunc igitur, virgo, tam multis larga placensque,
Tu mihi non unam morigerere vicem?
Quodne alii cupiunt gratum fatearis id esse,
Sitque cupidinibus gratia nulla meis?
Pontus plenus aquis imbres capit, ille repletus
Immensis opibus, plus tamen addit opum;
Et tibi, si placeat tot amoribus addere nostrum,
Copia amatorum maxima maior erit.
Crede tuos unum – dum pars unius habebor – ,
Nullius at iustas reice dura preces.

CXXXVI

Si, prope quod veni, mussant, tua pectora caeca
Corripe, meque tuum finge fuisse virum.
Ille quidem, agnoscunt, recipi consuevit eodem;
O facias igitur quod meus orat amor.
Sic tua vota Venus felix impleverit, opto,
Plurimaque immiscens, inter et illa meum.
Grandis ubi numerus, sententia cuique probatur,
'Unus homo in turba vix numerandus erit.'
Tuque meum in multis patiare latescere nomen,
Non nihilum dum me vis retinere loci.
Me nihilum credas, nihili si voce notatur
Quod fieri exoptat dulce, puella, tibi.
Denique me sat ames si nomen amaveris ipsum,
Nam penitus quod eo significatur amas.[246]

---

[245] Anstelle von Shakespeares Wortspiel mit *Will* spricht Barton von zwei gleichnamigen Liebhabern der Cynthia.

[246] Mit dem letzten Distichon scheint Barton doch noch auf die obszöne Nebenbedeutung von Shakespeares Namen *Will (si nomen amaveris)* anzuspielen: *penitus* (ganz und gar, tief eindringend) klingt an *penis* an.

135

Whoever hath her wish, thou hast thy will,
And 'Will' to boot, and 'Will' in overplus;
More than enough am I that vex thee still,
To thy sweet will making addition thus.
Wilt thou, whose will is large and spacious,
Not once vouchsafe to hide my will in thine?
Shall will in others seem right gracious,
And in my will no fair acceptance shine?
The sea, all water, yet receives rain still
And in abundance addeth to his store;
So thou, being rich in will, add to thy will
One will of mine, to make thy large will more.
    Let no unkind 'No' fair beseechers kill;
    Think all but one, and me in that one 'Will'.

136

If thy soul check thee that I come so near,
Swear to thy blind soul that I was thy 'Will',
And will, thy soul knows, is admitted there;
Thus far for love my love-suit, sweet, fulfil.
Will will fulfil the treasure of thy love,
Ay, fill it full with wills, and my will one.
In things of great receipt with ease we prove
Among a number one is reckon'd none:
Then in the number let me pass untold,
Though in thy store's account I one must be;
For nothing hold me, though[247] it please thee, hold
That nothing me a something sweet to thee.
    Make but my name thy love, and love that still,
    And then thou lov'st me, for my name is 'Will'.

---

[247] Th.: *so.*

CXXXVII

Heu, quid in his oculis egisti, o caece Cupido,
Unde videre, at non noscere visa queunt?
Quid sit forma decens, et ubi, discernere callent,
Par tamen in pravis cernitur inque bonis.
Si specie blanda capto mihi devenit illum
Cymba sinum, qua iam navigat omnis homo,
Cur oculorum error velut hamo traxit adunco
Non minus et mentem iudiciumque meum?
Mens mea cur, inquam, quod apertum repperit orbi
Hospitium, id septo censeat esse loco?
Curve oculus spectans id dissimulaverit omne,
Detur ut impuris gratia ficta genis?
O procul a veris oculus pectusque vagati
Servitio falsae se dare pestis amant.

CXXXVIII

Veriloquam sese iurat dum Cynthia, falsam
Qui scio iuranti credere nempe volo,
Scilicet ut puerum credat facilemque regenti
Me sibi, et in fictis artibus illa rudem.
Sic puerum fingens ab ea me virgine credi,
Quae vegetos mihi iam sentit iisse dies,
Ipse quoque accipio falsae periuria linguae
Virginis, ac verum sentit uterque premi.
At[248] negat iniustam sese cur illa? Vicissim
Cur ego diffiteor dissimuloque senem?
O in amore bonum est species fidentis, et annos
Dinumerat nemo sponte senilis amans.
Sic ego cum domina fingo, mecum illa, suisque
Amborum vitiis ficta levamen habent.

---

[248] Harrower schreibt *et*. Eher dürfte das dem adversativen *but* Shakespeares entsprechende *at* gemeint sein.

137

Thou blind fool, Love, what dost thou to mine eyes,
That they behold, and see not what they see?
They know what beauty is, see where it lies,
Yet what the best is take the worst to be.
If eyes corrupt by over-partial looks
Be anchor'd in the bay where all men ride,
Why of eyes' falsehood hast thou forged hooks,
Whereto the judgement of my heart is tied?
Why should my heart think that a several plot
Which my heart knows the wide world's common place?
Or mine eyes seeing this, say this is not,
To put fair truth upon so foul a face?
    In things right true my heart and eyes have err'd,
    And to this false plague are they now transferr'd.

138

When my love swears that she is made of truth
I do believe her, though I know she lies,
That she might think me some untutor'd youth,
Unlearned in the world's false subtleties.
Thus vainly thinking that she thinks me young,
Although she knows my days are past the best,
Simply I credit her false-speaking tongue:
On both sides thus is simple truth suppress'd.
But wherefore says she not she is unjust?
And wherefore say not I that I am old?
O, love's best habit is in seeming trust,
And age in love loves not to have years told.
    Therefore I lie with her and she with me,
    And in our faults by lies we flatter'd be.

CXXXIX

O meritum noli[249] fari, me teste vocato,
Hoc iniustitiae quo mea corda premis.
Non oculo at lingua tua volnera dirige, virgo,
Usaque vi iusta parce necare dolo.
Sive 'alibi' causaris 'amo', me, cara, vidente
Non alium versus lumina flecte virum;
Ut ferias tune artis eges cum viribus istis,
Sistere quas contra vis mea pressa nequit?
Est ita te purgare: suis confixus ocellis
Ut misere fuerim Cynthia nostra videt;
Inde meo par hoc hostile avertit ab ore,
Iniciant aliis ut sua tela viris.
Sed nunquam facias, at ocellis paene peremptum
Conficias totum, meque dolore leves.

CXL

Sis sapiens, crudelis ut es, nolisque[250] superbe
Imposita haec linguae rumpere frena meae;
Inveniam ne verba miser, testantia quantus
Me cruciet, dum tu nil miserare, dolor.
Te sapere an doceam, virgo? si forsan amare
Non potes, at prudens fingere, cara, fuit.
Difficiles aegri quando mors imminet ipsa
A medici capiunt omnia laeta labro.
In furias agerer spe dempta, interque furorem
Fors reperirem in te posse maligna loqui.
Invida res vita est, et iniqua loquentibus aures
Invidiosorum mox habuere fidem.
Quod mihi ne fiat, nec tu violeris, ocellos
Contineas istos, sis vaga corde licet.

---

[249] Harrower schreibt *nolis*.

[250] Hier dürfte tatsächlich der Konjunktiv *nolis* gemeint sein – eine mil-dere Nüance des Verbots als mit dem Imperativ *noli*. Ein ähnlicher Unter-schied scheint bei Shakespeare zwischen dem strikten *call not, wound me not* in Sonett 139 und der Konstruktion mit Hilfsverb *do not press* in Sonett 140 zu bestehen.

139

O, call not me to justify the wrong
That thy unkindness lays upon my heart;
Wound me not with thine eye but with thy tongue;
Use power with power and slay me not by art.
Tell me thou lov'st elsewhere; but in my sight,
Dear heart, forbear to glance thine eyes[251] aside:
What need'st thou wound with cunning when thy might
Is more than my o'er-press'd defence can bide?
Let me excuse thee: ah! my love well knows
Her pretty looks have been mine enemies,
And therefore from my face she turns my foes,
That they elsewhere might dart their injuries:
    Yet do not so; but since I am near slain,
    Kill me outright with looks and rid my pain.

140

Be wise as thou art cruel; do not press
My tongue-tied patience with too much disdain;
Lest sorrow lend me words and words express
The manner of my pity-wanting pain.
If I might teach thee wit, better it were,
Though not to love, yet, love, to tell me so;
As testy sick men, when their deaths be near,
No news but health from their physicians know.
For if I should despair, I should grow mad,
And in my madness might speak ill of thee:
Now this ill-wresting world is grown so bad,
Mad slanderers by mad ears believed be.
    That I may not be so, nor thou belied,
    Bear thine eyes straight, though thy proud heart go wide.

---

[251] Th.: *eye* (siehe Anmerkungen).

CXLI

Certe non oculis te, Cynthia, ductus amavi:
Dispiciunt formae tot vitiosa tuae;
Sed mihi pectus amat visum offendentia, pectus
Nil oculis curans quid videatur amat.
Non capit has aures tua vox, nec corporis ullus
Sensus avet tecum quod sibi dulce frui;
Nulla mihi naris siqua est, aut siqua palati
Gratia, nec cupide tangere promptus amor;
Sed fatuum hoc pectus tibi ne deserviat, illud
Mens mea nec sensus quinque vetare valent.[252]
Quippe viri imperium linquit, fastidia demum
Ut tua pertoleret femineumque iugum.
Hoc tamen et noxae in tantum prodesse videtur:
Quod mihi quae suadet, vindicat illa, nefas.

CXLII

Crimen amare meum est; tua virtus crimen amandi
Odit, ais, metuens ut sit honestus amor.
O misera, amborum vitas inquirere si vis,
Facta cito invenies irreprehensa meae.
Sin aliter, vix sint istis carpenda labellis,
Purpureus quorum non sine labe rubor;
Quae pepigere meis haud rarius improba furta,
Iuraque legitimis surripuere toris.
Tu iuvenes ut amas, mihi ius te detur amandi;
Si petis hos oculis, et mihi fas sit idem.
Fac pietas in te radicem agat, auctaque cum sit,
Tunc alios miserans tale merere queas.
Vaticinor: quae danda negas si poscis habenda,
Sit tibi ab exemplo nata repulsa tuo.

---

[252] Eigentlich müsste es heissen *nec mens mea nec sensus quinque vetare valent* („weder mein Verstand noch meine fünf Sinne können verhindern...“); die Weglassung des ersten *nec* in Bartons Text entspricht der wahrschein-lich fehlerhaft verkürzten Ausdrucksweise im Thorpe-Text *but my five wits nor my five senses can ...*

141

In faith, I do not love thee with mine eyes,
For they in thee a thousand errors note;
But 't is my heart that loves what they despise,
Who in despite of view is pleas'd to dote;
Nor are mine ears with thy tongue's tune delighted;
Nor tender feeling to base touches prone,
Nor taste, nor smell, desire to be invited
To any sensual feast with thee alone:
Nor[253] my five wits nor my five senses can
Dissuade one foolish heart from serving thee,
Who leaves unsway'd the likeness of a man,
Thy proud heart's slave and vassal wretch to be.
　　Only my plague thus far I count my gain:
　　That she that makes me sin awards me pain.

142

Love is my sin, and thy dear virtue hate,
Hate of my sin, grounded on sinful loving:
O, but with mine compare thou thine own state,
And thou shalt find I merit[254] not reproving;
Or, if I[255] do, not from those lips of thine,
That have profan'd their scarlet ornaments,
And seal'd false bonds of love as oft as mine,
Robb'd others' beds' revenues of their rents.
Be it lawful I love thee, as thou lov'st those
Whom thine eyes woo as mine importune thee:
Root pity in thy heart, that when it grows,
Thy pity may deserve to pitied be.
　　If thou dost seek to have what thou dost hide,
　　By self-example mayst thou be denied!

---

[253] Th.: *But* (siehe Fussnote 252).
[254] Th.: *it merrits* (siehe Anmerkungen).
[255] Th.: *it* (siehe Anmerkungen).

CXLIII

Villica siquando servandis sedula rebus
Volt capere elapsam claustra cohortis avem,
E gremio infantem deponit, nilque morata
Id sequitur solum quod revocasse cupit.
Parvulus interea desertus tentat et illam
Pone sequi, implorans voce manuque moras.
Mater, avem sectata fugas ante ora petentem
Assidue, nescit quid fleat ille miser.
Persequeris sic tu, virgo, quod te fugit usque;
Teque, infans veluti, sic ego pone sequor.
Si capies tua vota, mihi te redde, vicemque
Matris agens, labris imprime labra meis.
Sic habeas quod aves[256], ad me si currere retro
Vagitusque meos sistere blanda velis.

CXLIV

Binus amor variis animum solatur et angit
Imperiis, vitae numen et ira meae;
Hic meliora monet, vir casto candidus ore;
Furva est virgineis vox malesuada genis.
Quoque magis peream, traxit mihi numen amicum
A latere[257] illecebris ira maligna suis;
Scilicet in furiam sanctum mihi vertere numen
Volt, et in obscaenum sollicitare nefas.
In furiamne abeat de numine, multa vereri
Hoc super est, necdum cernere vera queo;
Quod tamen ambo absunt, ac se sunt inter amici,
Caelum in Tartareos suspicor isse locos.
Nec sciero verum, donec mihi sanctius illud
Ex animo flammis invida pestis aget.

---

[256] *quod aves* („was du begehrst") ist der Vogel *(avis)*, dem die Mutter nach-
läuft – offenbar eine Nachahmung des Shakespeare'schen Wortspiels im
gleichen Vers 13 *thou mayst have thy Will.*
[257] *(mihi) a latere* entspricht der Emendation *from my side* (Th.: *from my sight*). In
mehreren früheren Fassungen schreibt Barton *ab latere.*

143

Lo! as a careful huswife runs to catch
One of her feather'd creatures broke away,
Sets down her babe, and makes all swift dispatch
In pursuit of the thing she would have stay;
Whilst her neglected child holds her in chase,
And cries to her[258] whose busy care is bent
To follow that which flies before her face,
Not prizing her poor infant's discontent:
So runn'st thou after that which flees[259] from thee,
Whilst I, thy babe, chase thee afar behind;
But if thou catch thy hope, turn back to me,
And play the mother's part, kiss me, be kind.
   So will I pray that thou mayst have thy *Will*,
   If thou turn back, and my loud crying still.

144

Two loves I have, of comfort and despair,
Which like two spirits do suggest me still:
The better angel is a man right fair,
The worser spirit a woman colour'd ill.
To win me soon to hell, my female evil
Tempteth my better angel from my side,
And would corrupt my saint to be a devil,
Wooing his purity with her foul pride.
And whether that my angel be turn'd fiend
Suspect I may, yet not directly tell;
But being both from me, both to each friend,
I guess one angel in another's hell:
   Yet this shall I ne'er know, but live in doubt,
   Till my bad angel fire my good one out.

---

[258] Th.: *Cries to catch her.*
[259] Th.: *flies.*

CXLV

Labra manu ipsius formata cupidinis 'odi'
Sunt mihi, vel similem, reddere visa sonum.
Id penitus movit me, virginis eius amantem,
Ni simulac sensit me miserata foret.
Increpuit linguam, cui munus amabile, dixit,
Blanda etiam spretis reddere verba procis.
Alloquiis uti melioribus inde docetur,
Ac nova post 'odi' clausula iussa sequi;
Et sequitur, qualis noctem lux candida nigram,
Quando Erebum caelo pestis abacta volat.
Optima virgo 'odi' sensu purgarat amaro
'Non te' subiciens, quae mihi verba salus.[260]

CXLVI

O anima infelix, terrenis insita membris,
Serva sub induti corporis imperio,[261]
Cur mihi, dum langues intus tam pauper inopsque,
Extera sic fucis haec tua praeniteant?
Cur adeo impensam brevis incola ponis in ista
Tecta, per internam putria perniciem?
An nimium hoc sumptus, ut linquas omne vorandum
Vermibus? hanc finem corpus ut inveniat?
O anima, ut vivas, utare malignius ipso
Corpore, sis servi dives ab esurie.
Horas vende breves annos emptura deorum;
His satura, externas neglige delicias.
Mors hominum victrix ita vincitur; illaque victa
Si sit, habes vitam vivere perpetuam.

---

[260] Wie die Elegie CXXVI enthält dieses Gedicht nur sechs statt sieben
Distichen – hier entsprechend den nur vier- (statt fünf-)hebigen Versen des
Sonetts 145.
[261] Die ungewöhnlichen Pentameterschlüsse mit viersilbigen Wörtern
(wie in den Elegien LXIV und CXXII) sind hier vielleicht durch den
im Thorpe-Text sechs- statt fünfhebigen Vers 2 angeregt.

145

Those lips that Love's own hand did make
Breath'd forth the sound that said "I hate"
To me that languish'd for her sake;
But when she saw my woeful state,
Straight in her heart did mercy come,
Chiding that tongue that ever sweet
Was us'd in giving gentle doom,
And taught it thus anew to greet;
'I hate' she alter'd with an end,
That follow'd it as gentle day
Doth follow night, who like a fiend
From heaven to hell is flown away;
  'I hate' from hate away she flew[262],
  And sav'd my life, saying 'not you.'

146

Poor soul, the centre of my sinful earth,
My sinful earth, these rebel powers' array,[263]
Why dost thou pine within and suffer dearth,
Painting thy outward walls so costly gay?
Why cost so large[264], having so short a lease,
Dost thou upon thy fading mansion spend?
Shall worms, inheritors of this excess,
Eat up thy charge? This is thy body's end![265]
Then, soul, live thou upon thy servant's loss,
And let him[266] pine to aggravate thy store,
Buy terms divine in selling hours of dross;
Within be fed, without be rich no more.
  So shalt thou feed on Death, that feeds on men -
  And Death once dead, there's no more dying then.

---

[262] Th.: *threw.*
[263] Th.: *My sinfull earth these rebbell powres that thee array.*
[264] Th.: *Why so large cost.*
[265] Th.: *Is this thy body's end?*
[266] Th.: *that.*

CXLVII

Febris amor meus est, adeo desiderat ille
Cuncta quibus possit perpetuare malum;
Semper uterque etenim vel nutrimenta doloris
Appetit, incertae si placuere gulae.
Nam ratio, tantis in amoribus una medela[267],
Consilia indignans me data nulla sequi,
Cessit, et agnosco letale cupidinis omen
Esse, medelarum reicientis opem.
Sic ratio victa est, nec restat cura salutis
Ulla, sed huc illuc irrequietus agor;
Ac velut insani mea sensa ac verba vagantur
Longius a veris, ut sine mente sonus;
Nam mihi nonnunquam tu visa es dictaque, virgo,
Candida, quae tanquam Nox Erebusque nigras.

CXLVIII

Hei mihi, cum vero quam discordantia visu
Huic capiti inseruit lumina saevus amor!
Sive aliter, quonam sententia mentis aberrat
Falsa notans ea quae verius illa vident?
Si facies oculos mihi vere candida cepit,
Esse aliter volgus quo mihi iure putat?
Si specie fallebar, amor demonstrat aperte
Non sibi sed volgo noscere vera dari.
Quo potuit pacto? quid veri dispicit ille
Qui miser in lacrimis pervigilavit amans?
Haud igitur mirum, species me siqua fefellit;
Nubila dum purget sol videt ipse nihil.
Lumina, amor, lacrima mihi caecas, improbe, multa,
Ne videant clare quam tua falsa fides.

---

[267] Shakespeare vergleicht die hier als das einzige Heilmittel *(una medela)* der Liebe erklärte Vernunft *(reason, ratio)* mit einem Arzt *(physician,* Th.: *phisition).*

147

My love is as a fever, longing still
For that which longer nurseth the disease;
Feeding on that which doth preserve the ill,
The uncertain sickly appetite to please.
My reason, the physician to my love,
Angry that his prescriptions are not kept,
Hath left me, and I desperate now approve
Desire is death, which physic did except.
Past cure I am, now reason is past care,
And frantic-mad with evermore unrest;
My thoughts and my discourse as madmen's are,
At random from the truth vainly express'd:
  For I have sworn thee fair, and thought thee bright,
  Who art as black as hell, as dark as night.

148

O me, what eyes hath Love put in my head,
Which have no correspondence with true sight!
Or, if they have, where is my judgement fled,
That censures falsely what they see aright?
If that be fair whereon my false eyes dote,
What means the world to say it is not so?
If it be not, then Love doth well denote
Love's eye is *not* true – as all men do know[268].
How can it? O, how can Love's eye be true,
That is so vex'd with watching and with tears?
No marvel then though I mistake my view:
The sun itself sees not till heaven clears.
  O cunning Love! with tears thou keep'st me blind,
  Lest eyes well-seeing thy foul faults should find.

---

[268] Th.: *Loves eye is not so true as all mens: no* (siehe Anmerkungen).

CXLIX

Tene negas a me, virgo crudelis, amari,
Antefero nostris qui tua cuncta bonis?
Nilne tui memini? cuius, nimis improba, causa
Immemorem ipsius me iuvat esse mei.
Quisne tibi invisus mihi compellatur amice?
Quos, ubi tu frontem ducis, adulor ego?
Quin, mihi si voltu sis aspera, memet ab ipso
Supplicium praesens exigit ipse dolor.
Quid meritorum in me videor maioris habere,
Unde tuum nolim despiciamve iugum?
Optima nostra tui vitium venerantur et omne,
Quippe coacta oculis, imperiosa, tuis.
Sed perge irasci, quid agas scio: vera videntes
Tu colis; hos oculos, scis bene, caecat amor.

CL

O quibus unde datis a viribus, artis opisque
Indiga nativae, tu mea corda regis,
Meque fidem his oculis ipsius demere cogis
Iurando nitidam luce carere diem?
Unde in flagitiis haec te commendat agendi
Gratia, dum tentas infima quaeque mali?
Nam ingenio[269] sive arte valent, tua pessima, virgo,
Iudice me cunctis sunt potiora bonis.
Admonuit quisnam fore te mihi pluris habendam,
Quo plura acciperem cur odiosa fores?
O si ludificent alii quod amabile duco,
Non ideo tibi sum ludificandus ego.
Si non digna meum movisti cordis amorem,
Propterea fuerim dignior ipse tuo.

---

[269] Harrower schreibt *nam genio*. Die Antithese *ingenium – ars*, wie sie bei
Horaz und Ovid vorkommt, entspricht hier offenbar den beiden Begriffen
strength und *warrantise of skill*.

149

Canst thou, o cruel, say I love thee not,
When I against myself with thee partake?
Do I not think on thee, when I forgot
Am of myself, all-tyrant, for thy sake?
Who hateth thee that I do call my friend?
On whom frown'st thou that I do fawn upon?
Nay, if thou lour'st on me, do I not spend
Revenge upon myself with present moan?
What merit do I in myself respect,
That is so proud thy service to despise,
When all my best doth worship thy defect,
Commanded by the motion of thine eyes?
  But, love, hate on, for now I know thy mind:
  Those that can see thou lov'st, and I am blind.

150

O, from what power hast thou this powerful might
With insufficiency my heart to sway?
To make me give the lie to my true sight,
And swear that brightness doth not grace the day?
Whence hast thou this becoming of things ill,
That in the very refuse of thy deeds
There is such strength and warrantise of skill
That in my mind thy worst all best exceeds?
Who taught thee how to make me love thee more
The more I hear and see just cause of hate?
O, though I love what others do abhor,
With others thou shouldst not abhor my state.
  If thy unworthiness rais'd love in me,
  More worthy I to be belov'd of thee.

CLI

Si puer insipiens amor est nescitque pudorem,
Hunc ab eo genitum quis mihi nescit homo?
Blanditiis igitur nihil in me sequius urge,
Cara, meae et fraudis ne videare caput.
Proditus a te nam prodo simul ipse, puella,
Omnia naturae nobiliora meae.
Principio hoc pectus[270] mens improba concitat, esse
Significans in qua dulce triumphet amor;
Ille[271] tuum ad nomen surgit, nec plura moratus
Ut spolium felix te sibi deinde notat;
Quo tumidus fastu, contentus ad infima servit
Ille tibi, obsequiis stetve cadatve tuis.
Nec pudet illorum, carissima donec habetur
Haec mihi, cui iusto munere fungor amans.

CLII

Si, quod habes notum, te sum periurus amando,
Bis tuus in me fit, Cynthia, falsus amor;
Primum ob iura tori violata iugalia, deinde
Per nova pacta odiis iam temerata novis.
Cur tamen haec in te periuria bina notavi
Ad mea viginti? falsior ipse fui.
Ludibrii causa tibi vota mea omnia dixi,
Pectore sic erga te mihi lapsa fides!
Quae mihi non conficta tuo de corde benigno,
Deque fide ingenua, vel pietate tua?
Te magis et clarans habui mea lumina clausa,
Vel potius visus infitiata suos;
Namque tua in specie iuravi multa: nefandum
Ludibrio veri sic adiisse deos!

---

[270] Statt *pectus* (Herz) wäre das metrisch gleichwertige Wort *corpus* die genauere Übersetzung von *body*, aber *pectus* dürfte mit Bedacht gewählt sein.
[271] *ille* in den Versen 9 und 12 scheint zunächst für *amor* zu stehen; die obszöne Bedeutung (die bei Shakespeare schon für *body* gilt) geht aber aus *surgit, tumidus fastu, stetve cadatve* („er erhebt sich", „stolz angeschwollen", „er steht oder fällt") deutlich hervor.

151

Love is too young to know what conscience is;
Yet who knows not conscience is born of Love?
Then, gentle cheater, urge not my amiss,
Lest guilty of my faults thy sweet self prove.
For, thou betraying me, I do betray
My nobler part to my gross body's treason;
My soul doth tell my body that he may
Triumph in love; flesh stays no farther reason,
But, rising at thy name, doth point out thee
As his triumphant prize. Proud of this pride,
He is contented thy poor drudge to be,
To stand in thy affairs, fall by thy side.
    No want of conscience hold it that I call
    Her 'love' for whose dear love I rise and fall.

152

In loving thee thou know'st I am forsworn,
But thou art twice forsworn, to me love swearing -
In act: thy bed-vow broke and new faith borne[272];
In vowing: new hate after new love bearing.
But why of two oaths' breach do I accuse thee,
When I break twenty? I am perjur'd most;
For all my vows are oaths but to misuse thee,
And all my honest faith in thee is lost.
For I have sworn deep oaths of thy deep kindness,
Oaths of thy love, thy truth, thy constancy;
And to enlighten thee gave eyes to blindness,
Or made them swear against the thing they see.
    For I have sworn thee fair; more perjur'd I,
    To swear against the truth so foul a lie!

---

[272] Th.: *torn* (Siehe Anmerkungen).

CLIII

Deposita taeda sopitum invenit Amorem
Silvia, Dianae fida ministra deae[273];
Nec mora, confestim gelidae convallis in imo
Fonte cupidineam deprimit illa facem.
Cuius ab igne aliquid trahit immortale caloris
Fontis aqua in sese, perpetuumque tenet;
Crevit Aquis nomen Calidis[274], divinaque lymphae
Ad nova morborum fertur inesse salus.
Igne meae ex oculis dominae fax ipsa novatur,
Quam puer experiens ad mea corda movet;
Aeger opem fontis cupio, morosus et hospes
Huc feror, at nihilum suppeditatur opis.
Unde Cupido ignem petiit, fons ille salutis
Unus erit: dominae lumina nempe meae.

CLIV

Parvus Amor fertur somno cubuisse, sibique
Ad latus igniferam deposuisse facem;
Multaque nympha, quibus decretum vivere caste,
Praeteriisse; harum pulchrior una fuit,
Illaque virgineis capit ignem interrita palmis
Qui calefecisset pectora mille virûm;
Sic ardoris inexpleti dominumque ducemque
Per somnum exarmat virginis una manus!
Fonte face exstincta caluit fons tempus in omne,
Lymphaque morbosis inde salubris iit.
A domina laesus veni medicandus ad ora[275]
Ipse, quod expertus certa referre queo:
Non ope lympharum possis exstinguere amorem,
Eius enim gelidas calfacit ardor aquas.

---

[273] *Silvia,* Dienerin der Göttin Diana, ist bei Shakespeare namenlos.
[274] Mit *nomen* und mit der Grossschreibung *Aquis Calidis* scheint Barton auf einen bestimmten Badeort anzuspielen.
[275] Harrower schreibt *oram* (Akkusativ von *ora*, die Küste oder Himmelsgegend). Gemeint ist wohl *ora*, die Quellen.

153

Cupid laid by his brand, and fell asleep:
A maid of Dian's this advantage found,
And his love-kindling fire did quickly steep
In a cold valley-fountain of that ground;
Which borrow'd from this holy fire of Love
A dateless lively heat, still to endure,
And grew a seething bath, which yet men prove
Against strong[276] maladies a sovereign cure.
But as[277] my mistress' eyes[278] Love's brand new fired,
The boy for trial needs would touch my breast;
I, sick withal, the help of bath desired,
And thither hied, a sad distemper'd guest,
   But found no cure: the bath for my help lies
   Where Cupid got fire – in my mistress' eyes[279].

154

The little Love-god lying once asleep
Laid by his side his heart-inflaming brand,
Whilst many nymphs that vow'd chaste life to keep
Came tripping by; but in her maiden hand
The fairest votary took up that fire
Which many legions of true hearts had warm'd;
And so the general of hot desire
Was sleeping, by a virgin hand disarm'd.
This brand she quenched in a cool well by,
Which from Love's fire took heat perpetual,
Growing a bath and healthful remedy
For men diseas'd; but I, my mistress' thrall,
   Came there for cure, and this by that I prove:
   Love's fire heats water, water cools not love.

---

[276] Th.: *strang.*
[277] Th.: *at.*
[278] Th.: *eye* (siehe Anmerkungen).
[279] Th.: *Where Cupid got new fire; my mistres eye* (siehe Anmerkungen).

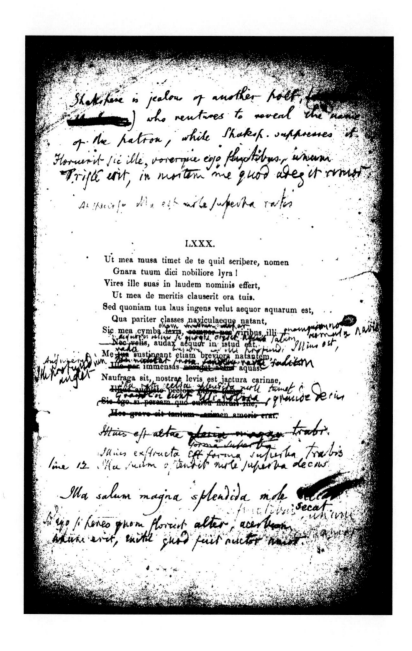

Sonett / Elegie 80. Manuskriptseite von Alfred Thomas Barton.

ANMERKUNGEN

1

Während Vers 3 im Thorpe-Text widersinnig mit *but* beginnt, schliesst sich dieser Vers bei Barton logisch korrekt mit *et* an Vers 2 an, dessen Aussage er bekräftigt, *(et quotiens acto pereat maturior aevo,* „und sooft ein nach vollendeter Lebenszeit Gereifter stirbt"). Auch die im Thorpe-Text eher unklare Aussage des Schlussverses *the world's due, by the grave and thee* ist in Bartons Schlussdistichon *...aut...quod patriae debes, fac Libitina voret* („...oder lass den Tod verzehren, was du der Mitwelt schuldest") klar verständlich.

2

Im Thorpe-Text sind Zitate direkter Reden nie als solche gekennzeichnet; auch dieses Gedicht enthält bei Thorpe keine Anführungszeichen. Von den beiden Antworten an einen fiktiven Fragesteller in den Versen 7 und 10/11 wird daher meist nur die zweite als direkte, die erste dagegen als indirekte Rede aufgefasst, wobei mit *thine own deep-sunken eyes* die Augen des antwortenden Freundes gemeint wären. Dabei deutet allein schon das betonte *thine own* darauf hin, dass die eigenen Augen des Fragestellers (bzw. dessen optische Erinnerung) gemeint sind. So hat es jedenfalls Barton verstanden – allerdings auch nicht von Anfang an. In einer früheren Version seines Texts lauten die Verse 7/8 *Dicere sub rugis oculorum haec esse sepulta / dedecus immodicum laesaque fama fuit* („Zu sagen, dies alles sei unter den Runzeln der Augenlider begraben, wäre eine nicht geringe Schmach").

3

Bartons Verse 7/8 *quisve suum in sese sepelit vesanus amorem / contentus clausa posteritate mori* („wer wäre so töricht, seine Liebe in sich selbst zu begraben und sich damit zufrieden zu geben, ohne Aussicht auf eigene Nachkommenschaft zu sterben") sind im Unterschied zu den entsprechenden Versen des Thorpe-Texts *(or who is he so fond will be the tomb / of his self-love to stop posterity)* sinnvoll und klar verständlich. Der Kern der Aussage ist zweifellos „wer wäre so töricht, sich der Aussicht auf eigene Nachkommenschaft zu berauben", also *who will be so fond to stop posterity;* als Apposition zu *posterity* und ebenfalls Objekt zu *stop* kommt nun offenbar hinzu *the tomb of (his) self-love:* Nachkommenschaft ist gleichbedeutend mit dem Ende (oder Grab) übertriebener Selbstliebe. Allerdings passt das Verb *stop* (aufhalten, zurückhalten) zwar zu Tod oder Untergang, nicht aber zum Grab. Es kann daher vermutet werden, dass hier – wie häufig im Thorpe-Text – ein Wort mit einem klangähnlichen anderen Wort verwechselt ist, nämlich *tomb* mit *doom*.

6

Die Klangwiederholung in Bartons Versen 2/4 *ante...quam spoliarit* – *ante...quam moriantur* entspricht dem Anklang *ere thou be distill'd* – *ere it be self-kill'd* in Shakespeares Sonett. Das wiederholte *ere* zeigt dabei, dass es hier auf rasches Handeln, also eher auf *swiftness* als auf *sweetness* ankommt. Im Übrigen ist das „süsse Gefäss" des Thorpe-Texts ein Unding, und auch die seltsame Konstruktion *make sweet some vial* legt den Verdacht auf eine Verfälschung des authentischen Wortlauts nahe. Bartons *imple vas aliquod dulcedine* („fülle irgend ein Gefäss mit Süsse") weicht von Thorpes Formulierung deutlich ab. Dagegen scheint in Bartons Text das mit dem Imperativ *reconde* verbundene *tu* dem pleonastischen, ebenfalls fragwürdigen *thou* des Thorpe-Texts *(treasure thou some place)* nachgebildet zu sein.

14

Im Thorpe-Text ist *saepe* („oft") normal als Adverb verwendet *(saepe requirendo praescia signa poli,* „oft Vorzeichen am Himmel suchend"). Dagegen ist *by oft predict* im Thorpe-Text (mit *oft* als Adjektiv und *predict* als Substantiv?) eine seltsame Ausdrucksweise. Merkwürdig ist hier allein schon, dass von „oft" bzw. „nicht oft" die Rede ist, wenn doch das lyrische Ich überhaupt nichts mit Himmelskunde zu schaffen haben will. Bei Barton besteht kein solcher Widerspruch: sein lyrisches Ich sagt nur *non vaticinor...,* „ich mache keine Prophezeiungen und pflege keine Vorzeichen am Himmel zu suchen". Die Wahrscheinlichkeit ist gross, dass hier wiederum – wie häufig im Thorpe-Text – zwei klangähnliche Worte verwechselt sind: eigentlich müsste es wohl heissen *Nor can I say... by aught predict that I in heaven find* („noch kann ich aufgrund irgend eines Vorzeichens, das ich am Himmel finde, wahrsagen").

21

Was Barton in Vers 6 sagt (*quasve parit gemmas terra vadumque maris,* „oder was für Edelsteine die Erde und der Meeresgrund hervorbringen"), ist zweifellos auch von Shakespeare gemeint; es dürfte also zu lesen sein *with earth's* (Th.: *earth*) *and sea's rich gems.* Hingegen weicht Barton in den Versen 11/12 deutlich von Shakespeare ab, indem er hier von der Mehrdeutigkeit des Worts *lumina* (Augen, Lichter, Sterne) Gebrauch macht (*nil facie superat, quanquam superare nitore aurea per caelum lumina mille puto,* „er zeichnet sich mit seinem Aussehen vor nichts anderem aus, obschon er mir mit dem Glanz seiner Augen tausend goldene Sterne am Himmel zu überstrahlen scheint").

23

Vers 9 lautet bei Thorpe *O let my books be then the eloquence...* Diese Version wird bis heute oft gegen die einleuchtende Emendation *looks* (Sewell) verteidigt. Barton nimmt mit seiner Übersetzung *O igitur sine me voltu mea sensa profari* („O lass mich mit meinem Blick meine Gefühle zum Ausdruck bringen") klar zugunsten von *looks* Stellung.

24

Durch den häufigen Wechsel der Possessivpronomina *my, thy, mine, thine, your* in diesem Sonett war Thorpe (bzw. sein Setzer) offensichtlich überfordert. *Your* in Zeile 6 dürfte durch *thy* zu ersetzen sein (der Adressat wird in diesem Gedicht sonst mit *thy* angesprochen), während das wohl unpersönlich gemeinte *you* in Zeile 5 wahrscheinlich richtig ist. In Zeile 8 müssen des Dichters eigene Augen (d.h. der Maler des Freundesbildnisses) gemeint sein, durch die (oder den) der Freund hindurchschauen muss, um sein Bild zu sehen.

25

Im Thorpe-Text fehlt der Reim zwischen den Zeilen 9 und 11 (Endwörter *worth* – *quite*); dies hat dazu geführt, dass entweder in Vers 9 *fight* oder in Vers 11 *forth* als neues Endwort konjiziert wurde. Für die zweite Lösung spricht, dass der Reim *worth-forth* auch in den Sonetten 38 und 72 vorkommt. Barton hat sich jedoch für die erstere Lösung entschieden – vielleicht aus Freude an dem Wortspiel in den Versen 11/12 *omnino-nomen-hon-omnia*. (Auch Shakespeare scheint derartige Wortspiele geliebt zu haben, z.B. *leaving thee living* in Sonett 6.)

27

In Bartons Vers 2 *dulce fatigatis membra labore viae* („angenehm für die von der Mühsal der Reise in ihren Gliedern Ermüdeten") ist *membra* ein Accusativus graecus (die einfachere Konstruktion mit dem Dativ *fatigatis membris* wäre hier metrisch nicht möglich), während *viae* (des Wegs, der Reise) wahrscheinlich auf einem Missverständnis beruht. Im Thorpe-Text lautet Vers 2 *The deare repose for lims with travaill tired,* wobei *travail* (mühevolle Arbeit, etwa gleichbedeutend mit *toil* in Vers 1) wohl zu Unrecht zu *travel* (Reise) emendiert wurde. Barton hält jedoch an der Deutung „Reise" auch noch in dem eine inhaltliche Fortsetzung bildenden folgenden Gedicht fest.

28

Das Gedicht knüpft offensichtlich an das vorangehende an, wobei Barton Shakespeares *return in happy plight* als Heimkehr von einer Reise *(domum reditus)* deutet. Erneut erwähnt Barton jene vermeintliche Reise in Vers 7, wo im Thorpe-Text lediglich von *toil* die Rede ist *(huic iter urgendum curae est,* „diesem liegt daran, mich auf die Reise zu schicken"). Im Thorpe-Text ist allerdings in Vers 8 schon wieder von *toil* die Rede, was kaum authentisch sein dürfte: die in den Sonetten 27 und 28 beschriebenen Plagen des Tages und der Nacht *(by day my limbs, by night my mind)* sind klar voneinander zu unterscheiden. Offenbar sind *toil* und *travail* die Plagen des Tages, während der Trennungsschmerz *(from far where I abide, still farther off from thee)* die Nacht beherrscht. *Toil* in Vers 8 dürfte daher mit dem klangähnlichen *dwell (to complain how far I dwell)* verwechselt sein. Die beiden in ihrer feindseligen Haltung miteinander verbündeten Mächte Tag und Nacht versucht das lyrische Ich mit Schmeichelreden zu besänftigen. Dies wird deutlich, wenn *thou art bright* und *thou gild'st the even* als Komplimente in direkter Rede gelesen werden. Barton hat in Vers 9 (*voce diem solor tristem*, „ich tröste den traurigen Tag") die entsprechenden Worte *I tell the day to please him* leicht abgewandelt – wohl in der richtigen Meinung, dass es keine besondere Wohltat für den Tag bedeutet, wenn ihm der Freund des Dichters als schön angepriesen wird.

29

Barton bringt in Vers 10 mit *laetaque cuncta reor* („und alles scheint mir erfreulich zu sein") den freudigen Stimmungsumschwung beim Gedanken an den Freund gut zum Ausdruck; dagegen kann die entsprechende Stelle des Thorpe-Texts *(and then my state)* wohl kaum richtig sein. (*My state* ist in den Zeilen 2 und 14 sinnvoll, dagegen wird es in Zeile 10 zum unpassenden Subjekt von *sings hymns*). Auch in den Versen 11 und 12 ist der Gedanke bei Barton klar (*feror in cantus ut cantat alauda* – „ich beginne zu singen wie die Lerche singt"), während im Thorpe-Text das Lerchengleichnis und die eigentliche Aussage miteinander vermischt sind.

32

In Vers 10 ist Bartons Anspielung auf die Versfüsse (*aptius et iunctos fecerat ire pedes* – „und er hätte die miteinander verbundenen Füsse geschickter laufen lassen") eine geistreiche Abwandlung von Shakespeares *to march in ranks of better equipage*.

34

Bei Barton erinnert *nubes obscaena* („hässliche Wolke") in Vers 3 an *nimborum obscaena agmina* („hässliche Wolkenzüge") im vorangehenden Gedicht. In ähnlicher Weise ist bei Shakespeare die Zusammengehörigkeit der Sonette 33 und 34 durch die Wortwiederholung *basest clouds* – *base clouds* betont; dazu kommt der wiederholte Reim *face-disgrace* in den Zeilen 6 und 8 beider Sonette.

In den beiden Schlussversen des Thorpe-Texts ist der poetische Vergleich Tränen-Perlen dadurch zerstört, dass bei *pearl* – wie bei Thorpe häufig – das den Plural bezeichnende Schluss-s fehlt, sodass die Tränen mit Perlmutt statt mit Perlen verglichen zu sein scheinen. Von diesem verdorbenen Vergleich hat sich Barton gänzlich abgewandt: *lacrimae pietas est aurea* bedeutet etwa „in der Träne zeigt sich eine goldene Gesinnung".

35

In Bartons Vers 10 dürfte anstelle des Genitivs *partis* der Dativ *parti (oppositae parti opem gratificatus sum,* „ich habe der Gegenpartei willig Hilfe geleistet") zu lesen sein. Dabei besteht diese Hilfeleistung offenbar darin, dass das lyrische Ich eine Verfehlung des Freundes *in amore* – also wohl eine Untreue – gerade mit dessen Liebesleidenschaft entschuldigt *(causor amorem).* Dies ist jedenfalls eine klarere Aussage als die entsprechende des Thorpe-Texts *to thy sensual fault I bring in sense.* Im Unterschied etwa zum *sensual feast* in Sonett 141 kann man sich unter einem „sinnlichen Fehler" nichts Konkretes vorstellen. Vermutlich meinte Shakespeare eher einen „sinnlosen Fehler", also irgendeine unüberlegte Fehlhandlung, in der das lyrische Ich zur Entschuldigung wenigstens einen gewissen Sinn zu erkennen sucht.

37

Während Shakespeare hier wie später in Sonett 90 von einem einzelnen, anscheinend besonders schweren Schicksalsschlag *(Fortune's dearest spite)* spricht, erwähnt Barton mehr allgemein die vom lyrischen Ich erlittenen Schicksalsschläge im Plural *(tela fortunae),* wobei er auf eine Wiedergabe des schwer erklärbaren Adjektivs *dearest* verzichtet. Da hier wohl kaum an Ironie zu denken ist, dürfte mit *dearest* ein anderes im Superlativ stehendes Adjektiv *(meanest? nearest* im Sinne von *latest?)* verfälscht sein.

40

Mit dem Plural *oblata* in Vers 5 (*si oblata receperis* „wenn du die dir dargebotenen Gelegenheiten entgegennimmst") und *quae* in Vers 6 bezieht sich Barton auf *meos amores cunctos* („alle meine Liebesbeziehungen") in Vers 1. Zweifellos meinte auch Shakespeare in den Versen 5 und 6 *if thou my loves receivest, for my loves thou usest,* während bei Thorpe hier *love* jeweils im Singular steht.

41

In Vers 8 umgeht Barton mit den Worten *reicietve preces* („oder wird er ihre Bitten zurückweisen") eine wörtliche Übersetzung der unklaren zweiten Hälfte dieses Verses im Thorpe-Text (*till he have prevailed,* von Tyrwhitt emendiert zu *till she have prevailed*).

44

Bartons Verse 13 f. *Nam lacrimas tantum mihi rerum sufficit illud / par grave* („denn nur Tränen über den Zustand der Dinge beschert mir jenes Paar von schweren Elementen") erinnern an Vergils berühmte Worte *sunt lacrimae rerum* (Aeneis 1.462; siehe auch S. 9).

51

Mit den auf *ardor* (Eifer, Liebesglut) sich beziehenden Worten in Vers 11 *Hinniet hic, non lenta pecus* („dieser wird wiehern, nicht ein träges Tier") schliesst sich Barton wie die Mehrzahl der neueren Herausgeber der reichlich absurden Version des Thorpe-Texts *Therefore desire...shall naigh noe dull flesh* an. Immerhin hat Thorpe kein Komma nach *neigh*; dies deutet darauf hin, dass statt *neigh* ein transitives Verb mit *dull flesh* oder *desire* als Objekt stehen müsste. Von *dull (substance of) flesh* wie auch von *desire* spricht Shakespeare in ähnlichem Sinn wie hier schon in den beiden zusammengehörigen Sonetten 44 und 45: auch dort malt er sich aus, wie die Sehnsucht ohne das träge Fleisch weite Strecken wie im Fluge überwinden könnte. Höchstwahrscheinlich ist dies auch hier der herrschende Gedanke; vielleicht ist *weigh* (im Sinne von beschweren, niederdrücken oder von wichtignehmen) statt *neigh* zu lesen.

Im Unterschied zu Vers 6 im Thorpe-Text *(th' imprison'd absence of your libertie)* ist Bartons Aussage *absentia...quae tibi libertas, si mihi carcer erit* („deine Abwesenheit, die für dich Freiheit bedeutet, auch wenn sie für mich der Kerker sein wird") klar verständlich. Mit *absence of liberty* kann ja eigentlich nur das Fehlen von Freiheit auf Seiten des lyrischen Ichs gemeint sein; es muss also wohl heissen *let me suffer... the imprison'd absence of my liberty.* Offenbar sind hier wiederum – wie oft im Thorpe-Text – Possessivpronomina verwechselt.

In den Versen 10/11 *sis ubi vis, id iuris habes ut tempora rebus / partiri possis quae quibus ipse velis* („Halte dich auf, wo du willst; du hast das Recht, deine Zeit so zu verteilen wie du möchtest") übernimmt Barton die zu einem ungewöhnlichen Enjambement führende Thorpe'sche Lesart *That you yourself may privilege your time / to what you will.* Wahrscheinlich ist aber Vers 11 als eine mit *do* statt *to* beginnende, mit Vers 9 parallelisierte neue Periode zu lesen *(Be where you list... – Do what you will..);* durch diese betonte Parallelisierung und den damit verbundenen Wiederholungseffekt wird die Wirkung der beiden Aufforderungen verstärkt.

60

Indem Barton Shakespeares abstrakte *nativity* durch die neugeborene Sonne *(natus sol ingens)* ersetzt, vermeidet er den im Thorpe-Text bestehenden Widerspruch zwischen *nativity* und dem zugehörigen männlichen Pronomen *his* in Vers 7 *(his glory).* Shakespeare meinte möglicherweise *this glory,* im Übrigen scheint auch er bei seinem Gleichnis an den Tageslauf der Sonne gedacht zu haben.

63

Bartons Formulierung der Verse 11/12 *Ne faciem humanis hanc cordibus exsecet umquam, e vita fuerit cum mihi raptus amor* („damit sie nie die Erinnerung an diese Schönheit aus den Herzen der Menschen tilge, wenn meine Liebe dem Leben entrissen sein wird") vermeidet die Ungeschicklichkeit der entsprechenden Verse des Thorpe-Texts, denen man entnehmen könnte, der Tod des zugleich als *love* und als *lover* bezeichneten Freundes sei geradezu erwünscht *(that he shall never cut from memory my sweet loves beauty, though my lovers life)*. Wahrscheinlich handelt es sich aber bei *my lover* wieder um eine der für den Thorpe-Text typischen Verwechslungen von Pronomina. Als *lover* ist den Sonetten sonst immer nur das lyrische Ich bezeichnet – nicht dessen Freund, der hier im gleichen Vers bereits als *my sweet love* erwähnt ist. Ihm ist der wie in anderen Gedichten als bereits verstorben gedachte Dichter offenbar als *his lover* gegenübergestellt.

66

Zeile 8 des Thorpe-Texts *and strength by limping sway disabled* scheint metrisch unkorrekt zu sein; ausserdem reimt sich das Endwort *disabled* nur mangelhaft auf *strumpeted* in Zeile 6. Bei Barton sind dagegen die Verse 6 und 8 durch rhythmisch-klangliche Übereinstimmungen besonders eng verbunden *(virginibus – auspiciis, nomina laesa – debilitata)*.

69

Dieses Sonett scheint im Thorpe-Text besonders fehlerhaft wiedergegeben zu sein. Das falsch reimende Endwort *end* in Zeile 3 wurde von Tyrwhitt und Sewell zweifellos korrekt zu *due* emendiert. Mehrfach kommt hier die für Thorpe typische Verwechslung von *their* mit *thine* oder *thy* vor; ferner dürfte in Zeile 11 die burschikose Anrede *churl* (nicht *churls*) an den Freund, nicht an *those same tongues* gerichtet sein. Das überflüssige Adjektiv *rank* in Zeile 12 ergibt einen hypermetrischen oder zumindest holprigen Vers; wohl zu Recht hat Barton auf ein entsprechendes Attribut zu *foetor lolii (=smell of weeds)* verzichtet.

70

Bartons Schlussdistichon ist in der von Harrower überlieferten Form *si speciem obtegeret nullam tibi livida fama, / Tu regeres unus pectora cuncta virum* missverständlich: eigentlich müsste es wohl heissen *si nulla obtegeret speciem tibi livida fama...* („wenn kein schlechter Ruf deine Schönheit bedeckte, würdest du alle Herzen beherrschen"). Aber auch Thorpes Version dieser Stelle *if some suspect of ill mask'd not thy show* ist missverständlich: das Verb *mask* (maskieren, verschleiern) lässt an *show* als Subjekt und *suspect of ill* als Objekt denken; gemeint ist aber offenbar nicht das den Verdacht verschleiernde gute Aussehen des Freundes, sondern umgekehrt der üble Verdacht, der die Schönheit befleckt oder beeinträchtigt. Statt *mask'd* dürfte vielleicht eher *marr'd* oder *mark'd* zu lesen sein.

76

Vers 7 lautet im Thorpe-Text *That almost every word doth fel my name,* wobei *fel* in späteren Textausgaben zu *fell, spell* oder *tell* emendiert wurde. Bartons Vers 7 *paene meum ut nomen prodat vox altera quaeque* („dass fast jedes zweite Wort meinen Namen verrät") lässt an eine weitere Emendation *sell* (verkaufen, verraten, preisgeben) denken. Möglicherweise sind hier – wie mehrfach in Thorpes Druck – die ähnlichen Lettern für s und f verwechselt.

77

Auch bei diesem Sonett scheinen im Thorpe-Text neben weiteren Fehlern (*were* statt *wear* in Z. 1, *blacks* statt *blanks* in Z.10) insbesondere die Pronomina verwechselt zu sein.

Da hier offenbar von drei dem Adressaten überreichten Geschenken – einem Spiegel, einer Uhr und einem leeren Tagebuch – die Rede ist, dürfte in den Zeilen 1 und 2 *this glass, this dial* statt *thy glass, thy dial*, andrerseits in Zeile 4 *thy* statt *this learning* zu lesen sein. Mit der Wiederholung von *ora* (was sowohl Gesichtszüge wie Öffnungen oder Löcher bedeuten kann) verdeutlicht Barton in den Versen 5 und 6 Shakespeares nicht ohne weiteres einleuchtenden Gedanken, dass Runzeln im Gesicht an offene Gräber erinnern sollen *(the wrinkles...of mouthed graves will give you memory).*

84

Mit *utrane vox* („welche von diesen beiden Stimmen") knüpft Barton deutlicher als Shakespeare an das vorangehende Gedicht an, in dessen Schlussvers von zwei rivalisierenden Dichtern *(both your poets, par vatum)* die Rede ist. Der relative Anschluss *quod* in Bartons Vers 3 *(quod spatio breviore amplectitur omnia,* „was in engem

Raum alles umfasst") bezieht sich auf *illud laudis opimae* („jenes Wort reichsten Lobes") in Vers 1. Dem würde entsprechen, dass *in whose confine* auf *this rich praise* zu beziehen ist, was sinnvoller wäre als die Bezugnahme auf *you,* wie sie durch *whose* nahegelegt wird. Statt *whose* dürfte aber wahrscheinlich *those* zu lesen sein (*in those confines,* d.h. *in the confines of that rich praise*).

85

Wie in mehreren anderen Gedichten (vgl. 36/7), stellt hier Shakespeare den äusserlichen Effekten anderer Dichter seine eigene schlichte, aber auf echter Empfindung beruhende Dichtungsart gegenüber. Mit einiger Wahrscheinlichkeit dürfte daher als Endwort nicht *effect,* sondern *affect* (im Sinne von *affection*) zu lesen sein.

94

Shakespeares wiederholtes *weed, weeds* (Unkraut) gibt Barton in Vers 12 mit *gramen agreste* (Ackergras), in Vers 14 mit *lolia* (Lolch) wieder, was hier eine reizvolle Gegenüberstellung zu *lilia* und zugleich einen Anklang an Vers 8 *(aliis – loliis)* ergibt. Schon in der Elegie LXIX scheint das Wort *lolium* Barton zu einem Wortspiel angeregt zu haben *(lolium...oleat).*

101

In Vers 7 *nec calamis opus est ut formae gratia detur* („noch bedarf es eines Stifts, um den Reiz der Schönheit wiederzugeben") hält sich Barton an den Wortlaut des Thorpe-Texts *Beautie no pensell, beauties truth to lay.* Bei Thorpe scheint jedoch *to* mit *no* verwechselt zu sein; dadurch ist die Anapher *no colour, no pencil, no lay* zerstört, deren drittes Glied, *no lay,* das wichtigste wäre. Die hier als selber sprechend gedachte Muse ist ja eigentlich nicht für die Mal- oder Zeichenkunst zuständig; sie soll vielmehr jene Lieder *(lays)* wieder hervorbringen, von denen in den Sonetten 100 und 102 ebenfalls die Rede ist *(Sing to the ear that doth thy lays esteem; When I was wont to greet it with my lays).* Die gleiche Verwechslung von *to* und *no* liegt offenbar in Sonett 105 vor: dort muss es in Vers 10 wohl heissen *varying no other words.*

104

In diesem Sonett sind nur die Verse 1-12 an den mit *you* angesprochenen Freund gerichtet, während das Schlusscouplet eine Rede an die Zukunft *(age unbred)* ist. Durch diesen Wechsel des Adressaten und den damit verbundenen Wechsel der Pronomina war Thorpe offensichtlich überfordert: nach dem korrekten *thou* in Zeile 13 (abstrakte Grössen werden stets mit *thou* angeredet) kehrt er im immer noch an die Zukunft gerichteten Schlussvers zum *you* des Gedichtanfangs zurück. Bei Barton sind die auf die Zukunft *(venientia saecla)* bezogenen Pronomina *vos, vestra* im Schlussdistichon deutlich unterschieden von *te, tuus* im Anfangsteil.

106

In Bartons Vers 11 bringt das adversative *at* die Einführung eines neuen Gedankens besser zum Ausdruck als das *and* an der entsprechenden Stelle des Thorpe-Texts, das durch *yet* oder *but* zu ersetzen sein dürfte. Allerdings kehrt Barton Shakespeares Gedanken („doch weil sie dich nicht wirklich sahen, konnten sie dich nicht gebührend besingen") um, indem er sagt: „hätten sie nicht dich vorausgeschaut, wären sie kaum zu ihren Lobgesängen fähig gewesen".

107

Dieses Sonett scheint bei Thorpe wiederum besonders fehlerhaft wiedergegeben zu sein.
Offenbar mokiert sich Shakespeare über die nicht eingetroffenen Untergangsprophezeiungen selbsternannter Auguren anlässlich der Mondfinsternis von 1595; er will also wohl die von momentanen Ereignissen nicht berührte Unsterblichkeit des Mondes hervorheben und nicht seinerseits den Mond als sterblich erklären. In Vers 5 dürfte also *th' immortal moon* statt *the mortal moon* zu lesen sein; ferner muss es wohl heissen *those sad augurs mocks* (nicht *mock!) their own presage* und *peace proclaim* (nicht *proclaims!) olives.* Barton distanziert sich von der unsinnigen Bezeichnung *mortal moon* durch die Personifikation des Monds mit der unsterblichen Göttin Luna; ferner übernimmt er den Spott auf die Unheils-

propheten, indem er sie *terrifici senes* (schreckenerregende Greise) nennt, die ihre nicht eingetroffenen Prophezeiungen nun ins Gegenteil verkehren *(irrita vertunt omina)*. In Vers 8 ist es bei Barton der Ölzweig, der langdauernden Frieden verheisst *(oliva ducit inexhaustos dies pacis)*, nicht der Friede, der Ölzweige verheisst (Th.: *peace proclaims olives*).

109

Bartons Vers 3 *Non animam citius quam memet linquere possum* („nicht eher könnte ich die geliebte Seele verlassen als mich selber") mildert auf einfache Weise die Paradoxie der offenbar wiederum durch eine Verwechslung der Pronomina verfälschten Aussage des Thorpe-Texts *As easie might I from my selfe depart as from my soule*. Dass es nicht schwieriger ist, sich von sich selber zu trennen als von der eigenen Seele, ist ja wohl selbstverständlich; gemeint ist hier aber natürlich die Seele des Freundes, also *thy soul* oder *that soul which in thy breast doth lie*. Da *anima* im Lateinischen nicht nur Seele, sondern insbesondere geliebte Seele bedeutet, lässt Bartons ohne Possessivpronomen genannte *anima* zunächst an die Seele des Freundes denken.

111

Bartons *poena... domitum perdomitura malum* („eine Strafe, die das bereits bezwungene Übel noch gänzlich bezwingen wird") ist sinnvoll, während die entsprechende Formulierung im Thorpe-Text *penance to correct correction* lediglich ein sinnloses, ja sinnwidriges Wortspiel zu sein scheint. Hier dürfte allerdings – wie noch öfter im Thorpe-Text – *to* und *too* verwechselt sein. Die Aussage wird sinnvoll, wenn sie (in enger Anknüpfung an den vorangehenden Vers) lautet: *nor (will I think) double penance too correct correction* („ noch werde ich eine verdoppelte Strafe für eine allzu strenge Massnahme halten").

112

Auch in diesem Gedicht korrigiert Bartons Text einige Unklarheiten des Thorpe-Texts. So geben die Verse 7/8 *Vivit nemo mihi, nullique ego, ferrea sensa / qui queat haec in fas flectere sive nefas* („niemand anderer lebt für mich, noch lebe ich für irgendjemanden, der meinen verhärteten Sinn zum Guten oder Schlechten beugen könnte") einen Sinn wieder, der sich aus den Worten *None else to me, nor I to none alive, that my steel'd sence or changes right or wrong* nur ungefähr ableiten lässt. Insbesondere fehlt in Zeile 7 ein Verb; möglicherweise ist hier aber zu lesen *...nor I to no one live* statt *nor I to none alive*. Weitere Unklarheiten bestehen in den Zeilen 10/11 des Thorpe-Texts:... *my Adders sence / to crytick and to flatterer stopped are*. Das durch den Reim mit *care* gesicherte Endwort *are* passt nicht zum Singular *sense;* dieses Endwort des Verses 10 ist aber seinerseits gesichert durch den Reim mit *dispense*. Die fehlenden Artikel zu *critic* und *flatterer* lassen vermuten, dass hier eigentlich die Abstracta *critique* und *flattery* oder aber die Pluralbegriffe gemeint sind, denen – wie häufig bei Thorpe – das s am Wortende fehlt. In Bartons Text gibt es keine derartigen Probleme; bemerkenswert ist hier die Differenzierung zwischen *sensa* (Plural des substantivierten Partizips von *sentio* im Sinne von Meinung, Sinnesart) in Vers 7 und *sensus* (Sinnesempfindung) in Vers 11.

113

Analog den bei Barton in Vers 10 parallel gesetzten Adjektiven *distortum – egregium* dürfte im Originaltext zu lesen sein *the most sweet-favour'd* (Th.: *sweet-favor*) or *deformedst...* Anstelle des unverständlichen Schlussverses im Thorpe-Text *(my most true mind thus maketh mine untrue,* von Malone emendiert zu *...maketh mine eye untrue)* sagt Barton: „meine Treue zu einem Einzigen erlaubt meinem Herzen keine andere Treue".

114

Durch das Widerspiel zwischen Auge und Herz (oder Sinn, Geist) in den Sonetten 113 und 114 scheint der Setzer des Thorpe-Texts wiederum insbesondere bezüglich der Pronomina überfordert gewesen zu sein. Offenbar ist jeweils das unpersönliche *it* auf *eye,* dagegen *his* auf *mind* zu beziehen; diese Trennung ist jedoch nicht konsequent durchgeführt. So ist *it* in Vers 4 zweifellos auf *mind* in Vers 1, nicht auf *eye* in Vers 3 zu beziehen: hier wird ja die Möglichkeit erörtert, dass – entgegen der Hypothese vom durch falsche Angaben der Augen betörten Geist – der durch die Liebe verzauberte Geist die an sich richtigen Wahrnehmungen des Auges zu Idealbildern des Geliebten umdeutet. Anstelle von *it* in Zeile 4 dürfte also ein betontes *him* zu lesen sein. In Bartons Text *Anne oculum dicam de visis vera referre per magicen illi quam tuus addat amor* („oder soll ich sagen, dass das Auge die Wahrheit über das Gesehene mitteilt dank der Zauberkunst, die ihm die Liebe zu dir verleiht") bleibt die Paradoxie der Thorpe'schen Version erhalten.

115

Der Gedanke des Shakespeare'schen Couplets *Love is a babe – then might I not say so,/ to give full growth to that which still doth grow* wird von Barton in geistreicher Weise abgewandelt: *Sed quod Amor puer est* für *Love is a babe* spielt nicht nur auf den Knaben Amor, sondern zugleich auf den männlichen Geliebten an, der in diesen Gedichten oft *puer* genannt wird. Während Shakespeares lyrisches Ich seine fehlerhaften früheren Aussagen mit dem nicht vorhersehbaren Wachsen der Liebe rechtfertigt, betont Barton umgekehrt, es sei ein Irrtum gewesen, das stets noch wachsende Kind Liebe schon als ausgewachsen zu bezeichnen *(...errabat versus, adultum id memorans, crescit quod mihi quoque die*, „...es irrte der Vers, indem er das als ausgewachsen bezeichnete, was mir noch täglich wächst").

125

Bartons Verse 3 f. *illave in aeternum fundamina iacta putarem, / quae citius quam vis eruat ipsa cadunt* („soll ich glauben, dass jene Fundamente für die Ewigkeit gelegt sind, die schneller als durch äussere Gewalt von selbst verfallen") entspricht dem gewiss sinnvoll emendierten Text *laid great bases for eternity which prove* (Th.: *proves*) *more short than waste or ruining.* (Nach Thorpes Version wäre die Ewigkeit kürzer als endliche Zeitabschnitte.) Ein von Barton nicht korrigierter weiterer banaler Fehler dürfte in den Zeilen 5 und 7 des

Thorpe-Texts liegen: in deren Endworten *savour-favour* scheinen –
wie auch an anderen Stellen – die schwer unterscheidbaren An-
fangslettern vertauscht zu sein. *Savour* bezeichnet eher einen
raffinierten als einen einfachen Geschmack; andrerseits ist *simple
favour*, das einfache Gefühl echter Sympathie, dasjenige was auch
in anderen Sonetten der äusserlichen Brillanz entgegengestellt ist
(so etwa in Sonett 82 *truly sympathized in true plain words* oder – wie
oben besprochen – in Sonett 85 *dumb thoughts speaking in affect*).

126

Dieses Gedicht enthält als einziges des Zyklus nur 12 Verse; diese
sind bei Barton wie in den übrigen Elegien zu Distichen, bei Shakes-
peare zu 6 Reimpaaren zusammengefasst. Ähnlich wie beim 15
Verse umfassenden Sonett 99, auf welches der Musenanruf in
Sonett 100 folgt, scheint durch diese Abweichung von der Normal-
form eine Zäsur innerhalb des Gedichtzyklus markiert zu sein: mit
Sonett 127 beginnt die Reihe der „Dark Lady"-Gedichte.
Von den *arma temporis* (Waffen der Zeit) sind bei Barton nur Sichel und
Uhr genannt, während bei Shakespeare noch der Spiegel hinzukommt.
Allerdings ist Zeile 2 im Th.-Text *(...times fickle, glasse, his sickle, hower)*
wohl entstellt, wobei wiederum die Verwechslung der Lettern s
und f eine Rolle spielt: *fickle* passt eher zur fortwährend tickenden
Uhr als zum Spiegel, und an erster Stelle dürfte Shakespeare die
als Attribut der Zeit häufig erwähnte Sichel genannt haben.

131

Während Shakespeare unmittelbar nach der Aussage *thy black is
fairest* erklärt, schwarz sei die Geliebte einzig in ihren Taten, vermeidet Barton diesen Widerspruch, indem er sagt „ganz besonders
aber bist du schwarz in deinen Taten" *(praecipue vero factis es nigra)*.

132

Das hübsche Wortspiel *morning sun – mourning eyes* konnte Barton
natürlich nicht auf Lateinisch wiedergeben. Aber auch Thorpe
scheint damit Mühe gehabt zu haben: während er sonst *mourning*
(Trauer) korrekt mit *ou* buchstabiert, schreibt er hier in Zeile 9

falsch *morning eyes.* Hingegen wäre in Zeile 7 – sofern Shakepeare zur Charakterisierung des Abendhimmels das französische, im damaligen Englisch noch kaum bekannte Wort *sombre* verwendet hätte – die Verballhornung zu *sober* verzeihlich. Allerdings ist *sober* gerade in seiner Vieldeutigkeit nichtssagend und – wie schon *full star* im vorangehenden Vers – unanschaulich. Da ist Bartons griechisch-lateinische Bezeichnung für den Abendstern *(Hesperus)* als poetischer Vergleich mit den Augen der Geliebten gewiss passender.

139
Während im Thorpe-Text in den Versen 3 und 6 übereinstimmend *thine eye* („dein Auge" in Einzahl) steht, differenziert Barton zwischen *oculo* (Singular) in Vers 3 und *lumina* (Plural) in Vers 6. Bei der Vorstellung des Seitwärtsschauens in Vers 6 muss wohl auch Shakespeare an beide Augen, also *thine eyes,* gedacht haben, während für den Thorpe-Text ein fehlendes Schluss-s typisch wäre.

142
Bartons Verse 3/4 *O misera, amborum vitas inquirere si vis, / facta cito invenies irreprehensa meae* („Unglückselige, wenn du unser beider Taten prüfst, wirst du rasch sehen, dass mich kein Vorwurf trifft") sind im Unterschied zur Version des Thorpe-Texts *O, but with mine, compare thou thine own state, / And thou shalt finde it merrits not reprooving* unmissverständlich (*it* im Thorpe-Text scheint sinnwidrig auf *thine own state* bezogen zu sein – vielleicht meinte Shakespeare allerdings *I merit not reproving*).
Ebenfalls sind Bartons Verse 11/12 *Fac pietas in te radicem agat, auctaque cum sit, / tunc alios miserans tale merere queas* („Lass Mitleid in dir Wurzeln schlagen, damit du es, wenn es einst gewachsen sein wird, anderen entgegenbringen und dadurch selber Mitleid verdienen kannst") klarer verständlich als die entsprechenden Worte des Originals *root pity in thy heart, that when it grows, / thy pity may deserve to pitied be.*

148
Die Verse 7/8 klingen in Bartons Fassung *Si specie fallebar, amor demonstrat aperte / non sibi sed volgo noscere vera dari* („Wenn ich mich durch das Aussehen täuschen liess, so beweist die Liebe damit,

dass ihr die den Menschen im allgemeinen gegebene Fähigkeit, die Wahrheit zu erkennen, fehlt") weniger absonderlich als in Thorpes Version *Loves eye is not so true as all mens: no*. Abgesehen von der fragwürdigen Antithese *Love's eye* – *all men's eye* und dem unschön am Versende angehängten *no* dürfte *all men's eyes are true* kaum der Meinung Shakespeares entsprochen haben.

152

Klarer als im Thorpe-Text sind in Bartons Versen 3 f. *Primum ob iura tori violata iugalia, deinde / per nova pacta odiis iam temerata novis* („zuerst durch die Verletzung des Ehegelöbnisses, dann mit der Entweihung der neu eingegangenen Verbindung durch neuen Hass") die der Geliebten vorgeworfenen zwei Meineide auseinandergehalten. Möglicherweise beruht aber die Vermischung der beiden Fehltritte in Vers 3 des Thorpe-Texts *(thy bed-vow broke and new faith torne)* auf einem banalen Fehler: liest man hier *borne* statt *torn,* so ist eine mit ehelicher Untreue verbundene neue Liebe in Zeile 3 von der abermaligen Untreue in Zeile 4 klar getrennt. Dabei weist *after new love bearing* in Zeile 4 auf *new faith borne* in Zeile 3 zurück. Mit dem an Vers 7 *ludibrii causa...*(„nur um meines spielerischen Vergnügens willen...") anklingenden Schlusssatz *nefandum ludibrio veri sic adiisse deos* („es war sündhaft, mit einer solchen Verhöhnung der Wahrheit bei den Göttern geschworen zu haben") nimmt Barton klar zugunsten der Emendation *more perjur'd I* (Th.: *more perjur'd eye*) Stellung.

153

Bartons Ausdruck *nova morborum* („neuartige Krankheitserscheinungen") entspricht der Emendation *strange maladies* (Th.: *strang malladies*). Eher als *strange* dürfte jedoch hier *strong* gemeint sein (ähnlich z.B. *strong infection* in Sonett 111): die Liebe ist keine seltene, wohl aber eine schwere Krankheit. Während es im Thorpe-Text in Zeile 9 und im Schlussvers *my mistres eie* bzw. *eye* in Einzahl heisst, betont Barton an diesen beiden Stellen *(oculis dominae, dominae lumina)*, dass es sich jeweils um beide Augen handelt. Das Fehlen des Schluss-s geht bei *eye* in Vers 14 des Thorpe-Texts aus dem Reimwort *lies* klar hervor.

SHAKESPEARE IN KLASSISCHEM GEWANDE: GVLIELMI SHAKESPEARE CARMINA QUAE SONNETS NUNCUPANTUR

Essay von Markus Marti

Alfred Thomas Barton (1843–1912) war von 1865 bis zu seinem Tod als Tutor für Latein und Griechisch am Pembroke College in Oxford tätig. Wohl hauptsächlich zu seinem eigenen Vergnügen formte der wackere Schulmann[1] während diesen fast vierzig Jahren Shakespeares Sonette in lateinische Elegien um, und daraus wurde schliesslich sein hier vorliegendes Hauptwerk, das seine dankbaren Schüler und Kollegen 1913 postum in einer auf 150 Stück beschränkten Ausgabe[2] veröffentlichten. Die kleine Auflage erstaunt uns kaum, denn wer – wir natürlich ausgenommen – sollte Shakespeares Sonette ausgerechnet auf Lateinisch lesen wollen? Erstaunlicher ist, dass die Auflage bereits zehn Jahre später vergriffen war. Die dankbaren und wohlerzogenen Schüler ergatterten sich also tatsächlich das Werk ihres alten Lehrers, und John Harrower (1857–1933), ein Griechischprofessor aus Aberdeen, gab in einer zweiten Auflage 1923 zum dreihundertsten Todestag Shakespeares 525 weitere Exemplare heraus.

---

[1] Das Vorwort zur ersten Ausgabe seiner Sonettübertragung lobt ihn als einen Lehrer, der seinen Schülern mit Latein und Griechisch auch Sittsamkeit und Tugend vermittelte, wobei diese seinen Rotstift beinahe mehr als die (damals aus dem Schulwesen nicht wegzudenkende) Rute fürchteten: 'conversiones Latine minus feliciter compositas tam acriter castigabat ut cerulam ejus miniatam vix minus quam flagellum ipsum discipuli reformidarent. Sic vitam moresque eorum pariter atque indolem ad virtutem corroborabat: sic instituti, sic imbuti sunt ut ea reverentia quam adulescentes conceperant ne aetate quidem provectioribus usu familiari exolesceret.' (Praefatio, 1913)

[2] "Begun as a *parergon* to fill the spare hours of a busy life, it ended by being the most considerable piece of work left behind him by its author, and as such was first published, after his death, in 1913, at the instance of his grateful pupils to be a remembrance of his full and ripe scholarship." (Preface, 1923).

Übersetzungen dienen entweder dem *Export* oder dem *Import* von Texten, im Idealfall beidem. Sie erfüllen einen Zweck, wenn die Sprecher der einen Sprache den Sprechern der andern etwas mitzuteilen haben oder wenn unter den Sprechern der Zielsprache eine Nachfrage nach dieser Information besteht. So betrachtet, scheint Bartons Übersetzung zwecklos zu sein, ein Export in die falsche Richtung, ein Schuss ins Leere. Sollte man nicht das elisabethanische Englisch Shakespeares in ein moderneres Englisch übertragen, statt es in eine noch ältere Form zu giessen? Gab es anfangs des zwanzigsten Jahrhunderts eine Leserschaft, die ungeduldig auf Shakespeare in Latein wartete, oder war es nötig, dass eine solche Leserschaft ihn endlich kennen lernte?

Die ersten Übersetzungen von Shakespeares Stücken in andere Sprachen gehörten zur ‚Exportkategorie' und waren aus ganz praktischen Gründen entstanden: Englische Schauspielertruppen mussten sich verständlich machen, als sie auf dem Kontinent auftraten. Ihre Übersetzungen waren äusserst primitiv, aber sehr erfolgreich: In Deutschland erschien schon 1620 eine zweibändige Ausgabe der Stücke der ‚englischen Komödianten', noch drei Jahre vor der ersten Folio-Ausgabe von Shakespeares Stücken in England.[3]

Die Übersetzungen der Stücke ins Deutsche, Russische, Italienische, Französische, Holländische, Portugiesische, Tschechische, Ungarische und Spanische, die gegen Ende des 18. Jahrhunderts gemacht wurden, gehören zur ‚Importkategorie': Die Stücke waren Teil eines gesamteuropäischen Kanons geworden, sie in der eigenen Sprache zu ‚besitzen', war diesen Sprachgemeinschaften aus Prestigegründen wichtig, um die Bedeutung der eigenen Kultur zu betonen und von anderen Kulturen abzusetzen.

Im 19. Jahrhundert wurden Shakespeares Stücke allmählich in fast allen europäischen Sprachen erhältlich. Als die Stücke einmal übersetzt waren, wandte man sich auch den Sonetten zu, und seit der

---

[3] Neben Stücken meist anonymer Autoren findet sich dort *Titus Andronicus, Tugend- und Liebesstreit (Twelfth Night)* und *Der bestrafte Brudermord oder Prinz Hamlet aus Dänemark* (vgl. Creizenach).

Mitte des 19. Jahrhunderts ist das Übersetzen der Sonette vor allem im deutschen Sprachraum geradezu zu einem Volkssport geworden.[4] Schon 1871 beklagte man sich in einem deutschen Literaturmagazin, dass zu viele Sonettübersetzungen veröffentlicht würden, und dass praktisch jeder Schulmeister seine eigene Übersetzung in der Schublade hätte.[5] Es gibt mittlerweile mehr als 70 publizierte Gesamtübertragungen der Sonette ins Deutsche, und von den populärsten Sonetten gibt es mehr als 150 Übersetzungen.[6] Für andere Sprachen trifft dasselbe zu.[7] Nötig sind alle diese Übersetzungen kaum: Ihre Auflagen sind gewöhnlich sehr klein, sie werden nicht importiert zum Nutzen einer grösseren Gruppe, niemand hat auf sie gewartet. Sonette zu übersetzen, scheint es, ist zum Selbstzweck geworden.

---

[4] Christian Heinrich Schütze (1760–1820) war vermutlich der Erste, der 1784 die deutsche Übersetzung zweier Sonette (116 und 143) veröffentlichte. Die erste vollständige Übersetzung (bis auf drei Sonette) war diejenige Karl Lachmanns (1820), Teile von Dorothea Tiecks Übersetzung erschienen anonym 1825.

[5] Unter dem Titel *Shakespeares Sonette und die deutschen Uebersetzer* fragte man sich im *Magazin für die Literatur des Auslandes*, ob denn die Sonette tatsächlich „immer und immer wieder in unsere Muttersprache übersetzt" werden müssten, denn alles und jedes so und so oft zu übersetzen, führe beim „wahren Freund der Kunst" zum Überdruss: „In Deutschland [...] wirft sich jeder von Literatur und Poesie Angekränkelte auf's Übersetzen. Es giebt fast keinen Schulmeister, der nicht irgend eine Uebertragung wenigstens im Pulte hätte. Je länger daran herumgefeilt ist, desto mehr freut er sich in seinen Mussestunden bei seiner heimlichen Lectüre. Wir gönnen ja Jedem sein Vergnügen, rathen aber [...] den Meisten dieser Herren, das Pult wieder zu schliessen" (zitiert in Jansohn/Fertig).

[6] Jürgen Gutsch versammelt in seiner Anthologie „*...lesen, wie krass schön du bist konkret*" 155 Übertragungen von Sonett 18; U. Erckenbrecht veröffentlicht in *Shakespeare sechsundsechzig* 132 Versionen von Sonett 66. Eine Internet-Datenbank der Universität Bamberg (betreut von Christa Jansohn, zusammengestellt von Annette Leithner-Brauns und Elmar Fertig) dokumentiert alle bis jetzt publizierten deutschen Übersetzungen (siehe Bibliographie).

[7] Vgl. Marti, Markus (ed.) "Shakespeare Translations", *Sh:in: E. Shakespeare in Europe.* <http://pages.unibas.ch/shine/translators.htm>.

Was macht das Übersetzen von Shakespeares Sonetten so attraktiv für Liebhaber der Dichtkunst? Ein erster Grund ist natürlich die Kürze dieser Texte. Ein Sonett lässt sich in ein paar Stunden, Tagen oder Wochen übersetzen, so rasch zwischendurch, als Freizeitbeschäftigung wie ein Kreuzworträtsel. Dennoch ist eine gute Übersetzung keine Kleinigkeit. Ein kunstvolles Sonett selbst zu *verfassen* und sich dabei an Metrum und Reimschema zu halten, ist schwierig genug, lohnt aber kaum die Mühe. Die Sonettform ist seit dem 19. Jahrhundert aus der Mode. Ein Sonett zu *übersetzen* ist noch schwieriger, verspricht aber auch Gewinn: Sich so genau wie möglich an den Inhalt zu halten, die Wortspiele, Bilder und Klangmuster des Originals in einem durch Versmass und Reim vorgegebenen Rahmen nachzuahmen, ist so schwierig, dass ein Erfolg in diesem Sprachspiel schon Lohn genug ist, ein privates Vergnügen ohne schalen Nachgeschmack. Im Gegensatz zum Kreuzworträtsel, das, einmal gelöst, beiseite geworfen wird, kann auch an der vollendetsten Übersetzung noch weiter gefeilt werden, man kann sie immer wieder lesen, vielleicht sogar veröffentlichen. Doch auch ohne Veröffentlichung wird der Übersetzer Teil des illustren Kreises von Shakespeareübersetzern, er stellt sich einem direkten Vergleich mit seinen Vorgängern und Kollegen und mit dem Barden selbst. Das Resultat lässt sich objektiv vergleichen und ist jederzeit nachprüfbar. Jede Übersetzung ist in irgend einem Punkt genauer und besser als die andere, sogar besser als das Original. Bartons Übersetzung, zum Beispiel, ist eindeutig klassischer als Shakespeares Original. Da eine perfekte und endgültige Übersetzung nie möglich ist, gibt es immer Raum für eine neue, die in dem einen oder andern Punkte besser ist.

Sprachen und Kulturen wandeln sich ständig, Wörter in der Zielsprache können langsam ihre Bedeutung ändern oder plötzlich unpassende Konnotationen erhalten – ältere Übersetzungen werden deshalb zum Teil unverständlich oder wirken verstaubt wie unsere ‚klassische' romantische Schlegel-Tieck-Übersetzung der Dramen. Aber auch das Verständnis des Originaltexts ist von kulturbedingten Gewichtsverschiebungen betroffen, gewisse Aspekte können wichtiger oder unwichtiger werden. Neuübersetzungen tragen solchen sprachlichen und kulturellen Wechseln Rechnung. Auch im Englischen sind Shakespeares Werke schwer verständlich geworden, und eine Übersetzung ins moderne Englisch würde sich aufdrängen, wenn die Leser auf das Original verzichten könnten.[8] Ein Stück wie *Hamlet* zu modernisieren, ist aber kaum möglich, da so viele Verse sprichwörtlich geworden sind. Was in anderen Sprachen Neuübersetzungen, leisten im Englischen neu kommentierte Ausgaben. Die Herausgeber von Shakespeares Werken fügen seit der ersten ‚modernen‘ Ausgabe von Nicholas Rowe (1709) Emendationen ein und holen in Fussnoten zu Worterklärungen aus, um die Texte für die Allgemeinheit verständlich zu machen.

Neue Übersetzungen und Editionen können meist nur kurze Zeit mit dem Kultur- und Sprachwandel Schritt halten. Gerade *weil* es so viele gibt, wird es immer noch mehr geben *müssen*. Eine endgültige Version eines Textes, der so oft gelesen und interpretiert wird wie die Werke Shakespeares, ist nicht möglich. Neue Bearbeitungen, Übersetzungen und Editionen mit neuen Interpretationen machen das Werk laufend komplexer. Weil immer wieder neue Bedeutungen hineingelesen werden, gewinnt es weiter an internationaler Bedeutung und kulturellem Prestige, weshalb es dann erst recht wieder bearbeitet und benutzt wird im Dienst von nationalen, politischen, sozialen oder privaten Interessen.

Es ist kein Zufall, dass die Zahl von Übersetzungen Shakespeares in andere europäische Sprachen vor allem im Zeitalter der Nationalstaatenbildung, des Nationalismus und des Kolonialismus zunahm. Obwohl das Übersetzen (wie auch in Bartons Fall) in erster

---

[8] Die Romantiker Charles und Mary Lamb boten mit ihren *Tales from Shakespeare* kurze Nacherzählungen der Dramen als Geschichten für Kinder und Erwachsene. Auch Thomas Bowdlers von ‚unzüchtigen‘ Stellen gereinigten *Family Shakespeare* von 1807, der in viktorianischer Zeit weite Verbreitung fand, könnte man als kulturelle Übertragung der Werke Shakespeares in eine neuere Zeit betrachten. Die Übersetzungen ganzer Stücke in modernes Englisch von Walter Saunders, einem südafrikanischen Professor, haben jedoch in England selbst kaum Erfolg.

Linie ein Privatvergnügen ist, kommt der Übersetzung selbst immer auch eine soziale und politische Bedeutung zu. Junge Staaten und nationalistische Bewegungen definieren und legitimieren sich durch ihre Sprache und Kultur, wobei der Übersetzung von Shakespeares Werken häufig eine solch zentrale Rolle zukommt, dass sie sogar von Politikern persönlich in die Hand genommen wird.[9] Der Besitz von Shakespeares Werken in der eigenen Sprache soll helfen, die kulturelle Bedeutung und Eigenständigkeit einer Volksgruppe oder Nation zu beweisen. Eine Shakespeareübersetzung ist zu diesem Zweck oft wichtiger als ‚eigene' Werke, deren literarischer Wert umstritten sein kann. Allein schon die Möglichkeit eines Zugangs zum Werk Shakespeares in der eigenen Sprache verschafft den Sprechern Prestige, auch wenn sie selbst diese Werke nicht lesen. So skurril auch eine Übersetzung der Werke Shakespeares ins Klingonische erscheinen

---

[9] In Deutschland übersetzte 1812 ein Geheimrat und Minister für Bergbau *Romeo und Julia* für sein Hoftheater in Weimar, aber auch das ‚Junge Deutschland' gab 1872 eine Gesamtausgabe heraus, an der die ehemaligen Revolutionäre Freiligrath und Herwegh mitarbeiteten; in Russland übersetzte und bearbeitete die Zarin Katharina die Grosse die *Lustigen Weiber von Windsor* als Übung in der für sie noch fremden Sprache, aber auch mit der klaren politischen Absicht, ihr Land von Frankreich kulturell unabhängig zu machen, indem sie die Vorliebe der russischen Oberschicht für alles Französische karikierte; hundert Jahre später sollte eine Shakespeareübersetzung der finnischen Volksbewegung zum Erreichen ihrer kulturellen Selbstständigkeit und Freiheit von Russland dienen; Kaiserin Sisi (Sissi) von Österreich übersetzte einige Dramen ins Neugriechische; der liberale Politiker und frühere Ministerpräsident Fan Noli übersetzte Shakespeare im amerikanischen Exil ins Albanische; der heute als Nazikollaborateur umstrittene Führer der bretonischen Befreiungsfront Roparz Hemon war der erste Übersetzer ins Bretonische; Julius Nyerere, der erste Präsident Tansanias, übertrug Shakespeare ins Kisuaheli. Gegenwärtig helfen neue Ausgaben, Unterschiede zwischen Slowakisch und Tschechisch zu verdeutlichen; spanische Regionen wie Katalanien oder Galizien definieren die kulturelle Eigenständigkeit ihrer Dialekte mit Shakespeare-Übersetzungsprojekten, und eine Übersetzung ins Kurdische soll die Einheit und Selbstständigkeit der Kurden im Irak demonstrieren.

mag, so zeigt sie uns doch, dass durch diesen Prozess sogar eine fiktive Kultur zur virtuellen Realität werden kann.[10] Übersetzungen aus den Werken Shakespeares ins Lateinische im späten 19. und frühen 20. Jahrhundert mögen uns ähnlich skurril erscheinen, wir würden sie gerne als Kuriosa abtun, als Fingerübungen von Schulmeistern in ihrer Freizeit. Aber unter den Übersetzern finden sich berühmte und geachtete viktorianische Altphilologen wie Benjamin Hall Kennedy[11] (Sonnet 18, Auszüge aus *Macbeth*) und Hugh Andrew Jonstone Munro[12] (Auszüge aus *Hamlet* und *Midsummer Night's Dream*), und die Übersetzungen wurden in den Lateinlesebüchern für englische Mittelschulen ververöffentlicht.[13]

Auch Bartons Übersetzung ist deshalb nicht einfach nur eine weitere Übersetzung der Werke Shakespeares in noch eine weitere Sprache – wie privat seine Beschäftigung mit Shakespeare auch

---

[10] Die erste Ausgabe von *Hamlet, Prince of Denmark (The Restored Klingon Version)* war auf 1000 gebundene Exemplare limitiert und ist bereits vergriffen; eine zweite Ausgabe ist als Taschenbuch erhältlich (Pocket Books, 2000). Geplant sind ferner Ausgaben von *Much Ado About Nothing* und *Macbeth*. Nick Nicholas übersetzte Sonett 18: "qaDelmeH bov tuj pem vIlo'choHQo". Ausser Shakespeare ist auch das Gilgamesch-Epos in Klingonisch erhältlich, und es gibt ein Projekt, die Bibel zu übersetzen.

[11] Benjamin Hall Kennedy (1804–1880) war Rektor in Shrewsbury von 1836 bis 1866, danach Professor für alte Sprachen am St John's College, Cambridge.

[12] Hugh Andrew Johnstone Munro (1819–1885), einer von Benjamin Hall Kennedys ersten Schülern in Shrewsbury, war Lektor am Trinity College und wurde 1869 auf den Lehrstuhl für Latein in Cambridge berufen. Sein Hauptwerk ist eine kritische Ausgabe von Lukrez (2 Bde., 1864), er arbeitete aber auch mit am Lateinlesebuch *Sabrinae Corolla*. Seine *Translations into Latin and Greek Verse* erschienen 1884.

[13] Shakespeareübersetzungen erschienen in Lateinbüchern wie *Sabrinae Corolla* (London, 1850), *Nova Anthologia Oxoniensis* (1899), *Cambridge Compositions* (1899), *Flosculi Rossallienses* (Cambridge, 1916), *Liliorum Hortulus* (1926). Besonders *Sabrinae Corolla* war sehr weit und lange über Zeit verbreitet, Webseiten von Antiquariaten bieten heute noch Nachdrucke an von 1859 (2nd ed. Cambridge, Deighton, Bell et Soc.), 1890 (London, G. Bell & Sons) und sogar 1950 (Adnitt & Naughton).

gewesen sein mag, sein postum veröffentlichtes Werk hat als kulturelles Produkt seiner Zeit auch weiter reichende Bedeutung. Die ‚tote' Sprache Latein definiert seit dem Untergang des römischen Reiches keine Nation mehr, und den Vatikan und die katholische Kirche wird der Anglikaner Barton kaum als Leserschaft ins Auge gefasst haben.[14] Bartons Latein ist kein Kirchenlatein, er braucht nicht die gereimten Verse der mittelalterlichen Hymnen. Eher als den Papst mag sich Barton die Geister von Augustus, Maecenas, Horaz, Vergil und Propertius als Leser vorgestellt haben.

Aber Latein war nicht wirklich eine tote Sprache im viktorianischen England. Es war noch lebendig als säkularisierte heilige Sprache einer virtuellen Nation, der Gelehrtenwelt. Die Dozenten Kennedy, Hughe und Barton *exportierten* Shakespeare nicht ins Totenreich, sie *importieren* ihn in ihre eigene Welt, deren Sprache in den englischen *Public Schools* gelehrt und an den Universitäten von Cambridge und Oxford offiziell[15] noch gesprochen wurde.

Seit dem Mittelalter hatte Latein den Status einer weltweiten Gelehrtensprache, ironischerweise den Status, den das Englische heute zum Teil hat. Dass es diesen Status – der weitgehend zwar

---

[14] Barton könnte allerdings auch vom Oxford Movement inspiriert gewesen sein, einer anglikanischen Reformbewegung, die mit dem Katholizismus liebäugelte. Dieses Liebäugeln ging zwar nicht so weit, dass man Latein als Kirchen- oder gar Umgangssprache hätte einführen wollen. Aber immerhin war die von Charles Edward Appleton, einem Führer der Bewegung, 1869 gegründete Zeitschrift *Academy* einer der Hauptschauplätze, auf dem der akademische Disput über die korrekte Aussprache des Latein geführt wurde (Stray, S. 201).

[15] Latein blieb bis ins 20. Jahrhundert für zeremonielle Anlässe die offizielle Sprache in Cambridge and Oxford: Sir Arthur Quiller-Couch, der erste Professor für Englische Literatur in Cambridge, erwähnte noch 1918 in einer Vorlesung: "Our Vice-Chancellor, our Public Orator still talk Latin, securing for it what attention they can." Die Creweian Oration, eine Dankadresse an Spender, die der Professor of Poetry in Oxford jährlich zu halten hat, musste noch bis 1972 in Latein gehalten werden.

bloss ein Mythos war[16] – zu verlieren drohte, war seit dem 17. Jahrhundert zu spüren, aber dass es ihn an Englisch abtreten sollte, war noch keineswegs klar. Im Gegenteil, gegen Ende des 19. Jahrhunderts kam es – im Gefolge des eher bescheidenen Erfolgs künstlicher Sprachen wie Volapük und Esperanto, auch zu Versuchen, Latein wieder zur internationalen Sprache zu erklären, da Deutsch, Französisch oder Englisch aus politischen Gründen nicht durchsetzbar waren.[17] In einem gewissen Sinne leistet daher Bartons Übersetzung für die weltweite, zumindest aber für die englische Gemeinschaft der Gebildeten, was Shakespeare-Übersetzungen sonst für fremde Völker und Nationen leisten: Sie stärkt die um Anerkennung ringende und an Bedeutung verlierende Gemeinschaft der Lateiner psychisch und physisch. Indem sie allen Gebildeten den Zugang zu Shakespeare in der eigenen, akademischen Sprache ermöglicht, stiftet sie Identität. Damit diese kleine Gemeinschaft aber auch physisch stärker wird, müssten neue Mitglieder gewonnen werden, und zu diesem Zwecke können volkssprachliche Texte eines beliebten oder ‚modernen' Autors als Lockmittel dienen.

Niemand wird Latein studieren, um die Werke Shakespeares lesen zu können, aber wer Shakespeare liebt und Latein lernen muss, könnte dies auch tun, indem er seinen Lieblingsautor auf Lateinisch

---

[16] Françoise Waquet zeigt in ihrem Buch *Latin or the Empire of a Sign* über die Bedeutung des Latein vom 16. bis 20. Jahrhundert auf, dass es trotz aller pädagogischen Bemühungen mit dem tatsächlichen Beherrschen des Lateinischen unter den Gebildeten (und Lehrern) in ganz Europa eigentlich schon immer schlecht bestellt war. Stray (S. 200) erwähnt, dass schon ab 1850 die Kandidaten für Lehrstühle in Cambridge auf die lateinisch gestellten Fragen auf Englisch antworteten ('licet candidatis Anglice respondere').

[17] Der Vorschlag des Engländers George Henderson, eine *Societas Internationalis Latinitatis Modernae* zu gründen, erhielt 1891 grosse Unterstützung in Frankreich und Deutschland, doch Henderson gab seine Bemühungen zehn Jahre später wieder auf. Kongresse für ein ‚Lebendiges Latein' gab es bis 1976 (Waquet, 264ff). Ob es wohl freiwillige Mitarbeiter oder dazu gezwungene Schüler sind, die sich am Internetnachschlagewerk *Vicipaedia, libera encyclopaedia* mit mittlerweile 4000 Seiten beteiligen, um Latein auch auf der Höhe der heutigen Zeit zu erhalten?

liest. Ein ähnlicher Gedankengang bewog den Lateinprofessor Francis William Newman 1884, eine Übersetzung von Defoes *Robinson Crusoe (Rebili Crusonis Annalium)*[18] zu veröffentlichen. In seinem englischen Vorwort überlegt er sich dazu:

> Ich möchte hier noch einmal betonen, dass kein noch so genaues Lesen von kleinen Häppchen Latein je so wirksam sein wird wie das [oberflächlichere] Lesen vieler Texte; um den Massen mehr Lesestoff anzubieten, muss der Stil sehr einfach sein und der Inhalt attraktiv. Damit wir sprechen können, brauchen wir einen Wortschatz, der alle gewohnten Dinge umfasst, was uns die Schullektüre nicht bietet. Terenz, obwohl etwas schwierig, wäre von grossem Vorteil für die Lernenden, aber seine Stücke sind zu wenig gehaltvoll und alles andere als erbaulich. In naher Zukunft wird man nach einer gemeinsamen Sprache für die Gebildeten suchen müssen. Wenn Latein dann noch in England, Frankreich, Italien, Deutschland, Ungarn und Spanien gelernt wird, dann ist dies, wie vor dreihundert Jahren noch, zum Besten für die ganze Christenheit. Aber vielleicht wird ja auch Latein noch aus den Schulen geprügelt. [Übersetzung M.M.]

Newmans *Rebili Crusonis Annalium* war der Vorläufer einer grossen Zahl von Übersetzungen zeitgenössischer Werke zu didaktischen und ideologischen Zwecken. Noch heute bieten sich den Lateinschülern Werke der Kinder- und Jugendliteratur an wie *Asterix Gallus*[19], *Michael Musculus et Donaldus Anas, Popeius, Insuperabilis Snupius, Maximi et Mauritii malefacta, Alicia in Terra Mirabili, Winnie Ille Pu* und *Domus Anguli Puensis, Ursus nomine*

---

[18] Francis William Newman (1805–1897), der Bruder des Kardinals John Henry Newman, war Professor für Latein an der Universität London. Seine Übersetzung von *Robinson Crusoe (Rebili Crusonis Annalium* a F.W. Newman contractorum, Latine redditorum, ad pueros docendos accommodatorum anno MDCCCLXXXIV - Londini apud Trübner) ist im Internet verfügbar (s. Bibliographie).

[19] *Rubricastellanus* (Karl-Heinz Graf v. Rothenburg) hat bereits 22 der bisher 33 Bände der Asterix-Comics übersetzt.

Paddington, Fabula de Petro Cuniculo, Cattus Petasatus und *Harrius Potter et Philosophi Lapis.*[20]

So kindlich oder kindisch die meisten dieser latinisierten Werke scheinen mögen,[21] sie haben etwas gemeinsam mit Shakespeares Sonetten: Die Texte sind populär, sie sind entweder in Versen geschrieben oder bieten aus anderen Gründen (Wortspiele, Neologismen usw.) eine sprachliche Herausforderung[22] für die Übersetzer, die damit ihr Sprachgeschick beweisen können. Auch wenn es sich nur um ein Kinderbuch mit Abzählreimen handelt, so bietet doch die Zielsprache Prestige für Übersetzer und Leser. Der Zweck dieser Übersetzungen ist derselbe, den schon Newman in seinem Vorwort zu *Robinson Crusoe* gibt: Sie sollen beweisen, dass Latein keine tote Sprache sei, da sich auch moderne Inhalte damit ausgedrücken lassen; und um Latein am Leben zu erhalten, sollen junge Leser geködert werden mit Themen, von denen die Übersetzer denken, sie seien attraktiver als Caesars Kriege, Ciceros Reden oder die Gründungsmythen Roms.[23]

Da Latein in vielen Schulsystemen die erste Fremdsprache ist, wären die klassischen Originaltexte oft zu anspruchsvoll und überfordern die noch jungen Schülerinnen und Schüler. So vertraut man auf Snoopy, Mickey Mouse und Bären namens Puh oder Paddington, um den anämischen Kreis heutiger Latinisten mit frischem Blut zu versorgen. Obwohl die meisten dieser Bücher eine intellektuelle Unterforderung für die Jugendlichen dar-

---

[20] Eine Liste dieser und weiterer moderner Übersetzungen findet sich im Anhang.

[21] Aus der Reihe fällt nur Alexander Lenards Übersetzung von Françoise Sagans *Bonjour Tristesse.*

[22] „Wer möchte nicht die lateinischen Ausdrücke für ‚Marmeladensandwich' und ‚finsterstes Peru' lernen?", heisst es in der Werbung des Bloomsbury Bookshop.

[23] So ehrenwert die pädagogischen Ziele auch sein mögen, in gewisser Weise ist die Strategie auch kontraproduktiv. Die jungen Leser durchschauen den didaktischen Zweck und merken bald, dass der Zuckerguss sie nur verführen soll, eine bittere Pille zu schlucken. Zeigt die Wahl von Texten aus der eigenen Kultur nicht auch, dass die Verführer selbst die klassischen Texte zu wenig attraktiv finden? Warum sollte man aber dann eine tote Sprache lernen, die als Lektüre nichts Besseres zu bieten hat als Übersetzungen von Büchern aus der eigenen Kindheit?

stellen, sind sie von pädagogischem Wert, weil sie Spass machen (was sonst bei Originaltexten nicht der Fall zu sein scheint[24]) und weil die Lernenden keine Probleme haben zu verstehen, was sie schon seit ihrer Kindheit auswendig kennen. Sie gelangen so mit wenig Aufwand zu einem Erfolgserlebnis.

Newmans *Robinson Crusoe* richtete sich an eine solche Leserschaft in den englischen Mittelschulen. Die Leser, die Barton – falls er überhaupt an eine Publikation dachte – mit seinen Sonetten ins Auge gefasst haben könnte, hätten aber kaum zu dieser Altersgruppe gehört. Shakespeares Sonette sind nicht weniger anspruchsvoll als etwa die Elegien des Properz. Als Lockmittel könnten sie nur für eine reifere Leserschaft dienen, für Universitätsstudenten, vielleicht auch für junge poesieliebende Frauen aus dem Mittelstand oder für Arbeiter und Handwerker auf dem zweiten Bildungsweg. Diese Beispiele sind nicht willkürlich gewählt, denn Bartons und Newmans Übersetzungen widerspiegeln Entwicklungen im damaligen englischen Bildungssystem, die Diskussionen über liberale Erziehung und Debatten über das Angebot der Universitäten. Sowohl Newman wie Barton spürten, dass die Bedeutung des Lateins am Abnehmen war. Latein musste zwar noch nicht gerettet werden – man war noch weit davon entfernt, es „von den Schulen zu prügeln", aber es gab auch in England bereits neue Schulen, die kein Latein mehr anboten.

---

[24] Übersetzer und Kritiker betonen die Wichtigkeit des Spassfaktors: Peter Needham, der Übersetzer von *Paddington Bear* und *Harry Potter*, der 30 Jahre in Eton Lateinlehrer war, sagt in einem Interview: „Dies wird etwas Wunderbares sein für Kinder. Es hat lustige Dialoge. An der Schule, an der ich lehrte, hatten wir keine solchen modernen Übersetzungen. Es wird etwas sein, das zu besitzen Spass macht – die Art von Ding, die man seinem Vater auf Weihnachten schenkt." (*Harry Potter and the Latin master's tome take on Virgil*. Nigel Reynolds im *Telegraph* vom 03/12/2001) und eine Kritik von *Cattus Petasatus* verspricht: „Was für jedermann am wichtigsten ist: Latein wird zum Spass werden, und das ist ein seltener Erfolg!" (James B. Rives in *Amphora*. Vol. 4, Issue 1, Spring 2005). [Übersetzungen M.M.]

Das englische Schulsystem war im 19. Jahrhundert in einem desolaten Zustand. In den elitären *public schools*[25] lernten die Kinder der Oberschicht kaum etwas anderes als Latein, und die Abenteuer Robinson Crusoes mussten für Schüler und Lehrer eine willkommene Erweiterung eines Kanons von verstaubten Texten gewesen sein, so willkommen wie die Einführung von Kricket und Fussball in den Lehrplan von Rugby.[26] Schulreformer wie Dr. Samuel Butler in Shrewsbury und Thomas Arnold in Rugby setzten zwar auch moderne Sprachen, Geschichte und Mathematik auf den Lehrplan ihrer Schulen, aber offenbar so behutsam, dass Charles Darwin, ein unzufriedener Schüler aus Butlers Schule, dies nicht einmal bemerkte.[27]

Weiter reichende Reformen waren nicht nötig, da die *Public Schools* ihre Schüler auf die alten Universitäten von Oxford und Cambridge vorbereiteten, deren hauptsächlich auf den klassischen Sprachen fundierenden Curricula seit dem Mittelalter praktisch unverändert geblieben waren.[28]

Solange die Erziehung Sache der Kirche und Privater war, musste sich die Mittelschicht selbst helfen. Handwerker und Arbeiter be-

---

[25] Die Internatsschulen von Eton, Harrow, Westminster, Rugby, Winchester, Charterhouse und Shrewsbury, und zwei Londoner Tagesschulen, St. Pauls und Merchant Taylors', waren 1860 von der Erziehungsbehörde als *Public Schools* definiert worden.

[26] Thomas Arnold (1795–1842, der Vater von Matthew Arnold) hatte als Rektor von Rugby Sport und Spiele wie Fussball und Cricket in den Lehrplan seiner Eliteschule aufgenommen, mit dem Ziel, dem viktorianischen Gentleman christlichen Sportsgeist und Fairness einzuimpfen. Rugby wurde damit ein Vorbild für die anderen Eliteschulen und für die beiden Universitäten.

[27] Dr. Samuel Butler (1774–1839) war Rektor des Internats von Shrewsbury von 1798 bis 1836. „Nichts könnte schlechter gewesen sein für meine geistige Entwicklung als Dr. Butlers Schule – sie war strikt klassisch, sonst wurde nichts gelehrt, ausser vielleicht noch ein bisschen Geographie des Altertums und Geschichte. Die Schule als ein Erziehungsmittel blieb für mich ein unbeschriebenes Blatt." (*The Autobiography of Charles Darwin*, 1887). [Übersetzung M.M.]

[28] Der hauptsächliche Unterschied zwischen den beiden Universitäten war, dass Cambridge seit dem 18. Jahrhundert der Mathematik ein höheres Gewicht zumass.

gannen, sich in *Mechanics' Institutes* und *Working Men's Colleges* weiter zu bilden; für die Kinder des Mittelstands wurden Schulen gegründet, in denen praktischere Fächer wie Geographie, Biologie, Chemie, Physik und Technik gelehrt wurden. Als Ausgleich für diese Fächer hätten Latein und Griechisch zu viel Zeit verlangt. Der Vermittlung der als unverzichtbar erachteten ‚humanistischen Werte‘, die den zukünftigen Politikern, Priestern und Gentlemen in den *Public Schools* und den Universitäten mit dem Studium der lateinischen und griechischen Grammatik eingedrillt wurden, sollte deshalb ein neues Fach ‚Englische Literatur‘ dienen. Abgänger der neuen Mittelschulen konnten mangels Latein nicht an die altehrwürdigen Universitäten, aber die neuen ‚Backsteinuniversitäten‘[29], die vor allem für den Mittelstand gedacht waren, ermöglichten es jungen Männern und *Frauen*[30], auch ohne Latein einen Abschluss oder ein Diplom in einem der neuen Studienfächer zu erhalten.[31]

In der Folge der industriellen Revolution war ein grosser Teil der Bevölkerung verarmt, und Bildung war nicht für alle erschwinglich. Die Kinder der Arbeiterklasse konnten neben der Arbeit freiwillig Sonntagsschulen oder von Wohlfahrtsgesellschaften organisierte Abendschulen besuchen, wo sie hauptsächlich religiös indoktriniert wurden. Ein obligatorisches, staatlich gewährleistetes Schulsystem, das einer grösseren Zahl von Menschen aus allen Schichten eine zeitgemässe Bildung vermittelte, war nicht nur

---

[29] London, University College wurde 1826 gegründet, London, King's College 1829; London University 1836; Birmingham 1844.

[30] Bis 1871 mussten Studierende und Lehrer der Universitäten von Oxford und Cambridge praktizierende Mitglieder der anglikanischen Kirche sein. Die Universität von London dagegen gab Diplome ab an Mitglieder „aller Klassen und Konfessionen ... ohne irgendwelche Unterscheidung", ab 1878 wurden auch Frauen zu Diplomstudiengängen zugelassen, die ersten vier Frauen empfingen ihre Diplome 1880. Die ersten Colleges für Frauen in den alten Unversitäten wurden schon 1869 (Girton College, Cambridge) und 1879 (Sommerville und Lady Margaret Hall, Oxford) errichtet, Diplome gab es aber in Oxford erst nach 1920 und in Cambridge nach 1948.

[31] Fächer wie Chemie, Elektrotechnik, Geographie, Psychologie, Zoologie, Ägyptologie, Englisch, Französisch, Deutsch und Italienisch wurden zuerst nur an der Universität von London angeboten.

notwendig, um das industrielle Niveau des Landes zu erhalten, sondern auch, um eine drohende Revolution zu verhindern.[32] Staatliche Eingriffe brachten ab 1870 die dringend nötigen Reformen, und 1874 gab es bereits 5000 *neue* Schulen mit Englisch- statt Lateinunterricht für den Mittelstand.[33] Plötzlich brauchte es nun eine grosse Zahl Lehrer und Lehrerinnen für die neuen Fächer. Vor allem Frauen besuchten an der Londoner Universität Kurse in Englischer Literatur, um Englischlehrerinnen zu werden, und gegen Ende des Jahrhunderts begannen auch die alten Universitäten, Angebote für diese wachsende Nachfrage in Betracht zu ziehen. Der englische Schulinspektor und Bildungsreformer Matthew Arnold, der von 1857–1867 das Amt eines *Professors of Poetry* in Oxford inne hatte, war der Erste, der in diesem Amt einen Teil seiner Vorlesungen in Englisch hielt.[34]

Aber ob man nun wirklich einen Lehrstuhl für Englische Sprachwissenschaft und Literatur einrichten solle, und was Themen dieser Fächer sein könnten, war zu Bartons Zeit in Oxford noch völlig umstritten.[35]

---

[32] „Die Politiker sagen ‚Ihr müsst die Massen erziehen, denn sie werden die neuen Herren werden.' Der Klerus stimmt in diesen Ruf nach Bildung ein und versichert, die Leute würden aus den Kirchen und Kapellen verschwinden und sich dem finstersten Unglauben zuwenden. Die Fabrikanten und Kapitalisten stimmen herzhaft ein in den Chor und erklären, Unwissen mache schlechte Arbeiter; England werde bald nicht mehr fähig sein, Baumwollgüter oder Dampfmaschinen billiger zu produzieren als andere Nationen." (Thomas Huxley in *A Liberal Education and Where to Find It,* 1868.) [Übersetzung M.M.]

[33] 1880 wurde die allgemeine und kostenlose Schulpflicht für Kinder von 5 bis 10 Jahren eingeführt. Eine Reihe weiterer Erlasse musste folgen, bis 1918 die Kinder bis zum Alter von 14 schulpflichtig wurden.

[34] *Professor of Poetry* war ein Ehrenamt. Der Inhaber war zu drei Vorlesungen pro Jahr verpflichtet. Arnolds Vorgänger hatten diese jeweils in Latein gelesen. Die Creweian Oration, die auch zu diesem Amt gehörte, wurde bis 1972 in Latein abgehalten.

[35] Die Merton Professorship of English Language and Literature wurde 1885 eingerichtet. Der erste Prof. war Arthur Sampson Napier, ein Philologe und Spezialist in germanischen Sprachen. 1897 begann die Oxford English School, mit 4 Männern und 10 Frauen, die Examen ablegten. Bis 1906 (5 Männer, 22 Frauen) blieben die Frauen in der Überzahl. 1911 wurde Arthur Quiller-Couch der erste Professor für Englisch in Cambridge.

Barton und Newman mochten als Altphilologen in der drohenden Einführung von Englisch als Universitätsfach eine Gefährdung ihres eigenen Faches gesehen haben, aber die mittelständischen Abgänger aus den neuen Schulen wären vor deren Einführung ohnehin nie ihre Studenten geworden, die alten Universitäten verlangten weiterhin das Lateinstudium als Grundlage für alle weiteren Studien.

Indem Barton *Shakespeare* übersetzt, zeigt er, dass er im Disput um die Einführung des Englischen als Universitätsfach wie Arnold auf der Seite der liberal-humanistischen Reformer steht, die auch in den Werken der eigenen Nation universitär vermittelbare Werte sehen; Shakespeare wäre, falls es denn eingeführt würde, ein tauglicher Stoff des Faches Englische Literatur; indem Barton Shakespeare ins *Lateinische* übersetzt, zeigt er aber auch, dass er, wie Matthew Arnold und die meisten seiner Kollegen in Oxford, das Fach in Verbindung mit Sprachwissenschaft sieht, verbunden mit dem Studium der klassischen Sprachen und der Klassiker, vielleicht sogar mit Latein als Unterrichtssprache.[36]

Bartons Werk ist mehr als nur ein Köder, um eine reifere mittelständische Leserschaft zu Latein- und Englischkursen auf dem zweiten Bildungsweg zu locken. Es ist als seriöse Übersetzung auch eine Alternative zu einer genauen philologischen Edition, ein Gesellenstück, das zeigt, dass sein Autor fähig wäre, Englische Literatur zu unterrichten, wenn das Fach eingeführt werden sollte. Barton fixiert und konserviert Shakespeares Sonette für Lateinkundige auf dem Stand seiner Zeit und klärt dabei – wie jede Übersetzung das tun muss – auch semantisch diffuse Stellen.[37]

---

[36] Matthew Arnold war zwar für die Einführung eines Studienfaches Englische Literatur, aber nicht auf Kosten des Latein, während andere Reformer wie Thomas Henry Huxley die *humanities* einschränken wollten, um mehr Raum für die Naturwissenschaften zu erhalten.

[37] Als Vorlage zog er neben der ersten Ausgabe Thorpes von 1609 verschiedene zeitgenössische Editionen zu Rate.

Dass die Zielsprache der Übersetzung keine wirklich ‚lebendige'
Sprache mehr ist, hat den Vorteil, dass das Produkt keinen Ver-
änderungen mehr unterworfen ist. Shakespeares Englisch mag
unverständlich werden, moderne Sprachen sind ständig dem
Sprachwechsel unterworfen, aber das klassische Latein aus der
Blütezeit Roms wird immer bleiben, wie es ist – festgehalten in
einem abgeschlossenen Korpus klassischer Texte, der, abgesehen
von dieser Erweiterung durch die Shakespeareschen Sonette, unverändert bleiben wird. Die Übersetzung in die tote Sprache erlaubt es, den Inhalt von Shakespeares Text einzufrieren und dadurch ewig verfügbar zu machen für eine weltweite Gemeinschaft
von Lesern mit klassischer Bildung.

Barton geht es aber nicht nur um philologische und semantische
Festlegungen, es geht ihm auch um den künstlerischen Gesamt-
eindruck, um die formale Eigenart der einzelnen Gedichte, obwohl sich dabei eine exakte Wiedergabe in Sonettform aus histo-
risch-ästhetischen Gründen verbietet. Die Sonettform, die erst
im 13. Jahrhundert in Sizilien entstanden ist, wäre mit ihren
Reimen und metrischen Konventionen ein Anachronismus; eine
adäquate Übertragung in die klassische Sprache lässt sich nur mit
einer reimlosen klassischen Form und antikem Metrum bewerk-
stelligen, und so werden aus den gereimten jambischen Fünfhebern
im Lateinischen reimlose Distichen. Barton will nicht zeigen, wie
Shakespeare dichtete, er will zeigen, wie er gedichtet *hätte*, wenn
er zur Zeit Ovids gelebt hätte Barton *übersetzt* also nicht nur den
Text, er *versetzt* auch seinen Dichter, und macht aus dem elisabethanischen *Sonneteer* einen klassizistischen *Poeta Laureatus* mit Toga
und Lorbeerkranz.

Shakespeare mag – wie in den Übersetzungen in andere Sprachen
– dazu dienen, Sprache und Sprachgemeinschaft zu adeln, erneu-
ern und beleben, aber das Latein des klassische Altertums adelt
und immortalisiert im Gegenzug auch Shakespeare, dessen Übersetzer und seine Nation. Für die Viktorianer ist Latein noch immer die Sprache, die – *aere perennius* – die Zeiten überdauern
wird, die Sprache der Denkmäler und der auf klassizistische

Tempel gemeisselten Inschriften, die für die Ewigkeit gedacht sind. Mit Bartons Übertragung hält die britische Kultur, vertreten durch den nationalen und nunmehr unsterblichen Barden, ein weiteres Mal Einzug im Olymp.

Schon zu Lebzeiten Shakespeares hatte ein theaterbegeisterter Student namens Francis Meres in seiner Zitatensammlung *Palladis Tamia: Wit's Treasury* (1598) seinen Lieblingsautor als ebenbürtigen zeitgenössischen Dramatiker neben die lateinischen Klassiker gestellt: „Wie Plautus als bester Komödien- und Seneca als bester Tragödienschreiber der Römer gelten, so ist Shakespeare unter den Engländern der beste in beiden Gattungen".[38] *Translatio imperii* war ein Slogan in der politischen Propaganda unter Elisabeth I., in elisabethanischen Gründungsmythen wurde London als das von Brutus errichtete Neue Troja (Troynovant) dargestellt, die Schwesterstadt des alten Rom und das Herz des neuen Imperiums. Um diesen Anspruch zu legitimieren, brauchte die aufstrebende Weltmacht kulturelle Errungenschaften, die mit denjenigen Roms verglichen werden konnten. Die Idee, das elisabethanische England als eine dem antiken Rom ebenbürtige Kulturnation zu definieren, war also damals nicht neu, Meres war aber wohl der Erste, der *Shakespeare* benutzte, um die eigene Nationalliteratur bedeutungsvoll zu machen.

Barton vollendet, was Meres begann, indem er durch den Tatbeweis einer vollständigen Sonett-Übersetzung Shakespeare auch noch in einer dritten literarischen Disziplin als Klassiker der Lyrik neben Horaz, Ovid, Properz und Catull stellt. Wie Meres die gesamte elisabethanische Literatur aufwertet, indem er einen ihrer

---

[38] "As Plautus and Seneca are accounted the best for Comedy and Tragedy among the Latines: so Shakespeare among y' English is the most excellent in both kinds for the stage; for Comedy, witnes his *Ge'tleme' of Verona*, his *Errors*, his *Love labors lost*, his *Love labours wonne*, his *Midsummer night dreame*, & his *Merchant of Venice* : for Tragedy his *Richard the 2. Richard the 3. Henry the 4. King John, Titus Andronicus* and his *Romeo and Juliet*' [Übersetzung M.M.].
Ausser dem vermutlich verloren gegangenen *Love labours wonne* sind uns alle Stücke aus dem Kanon bekannt.

Vertreter als den römischen Klassikern ebenbürtig bezeichnet, so wertet Barton nun die viktorianische Kultur auf als eine Kultur, die nicht nur das Erbe Roms pflegt, sondern auch in der Lage ist, den klassischen Bildungsschatz durch eigene Beiträge zu erweitern. Das britische Empire wird so als kulturelle Wiedergeburt des römischen Imperiums legitimiert.

Nationalistische Propaganda wird sich Barton mit seiner Freizeitarbeit natürlich nicht bewusst zum Ziel gesetzt haben, aber der Einzelne ist sich kaum je bewusst, wie sehr er als kleines Rädchen im Getriebe mit seinem Wirken Teil ideologischer Prozesse ist. Bewusster waren dem Latein- und Griechischlehrer dagegen die auf dem humanistischen Bildungsideal des 19. Jahrhunderts basierenden erzieherischen Ziele, die auch sein Herausgeber Harrower im Vorwort zur zweiten Auflage von 1923 als Hauptgrund für eine Veröffentlichung nennt. Bartons Werk sei nämlich

> [...] für alle *homines venustiores* [klassisch Gebildete, Schöngeister] von ewigem Wert, weil es in monumentaler Form die fundamentale Identität des Denkens und Fühlens in der alten und neuen Welt bestätigt. Je genauer man es studiert, umso mehr wird deutlich, dass der Wissenschaftler mit durchdringendem Blick die essenzielle Gleichheit unter der nur scheinbaren Verschiedenheit englischer und römischer *humanitas* entdeckt hat. [Übersetzung M.M.]

Die Kombination von Latein und Shakespeare soll also beweisen, dass die englische und die römische *Humanitas* trotz verschiedener Sprachen auf demselben festen Felsen gründen, sie ist von ‚ewigem Wert', weil sie die ewigen humanistischen Grundwerte vermittelt, die dieselben hohen Gedanken und Gefühle nähren. Was die beiden Elemente für sich allein eigentlich schon garantieren sollten, muss, nach Harrowers Meinung, in ihrer sich gegenseitig verstärkenden Symbiose zur Gewissheit werden: Wenn die Beschäftigung mit nur einem der Elemente, mit Shakespeare oder mit Latein allein, schon zu einer Kultivierung des Geschmacks, zur Erziehung der Gefühle und zur Erweiterung des Geistes führt, muss dann die

Nation, die beide Elemente verbinden kann und Shakespeare in Latein liest, nicht auch eine bessere und kultiviertere Nation sein? Dass ein solcher Gebrauch von Nationaldichter und humanistischem Ideengut auch als intellektueller Überbau für Imperialismus und Kolonialismus dienen könnte, war kein Argument gegen die humanistischen Werte in den zwanziger Jahren, einer Zeit, als dieses Gedankengut noch dazu diente, zu zeigen, wie richtig die eigene Position und die eigenen Werte waren. Grossbritannien hatte den Weltkrieg nicht ausgelöst, und die demokratischen Kräfte hatten ihn am Schluss gewonnen, was sollte also am liberalen Humanismus nationalistischer Prägung falsch sein? Es brauchte einen zweiten Weltkrieg und viele weitere Kriege, um diese felsenfesten Überzeugungen zu erschüttern.

Natürlich waren es weder die 150 Büchlein der ersten Ausgabe, die zu den Gräueln des ersten Weltkriegs geführt hatten, noch waren es Harrowers 525 Exemplare von 1923, die dann zu Konzentrationslagern, Verfolgungen und millionenfachem Morden im zweiten Weltkrieg führen sollten, aber die Überzeugung einer ‚felsenfesten Identität‘ der eigenen Kultur mit einer idealisierten humanistischen Kultur treibt viele an sich harmlose Blüten, die, wenn man sie zusammenbindet, nicht mehr ganz so harmlos sind. Einen bescheidenen Beitrag zur Verbesserung der Welt möchte auch Claude Pavur, der Herausgeber von Bartons Übersetzung auf einer Webseite einer amerikanischen Universität leisten:

> Warum die Sonette Meister Shakespeares in Latein? Zur bessern Kenntnis beider Sprachen und auch zu einem besseren Verständnis von Dichtung. Und vielleicht auch, weil es von Tag zu Tag deutlicher wird: Die Welt braucht Latein. [Übersetzung M.M.] [39]

---

[39] "Why the Sonnets of 'Master Shakespeare' in Latin? For a better knowledge of both languages and for a better appreciation of the poetry as well. And perhaps because it is becoming clearer day by day that — *the world wants Latin*." Claude Pavur, S.J., Saint Louis University, 2004.

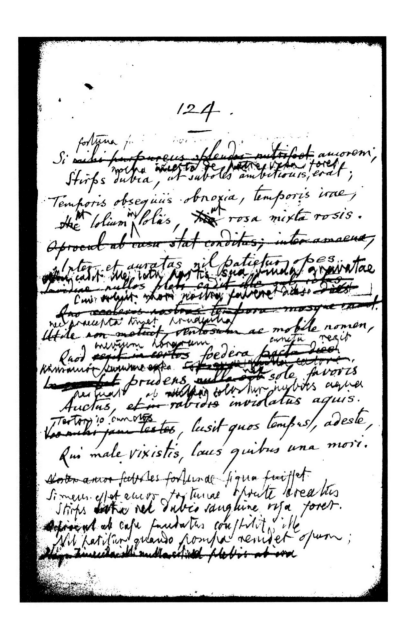

Sonett/Elegie 124. Manuskriptseite von Alfred Thomas Barton.

Dass die Welt Shakespeare und Latein in Kombination brauchen sollte, leuchtet uns heute kaum mehr ein. Unbestritten ist, dass viele Teile der Welt Shakespeare und die antiken Klassiker immer wieder zu Prestigegründen brauchen und missbrauchen; gegenüber dem gut gemeinten humanistischen Glauben, der Besitz des einen oder andern oder gar beider mache automatisch den Besitzer zum edleren Menschen, sind wir heute aber doch eher skeptisch eingestellt. Man kann verstehen, dass sich der Lateinlehrer Pavur wie der Übersetzer Barton und sein Herausgeber Harrower von Amtes wegen diesem Credo verpflichtet sehen. Uns reicht aber, was Harrower als nur ungenügenden Grund für eine Veröffentlichung angibt, nämlich dass Bartons Übersetzung ein Triumph der Ausdruckskraft sei, ein Fest des sprachlichen Einfallsreichtums. Wir sind zufrieden mit dem Vergnügen, das sich in den wohlklingenden und doch geschliffenen Ausdrücken und in einer klaren Sprache finden lässt. Shakespeare Sonette als lateinische Elegien sind für uns ein durchaus liebenswertes Kuriosum, das in seiner Art an andere Kuriosa der viktorianischen Zeit erinnert. Ironischerweise erhält Bartons Wahl der Elegie als Gedichtform dabei eine tiefere Bedeutung: Es sind Schwanengesänge aus einer Zeit, die an solche Werte glaubte.

SHAKESPEARE IN A ROMAN GARB
GULIELMI SHAKESPEARE CARMINA
QUAE SONNETS NUNCUPANTUR

Essay by Markus Marti

Alfred Thomas Barton (1843-1912) was a tutor of Latin and Greek at Pembroke College, Oxford, from 1865 till his death in 1912. In his spare time, the respected schoolmaster[1] translated Shakespeare's sonnets into Latin for his own pleasure, but after his death "grateful pupils" published the result as his "opus maximum" in an edition of 150 copies.[2] Such a small circulation is no surprise – who should read Shakespeare in Latin, one might ask. It is more astonishing that all copies had been sold ten years later, when John Harrower (1857-1933), a professor for Greek at Aberdeen, published an extra 525 copies in a second edition for the Shakespeare anniversary in 1923.

Translations are meant for the *export* or *import* of texts, and, ideally, for both. They help the speakers of one language to communicate their message to the speakers of the other, or satisfy a demand among the speakers of the target language. From such a practical point of view, Barton's translation may seem futile, a process in the wrong direction, an *export* to no-where. Was there a readership asking for Shakespeare's verses in Latin, or was it imperative that somebody got acquainted with such a rendering?

---

[1] The Latin preface to the first edition of his translations praises him as a teacher of morals, Greek and Latin, whose red pencil commanded as much respect as the birch: 'conversiones Latine minus feliciter compositas tam acriter castigabat ut cerulam ejus miniatam vix minus quam flagellum ipsum discipuli reformidarent. Sic vitam moresque eorum pariter atque indolem ad virtutem corroborabat: sic instituti, sic imbuti sunt ut ea reverentia quam adulescentes conceperant ne aetate quidem provectioribus usu familiari exolesceret.' (Praefatio, 1913).

[2] "Begun as a *parergon* to fill the spare hours of a busy life, it ended by being the most considerable piece of work left behind him by its author, and as such was first published, after his death, in 1913, at the instance of his grateful pupils to be a remembrance of his full and ripe scholarship." (Preface, 1923).

The first translations of Shakespeare's plays into other languages belonged to the *export* variety and served a practical purpose: English comedians had to make themselves understood on the stage if they wanted to be successful on the continent. Their translations, although rather primitive, *were* successful: A two-volume German edition of the plays that had been performed by "English comedians" appeared in Germany in 1620, three years before the first folio edition of Shakespeare's plays was published in England.[3]

The late 18th century translations of Shakespeare's plays into German, Russian, Italian, French, Dutch, Portuguese, Romanian, Czech, Hungarian and Spanish were of the second, the *import* variety: there was a growing demand for Shakespeare's plays in these countries. The plays had become part of a Pan-European canon, and it was essential to have them in one's own national language, often as a means of distinguishing one's own culture from another.

In the 19th century, translations of Shakespeare's plays were available in most European countries. Translating the sonnets seems to have been less urgent at the beginning, but once the plays were known, the sonnets got more attention, and translating them has become extremely popular since the middle of the 19th century.[4] Already in 1871, there was a complaint in a German literary magazine that too many new translations of Shakespeare's sonnets were being published, and that every schoolmaster had

---

[3] Among the plays were *Titus Andronicus, Tugend- und Liebesstreit (Twelfth Night), Der bestrafte Brudermord oder Prinz Hamlet aus Dänemark.* Creizenach also mentions a performance of *Von Romeo undt Julia,* 1604 at Nördlingen, and a *Teutsche Komedia der Jud von Venedig, auss dem engeländischen (Merchant of Venice)* (p. XL); in 1607 Captain Keeling's crew played *Hamlet* in Sierra Leone, on board the Red Dragon – with a running translation into Portuguese.

[4] The first to translate two sonnets (116 and 143) into German was probably Christian Heinrich Schütze (1760-1820) in 1784, the first translation of the complete sonnets by Karl Lachmann appeared in 1820, while Dorothea Tieck's translation was published (anonymously) in 1825; the French translation by François-Victor Hugo (the son of Victor Hugo) was completed in 1857.

his own version ready in his desk, waiting to be published.[5] More than 70 German translations of the cycle have been published up to now, and of the most popular sonnets there are more than 150 translations extant.[6] The situation in other countries is similar.[7] It can hardly be maintained that all these translations are necessary: their circulation is usually very small, they are no longer *imported* for the benefit of a larger group; translating sonnets, it seems, has become an end in itself.

What makes translating Shakespeare's sonnets such a popular occupation for amateurs of poetry? One reason is obviously the brevity of these texts. A sonnet may be translated in a couple of hours, in a day, a week, or a month, between other things, as a form of recreation. And yet, a good translation is not just a trifle. Writing your *own* sonnets by strictly observing metre and rhyme scheme is not an easy thing to do, but the result is not rewarding – the form has been in disrepute, out of fashion since the 19th century. Translating somebody else's sonnet is even harder but promises a higher reward: keeping as much of the original content as possible, imitating puns, rhetorical figures and sound patterns in a predetermined space restricted by metre and rhyme is so difficult that the success in such a language game is already its own reward, a solitary pleasure. Unlike a crossword puzzle that will be thrown away once it has been solved, the finished translation can still be improved, read and reread, eventually even published. The translators become part of the large community of Shakespeare translators and get into direct competition with

---

[5] *Magazin für die Literatur des Auslandes* (cf. bibliography, Jansohn, Christa und Eymar Fertig).

[6] Jürgen Gutsch collected in his anthology „*...lesen, wie krass schön du bist konkret"* 155 translations of sonnet 18; in his second edition of *Shakespeare sechsund-sechzig* U. Erckenbrecht published 132 versions of sonnet 66. Christa Jansohn's, Annette Leithner-Brauns' and Eymar Fertig's data bank *Shakes-peares Sonette in Deutschland* tries to record all the translations that have been published so far (cf. bibliography).

[7] For translations into German and other European languages, cf. Marti, Markus (ed.) "Shakespeare Translations", *Sh:in:E. Shakespeare in Europe.* <http://pages.unibas.ch/shine/translators.htm>.

their predecessors and colleagues, even with the bard himself. The results can be objectively compared, for everybody to see and judge. Each translation is in a certain way 'truer' to the original than the other, in some respects it will even be 'better' than the original. Barton's translation, for example, is definitely more classical than Shakespeare's original. As a perfect translation of an original text will never be possible, there is always room for a new one that is better in one aspect or other.

Languages and cultures change, older translations become dated and difficult to understand (an effect that can be noticed with the romantic German translation by Schlegel-Tieck). In some cases words in the *target language* may have changed their meanings or acquired unsuitable connotations; in other cases the reading of the *original text* may have changed because certain aspects have become more (or less) important to us. New translations can make up for such linguistic and cultural changes. In English, this is more difficult – many passages have become abstruse, and a translation into modern English might be a good idea if the readers were not so keen to read the original.[8] It would be difficult to modernize a play like *Hamlet*, in which so many lines have become proverbial. In English, the task of keeping pace with new interpretations and linguistic change can only be achieved by new editions. An ever increasing number of editors have added emendations, comments and annotations to Shakespeare's works in footnotes since the first 'modern' edition by Nicholas Rowe (1709).

New translations and new editions can only keep pace for a very short time. Ironically, it is because there are so many already that their number is still bound to increase. A final version of a text that is so widely read and interpreted is not possible. Every new

---

[8] With their *Tales from Shakespeare*, Charles and Mary Lamb offered something like a cultural translation for children, changing both genre and language, and Thomas Bowdler's *Family Shakespeare* of 1807 may also be seen as a cultural translation of Shakespeare's works for and into a more prudish time. The recent translation of Shakespeare's plays into modern English by Walter Saunders, a South African professor, seems to have no success in England.

edition or translation adds new meanings to its complexity. The more the text becomes loaded with new meanings, the more cultural prestige and international renown it wins from ensuing new editions and translations, and the more it will be adapted and used again for new meanings, serving national, political, social or private interests.

Translations of Shakespeare's works boomed especially in the 19th century, when many European countries began to define themselves as nations. Although translating may just be a private occupation of the translator (as in Barton's case), the translation itself always has a social and political meaning. Young nations or nationalist movements define themselves by their own language or culture, and translations of Shakespeare's works are given top priority in that process. State leaders and politicians ordered such translations or made them themselves: In Germany, Goethe, privy councellor and minister in the duchy of Weimar, translated *Romeo and Juliet* for the court theatre in 1812, and the group *Junges Deutschland* (among them the former revolutionaries Freiligrath and Herwegh) published the complete works in 1872; in 1780, Catherine the Great translated and adapted *The Merry Wives of Windsor* – partly as an exercise in Russian, which was not her mother tongue, but also with clear political intentions – providing Russia with a cultural identity independent from France; in turn, about 100 years later, the Finnish national move-ment created its cultural identity and freedom from Russia by a translation of Shakespeare into Finnish;[9] the Austrian empress Sisi (Sissi)

---

[9] "Translating Shakespeare can have enormous cultural and even political signi-ficance: in Finland, for example, the first transl. of Sh. in the 19th c. were an important part of a growing nationalist movement which eventually resulted in Finland's declaring her independence from the Russian Czar in 1917. Translating Sh. was a way of building cultural capital, of proving both to themselves and to others that Finns were capable of understanding and rendering into their own (oppressed) language the 'genius' of Sh. At the same time, Finns were collec-ting and celebrating their native literary achievements in *The Kalevala*. If this is partly what the Kurds are doing, shouldn't we offer to help rather than say 'forget about it' and tell them (and everyone else) to learn English?" (Nely Keinänen in a contribution to the *Shaksper* discussion forum, cf. bibliography).

translated *Hamlet, King Lear,* and *The Tempest* into Greek; the former prime minster Fan Noli translated Shakes-peare into Albanian during his exile in the United States; Roparz Hemon, a leader of the Breton liberation front (and a nazi collaborator), was the first to translate Shakespeare into Breton; Julius Nyerere, the first president of Tanzania, had Shakespeare translated into Swahili and translated some of the plays himself; currently, new editions should help to define the difference between Slovak and Czech, and Shakespeare translation projects help to define the cultural identity of Spanish regions such as Catalania and Galicia, and of the Kurdish people in Iraqi Kurdistan.[10]

As new nations and emergent groups usually define themselves by a common language or culture, they can show their cultural significance and independence if they 'own' Shakespeare's works in their own language. A translation of his works may be more important than the nation's own literary heritage. The vernacular literature of an emergent or challenged nation may be denigrated by dominant or oppositional groups, but the value of Shakespeare is indisputable. The accessibility of his works in any language provides prestige for the speakers even if they will never read any of his works, and even if the members of dominant groups sneer at their attempts. However whimsical the translation of Shakes-peare's works into the "Galaxy's fastest growing language", Klingon,[11] may seem to us, it shows that a fictitious culture can become a virtual reality in this process.

The translations of bits and pieces of Shakespeare's work into Latin in the late 19th and early 20th century may remind us of translations into Klingon – we may discount them as small

---

[10] cf. Dabrowska's article in KurdishMedia.com.

[11] The Klingon Shakespeare Restoration Project's first edition of *Hamlet, Prince of Denmark (The Restored Klingon Version)* (1996) a limited hardback edition of 1000 copies is out of print, but a second edition in paperback (Pocket Books, 2000) is now available. The publication of *Much Ado About Nothing* and *Macbeth* are planned. Nick Nicholas translated sonnet 18: "qaDelmeH bov tuj pem vIlo'choHQo". Besides Shakespeare, the epic of *Gilgamesh* is available in Klingon, and there is a Klingon Bible Translation Project.

curiosities, 'finger exercises' of linguists and schoolmasters in their free time. But they were made by eminent Victorian classicists like Benjamin Hall Kennedy[12] (Sonnet 18, excerpts from *Macbeth*) and Hugh Andrew Jonstone Munro[13] (parts from *Hamlet* and *Midsummer Night's Dream*), and they were published in Latin primers[14] that were used in public schools all over the country. Barton's translation of the whole sonnet cycle is not just one more translation of Shakespeare into yet another language; however private his occupation with Shakespeare, his work as a cultural product of his time also has further implications.

Since the decline of the Roman Empire the Latin language has not defined any nation except for the Vatican and the Catholic church, which Barton as an Anglican can hardly have envisaged as prospective readers;[15] his Latin is not Church Latin, he does not use the rhyming stanzas of medieval hymns. Rather than of the Pope, Barton might have thought of the ghosts of the

---

[12] Benjamin Hall Kennedy (1804-1880) was headmaster at Shrewsbury from 1836 till 1866, when he became a fellow and classical lecturer of St John's College, Cambridge.

[13] Hugh Andrew Johnstone Munro (1819-1885) was one of Benjamin Hall Kennedy's first pupils at Shrewsbury, classical lecturer at Trinity College and in 1869 elected to the newly-founded chair of Latin at Cambridge. His main work is an edition of Lucretius (2 vols, 1864). As a master of Greek and Latin verse composition he contributed to the famous volume of Shrewsbury verse, *Sabrinae Corolla*. His *Translations into Latin and Greek Verse* were privately printed in 1884.

[14] Translations of Shakespeare's texts were published in Latin primers such as *Sabrinae Corolla* (London, 1850), *Nova Anthologia Oxoniensis* (1899), *Cambridge Compositions* (1899), *Flosculi Rossallienses* (Cambridge, 1916), *Liliorum Hortulus* (1926). Especially *Sabrinae Corolla* remained very popular for a long time, websites of bookshops offer reprints from 1859 (2nd ed. Cambridge, Deighton, Bell et Soc.), 1890 (London, G. Bell & Sons) and even 1950 (Adnitt & Naughton).

[15] As a tutor in Oxford, Barton may have belonged to the Oxford Movement, but the sympathies of the Oxford Movement for Catholicism did not go so far as to reintroduce Latin into daily life – not even into church service. Nevertheless, in 1869 Charles Edward Appleton, one of the leaders of the Movement, founded *Academy*, a journal that provided a battle field for the ongoing debate about the correct pronunciation of Latin (Stray, S. 201).

emperor Augustus, of Maecenas, Horace, Vergil and Propertius as readers of his translation.

But Latin was not only a language of the dead in 19th-century England. It was also the secularized 'holy' language of a virtual nation, of the universal 'republic of letters'. Kennedy's, Hughe's and Barton's translations are not of the *export* variety, they *import* Shakespeare into their own language, the language of academia as taught in English public schools and as officially spoken in the ancient universities of Cambridge and Oxford.[16] Since the middle ages Latin had had the (mostly mythic)[17] status of a world language of the educated, ironically the status that English has today. That it was in danger of losing this status may have been felt, but that it should lose it to English was not clear yet. On the contrary, there were attempts to reintroduce Latin as a world language towards the end of the 19th century, in the wake of the poor performance of artificial languages like Volapük or Esperanto, as it was politically not advisable to declare English, German or French an international language.[18] Barton's translation does for this virtual commonwealth, the English Academia, what other Shakespeare translations do for foreign nations. It

[16] Latin remained the official ceremonial language in Cambridge and Oxford till late in the 20th century. In 1918, Sir Arthur Quiller-Couch, the first professor of English Literature at Cambridge, mentioned in his lecture that "our Vice-Chancellor, our Public Orator still talk Latin, securing for it what attention they can." The Creweian Oration, a speech of the Oxford professor of poetry in praise of university benefactors, was to be held in Latin till 1972.

[17] Françoise Waquet shows in *Latin or the Empire of a Sign* (a survey on the importance of Latin from the 16th to the 20th century) that despite all pedagogical efforts knowledge in Latin had always been very poor, even among teachers. In the 1853 contest for the chair of Greek in Cambridge, all the candidates prefered to answer in English to the questions that had been prepared for them in Latin. ('licet candidatis Anglice respondere', cf. Stray p. 200).

[18] A proposal of the Englishman George Henderson to set up a *Societas Internationalis Latinitatis Modernae* was well received in France and Germany in 1891, but Henderson had to give up 10 years later. Congresses of 'Living Latin' were held till 1976 (Waquet, 264ff). The people who have contributed to the 4000 Latin pages of the internet dictionary *Vicipaedia, libera encyclopaedia* may still entertain a similar dream, unless their teachers have forced them to participate... <http://la.wikipedia.org/wiki/Pagina_prima> (14.04.06).

216

strengthens the weakened community of Latinists both psychologically and physically by modernising and enlarging its corpus of literature.

Psychologically, the translation provides the community of English speakers of Latin with a stronger identity, granting them access to Shakespeare in their 'own' language if they should need it. To strengthen a community physically, new members have to be attracted, and for that purpose a vernacular text by a popular 'modern' author could serve well as bait. Nobody is going to study Latin to read Shakespeare, but people who love Shakespeare could learn Latin by reading their favourite works in Latin. John Henry Newman's brother Francis William Newman, who published a Latin translation of Defoe's *Robinson Crusoe (Rebili Crusonis Annalium)* in 1884,[19] explained the aims of such a practice in his preface:

> [...] to make extensive reading possible to the many, the style ought to be very easy and the matter attractive. To enable us to talk, we ought to have a vocabulary that includes all familiar objects [...]. In the near future, some universal tongue will be sought for by the educated. If Latin be still learned in England, France, Italy, Germany, Hungary, Spain, this is still, as three centuries ago, the best for all Christendom. But perhaps even Latin will be beaten out of the schools.[20]

Newman's *Rebili Crusonis Annalium* was the forerunner of a large number of translations of contemporary works with didactical and ideological aims. Today's students of Latin may read *Asterix*

---

[19] Francis William Newman (1805-1897) was professor of Latin at London University. His translation of *Robinson Crusoe (Rebili Crusonis Annalium* a F.W. Newman contractorum, Latine redditorum, ad pueros docendos accommodatorum anno MDCCCLXXXIV – Londini apud Trübner) is available on the internet (see bibliography).

[20] cf. [http://www.grexlat.com/biblio/rebilius/gl/praefatio.html] (Dec. 05).

Gallus,[21] *De Titini et Miluli facinoribus, Michael Musculus et Donaldus Anas, Popeius, Insuperabilis Snupius, Haegar Terribilis, Maximi et Mauritii malefacta, Vinnetu, Alicia in Terra Mirabili, Winnie Ille Pu* und *Domus Anguli Puensis, Ursus nomine Paddington, Regulus, Fabula de Petro Cuniculo, Cattus Petasatus* and *Harrius Potter et Philosophi Lapis.*[22] Childish as most of these 'modern' Latinized works may seem,[23] they have a great deal in common with Shakespeare's sonnets: the texts are popular, and they are either in verse or for other reasons (puns, neologisms etc.) linguistically challenging,[24] so that the translators can prove their linguistic skills. The target language provides prestige for the translators and the readers, even if the text is 'only' a book of nursery rhymes.

The main purpose is still that which is mentioned in Newman's preface to *Robinson Crusoe*: the translations should prove that Latin is not a 'dead' language because modern contents can be expressed in it, and to keep Latin 'alive', the translators want to attract younger people by topics they consider more attractive for them than Caesar's war reports, Cicero's speeches or the founding myths of Rome.[25]

---

[21] 22 of the 33 volumes of the Asterix comics are available in Latin, translated by *Rubricastellanus* (Karl-Heinz Graf v. Rothenburg).

[22] For a list of these modern translations see bibliography.

[23] An exception: Sagan, Françoise. *Tristitia Salve* (*Bonjour Tristesse*), tr. Alexander Lenard. Paris: Julliard, 1963.

[24] "Who can resist learning the Latin for 'marmalade sandwiches' and 'Darkest Peru'?" (*Ursus nomine Paddington*, Editorial review, Bloomsbury Bookshop).

[25] However honorable these aims, there is also something counter-productive in this strategy. Even young readers will discern the didactic purpose and presume that what attracts them is just the sugar that coats an obviously bitter pill. Does the choice of vernacular texts not suggest that the original literature is not considered attractive by these missionaries who want to find new disciples for their language community? Why should one learn a dead language that has obviously nothing better to offer than translations of one's own childhood books? There is even something perverse and obscene in this strategy: prostitution, zoophilia, pedophilia, and necrophilia come to one's mind, if one thinks that the little Latin bears, rabbits, dogs and ducks are used as teasers to seduce very young people to love a language that has died many centuries ago.

Because Latin is the first foreign language in many school systems, the classical texts are intellectually too demanding for the pupils. So it is up to Snoopy, Mickey Mouse and Paddington Bear to pump fresh blood into the anaemic circle of today's Latinists. Although most of these books are below the intellectual level of teenage students, they are pedagogically useful because they are fun (which seems not to be the case with original texts),[26] and because the learners have no problems in understanding what they have memorized in their own language since childhood. Very little effort will be needed to get a feeling of success.

Newman's *Robinson Crusoe* was directed at such a young readership in boarding schools. The readers Barton might have envisaged with his sonnets – if he thought of a publication at all – could not have been adolescents, though. Shakespeare's sonnets are not less demanding than Propertius' *Elegies*. As teasers they would only have worked for a more mature readership, for university students, maybe for young middle-class women who loved poetry, maybe also for adult workers or mechanics looking for a second-chance education in one of the Mechanics' Institutes and Working Men's Colleges.

Barton's and Newman's translations thus reflect the ongoing discourse about the English educational system, about a 'liberal education' and the syllabi of universities in the Victorian age. Both Newman and Barton may have felt that the importance of Latin was beginning to shrink a little. Latin did not yet need to be

---

[26] The fun factor is stressed by translators and critics: Peter Needham, the translator of *Paddington Bear* and *Harry Potter*, who had taught Classics at Eton for over 30 years, said in an interview: "This is going to be a wonderful thing for children. It has got very witty dialogue. At the school I taught at we didn't have modern translations of this sort. But I also think its going to be a fun thing for intelligent people to have – the sort of thing you give your father for Christmas." (*Harry Potter and the Latin master's tome take on Virgil*. Nigel Reynolds, *Telegraph* 03/12/2001) and a review of *Cattus Petasatus* promises: "Most importantly, for everyone, it will make Latin fun, and that is a rare achievement." (James B. Rives in *Amphora*. Vol. 4, Issue 1, Spring 2005).

saved, it was not going to be "beaten out of the schools", but many *new* schools were being founded which no longer offered Latin.

The English school system had been in a bad state in the beginning of the 19th century. In the so-called *public schools*,[27] the children of the upper classes learnt hardly anything but Latin, and the addition of Defoe's *Robinson Crusoe* to the set canon of reputedly dull texts was certainly more than welcome, as welcome as the introduction of cricket and football into the curriculum at Rugby.[28] The reformers Dr Samuel Butler and Thomas Arnold put modern languages, history and mathematics on the syllabus of their schools, but in such homoeopathic doses that Charles Darwin, a pupil of *Butler's School*, did not even notice it.[29] More substantial reforms did not seem necessary, as the public schools had to prepare their students for the ancient universities of Oxford or Cambridge, which still offered an essentially medieval syllabus of classics, divinity and mathematics, with sports as an essential addition to the curriculum.[30]

The middle classes needed a more practical education, but since education was private or in the hands of the church, they had to look after themselves. For artisans and workers, a second-chance education was provided by the Mechanics' Institutes and

---

[27] The elite boarding schools of Eton, Harrow, Westminster, Rugby, Winchester, Charterhouse and Shrewsbury, and two London day schools, St. Pauls and Merchant Taylors', had been defined as *Public Schools* in the 1860s by the educational Clarendon commission.

[28] Thomas Arnold (1795-1842, Matthew Arnold's father) added sports and games like football and cricket to the curriculum at Rugby – with the aim of forming the Victorian gentleman as a 'muscular Christian' and sportsman. Rugby became a model for other public schools and the universities.

[29] Dr. Samuel Butler (1774-1839) was headmaster of the Shrewsbury School from 1798 till 1836. "Nothing could have been worse for the development of my mind than Dr. Butler's school, as it was strictly classical, nothing else being taught, except a little ancient geography and history. The school as a means of education to me was simply a blank."(*The Autobiography of Charles Darwin*, 1887).

[30] The main difference between the two ancient universities was that mathematics had become more important in Cambridge since Newton's times.

Working Men's Colleges; for children, schools that taught modern languages, geography, biology, chemistry, physics and engineering were founded. As a counterweight to the technical learning, Latin and Greek would have taken up too much time in basic linguistic drilling. The so-called humanist values, which had always been the reason for teaching Latin and Greek to the future gentlemen in public schools and universities, were now to be imparted by the teaching of English Literature. The graduates of these schools could not go to the ancient universities, but the new 'red brick' universities[31] offered the chance for young men *and women*[32] to get a degree, a title or a diploma without Latin in new and more practical subjects.[33]

The industrialisation of both labour and production resulted in a large part of the population becoming poor. The children of the lower classes had to work and often merely attended Sunday schools or charity schools which offered mainly religious indoctrination. A school system that provided a modern education to a greater number of people on all levels seemed not only necessary to maintain the country's industrial standard, but also to prevent a revolution.[34] From 1870 onwards, the state started to bring things

---

[31] London, University College was founded in 1826, London, King's College in 1829; London University in 1836; Birmingham in 1844.

[32] Till the University Test Act in 1871, students and teachers of the ancient Universities had to be members of the Anglican Church. London University awarded degrees to (male) members of "all classes and denominations ... without any distinction whatsoever", and from 1878 onwards also to women, the first four women got their degrees in 1880. The first women's colleges in the ancient universities were founded in 1869 (Girton College, Cambridge, first students entered in 1870) and 1879 (Sommerville and Lady Margaret Hall College, Oxford), but degrees were only given after 1920 in Oxford and 1948 in Cambridge.

[33] University College, London was the first to offer subjects like chemistry, chemical engineering, electrical engineering, geography, psychology, zoology, Egyptology, English, French, German, and Italian.

[34] "The politicians tell us, 'You must educate the masses because they are going to be masters'. The clergy join in the cry for education, for they affirm that the people are drifting away from church and chapel into the broadest in-fidelity. The manufacturers and the capitalists swell the chorus lustily. They declare that ignorance makes bad workmen; that England will soon be unable to turn out cotton goods, or steam engines, cheaper than other people." Thomas Huxley, *A Liberal Education and Where to Find It* (1868).

under control with a series of Education Acts; by 1874, over 5,000 *new* schools, in which English was taught instead of Latin, had been founded.[35] Because of these rapid developments, there was an immediate need for a very large number of teachers in the new subjects. Women especially attended courses in English Literature to become teachers in the new schools. It was only towards the end of the century that the ancient universities began to consider whether they should not offer courses for this growing demand. The English school inspector and reformer Matthew Arnold, who held the chair in poetry at Oxford from 1857-67, was the first professor to hold his lectures in English.[36] But whether or not to introduce a proper chair for English Linguistics and English Literature, and what the topics of these subjects should be, was still in dispute during the time that our Latin translator, Barton, was at Oxford.[37]

Barton and Newman as teachers of the Classics might have seen in the impending introduction of English as a university subject a potential danger for their own subject, but the pupils of the new schools would have never been their students before, and the ancient universities still insisted on a classical education as a base for further studies. By choosing to translate *Shakespeare*, Barton shows that he is not entirely opposed to the liberal-humanist reforms. Shakespeare could well have been a topic if English Literature were to be introduced as a subject. But by translating Shakespeare's verses into *Latin*, Barton shows that he, like

---

[35] In 1880 elementary school from the age of 5 to 10 became compulsory and free. A number of further Education Acts followed till elementary and secondary education became compulsory for everybody up to the age of 14 in 1918.

[36] *Professor of Poetry* was a honorary position that demanded three lectures of one hour a year. Matthew Arnold's predecessors had only lectured in Latin. The Creweian Oration, a speech in praise of the unversity's benefactors, had been held in Latin till 1972.

[37] The Merton Professorship of English Language and Literature was established in 1885. The first professor was Arthur Sampson Napier, a philologist with interest in the Germanic languages. In 1897 the Oxford English School started, with 4 men and 10 women taken the Honours examination. Till 1906 (5 men, 22 women), students were mainly women. Arthur Quiller-Couch became the first professor of English in Cambridge in 1911.

Matthew Arnold and most of his colleagues in Oxford, would have liked to see this subject linked with philology and connected with the study of the classics, maybe even taught in Latin.[38]

From a scholarly point of view, Barton's work is more than just a teaser to attract a mature or maybe even female middle-class readership to second-chance Latin courses; as a serious academic translation, it is also an alternative to a philological edition. It could be seen as a test-piece or masterpiece to show his ability to teach English Literature; his translation fixes and conserves the 'modern', 19th century understanding of Shakespeare, the state of the art of his time,[39] and it is of a remarkable semantic precision. That the target language of his translation is not a 'living language' has the advantage that the work is not affected by change. Shakespeare's English may become incomprehensible, contemporary languages may change, but the classical Latin of the Roman Augustan period will remain forever as it is – fixed and stored in a corpus of classical texts which is available all over the world and will remain unchanged, except for this addition of Shakespeare's sonnets. The translation into a dead language allows to the content of Shakespeare's text to be deep frozen, to be kept eternally available for a worldwide communion of readers with a classical education.

But Barton's aim was not only a philological and semantic denotation of Shakespeare's text; his translation also shows aesthetic and poetic ambitions. Stylistically, the sonnet form, developed in 13th century Sicily, would not fit into a classical corpus. End rhymes are a feature of the Middle Ages; they were not used by the Roman poets in the Augustan age. To avoid this anachronism, Barton uses rhymeless dystichs instead of rhymed iambic pentameter, and Shakespeare's sonnets become elegies.

---

[38] Matthew Arnold was in favour of having English Literature as a subject, but not at the expense of the classics, whereas other reformers like Thomas Henry Huxley were for diminishing the humanities to get more space for the study of Science.

[39] Apart from Thorpe's edition of 1609 he must have used several contemporary Victorian editions to work from.

Barton does not show how Shakespeare wrote, he shows how Shakespeare would (or should) have written, had he lived in ancient Rome. He does not only translate the text, he 'translates' its author as well, turning the Elizabethan *sonetteer* into a classicist 'Roman' *poeta laureatus*, clad in a toga and wearing a laurel wreath.

Shakespeare may – as in other translations – serve to ennoble, renew or revive Latin, but Latin with its humanist connotations of classical antiquity and ancient Rome also ennobles and immortalizes Shakespeare, his translator Barton, and his nation. For the late Victorians, Latin is the language which – *aere perennius* – will survive the times, the language of memorial plates and inscriptions like „Victoria Regina Imperatrix" chiselled on classicist buildings that are meant for eternity. With Barton's translation British culture, represented by the latinized and thus immortalized bard, enters Olympus a second time.

An Elizabethan theatre-goer, the young student Francis Meres, had already put Shakespeare as a contemporary representative on two Olympic pedestals, praising his favourite playwright as the best writer of comedies and tragedies, equal to the Latin classics. In his commonplace book *Palladis Tamia: Wit's Treasury* (1598) he wrote: "As Plautus and Seneca are accounted the best for Comedy and Tragedy among the Latines: so Shakespeare among y' English is the most excellent in both kinds for the stage ...".[40]

Meres wants to upgrade the literature of his own time, implying that Elizabethan England is an Empire of a cultural standard equal to ancient Rome. *Translatio imperii* was a slogan in Elizabethan political propaganda – in founding myths, London was presented as Brute's New Troy (Troynovant), ancient Rome's sister, the centre of the new Empire. To legitimize this claim, the emerging world power needed cultural achievements that could

---

[40] "... for Comedy, witnes his *Ge'tleme' of Verona*, his *Errors*, his *Love labors lost*, his *Love labours wonne*, his *Midsummer night dreame*, & his *Merchant of Venice* : for Tragedy his *Richard the 2. Richard the 3. Henry the 4. King John, Titus Andronicus* and his *Romeo and Juliet*' Apart from the lost *Love labours wonne* all the plays are still in our canon.

be compared to the achievements of ancient Rome. Meres' idea was not new, therefore, but Meres was probably the first to use Shakespeare for this purpose. Barton now only completes what Meres began: With the evidence of his own translation he puts the author, who has already become an universally acknowledged 'classic' in comedy and tragedy, on the pedestal in a third literary discipline, as a classic poet equal to Horace, Ovid, Propertius and Catull, implying again that the British Empire is the reincarnation of the Roman Empire. In its culture, this Empire does not only cultivate and propagate the classical heritage, it is also able to *extend* and *complete* the classic canon with its own literature.

Nationalist propaganda was hardly the aim of Barton's leisure time activity, but the individual never knows how much or what he or she contributes as a small wheel in larger ideological processes. As a teacher of the classics, Barton would not have contradicted that the value of his own work was based on what his editor Harrower offers as the reason for the second edition in 1923:

> What gives it permanent value for all *homines venustiores* is that it asserts in monumental form the bedrock identity of thought and feeling in the old world and the new. The closer it is studied the more apparent will be the penetrating insight of the scholar which detected the essential likeness under the semblance of diversity between the English and the Roman *humanitas*.

The combination of Latin and Shakespeare shows that Rome and Britain are founded on the same rock and are nurtured by the same *humanitas*, the same elevating feelings and thoughts. What both elements are supposed to grant by themselves, must become a certainty in their symbiosis: if, according to the liberal-humanist creed, the occupation with one of the elements, with Shakespeare or Latin alone, will lead to a cultivation of one's taste, provide a sentimental education and an enhancement of one's spirit, how should a nation that combines the two elements and reads Shakespeare in Latin not be a better and more cultivated nation? That such a nationalist use of Shakespeare and the humanities may serve as an intellectual superstructure for imperialism and colonialism, was not considered an argument against humanist values in the twenties, when these very ideas still served to justify one's own position and one's values. Great Britain had not started the war, and the democratic powers had won it in the end, so what was wrong with liberal humanism? It needed a second world war and some more to shake these adamant convictions.

It was, of course, neither the 150 copies of the 1913 edition of Shakespeare in Latin that had led to the atrocities of the First World War, nor Harrower's 525 copies in 1923 that led to the concentration camps, to the persecution and the killing of many more millions of people in the second war, but the conviction of a 'bedrock identity' between one's own culture and an idealized humanist one may have many sprouts, which, taken together, are not all that harmless.

Just a small contribution to make this world a better one, is also what Claude Pavur, the editor of Barton's translation on the internet, has in mind:

> Why the Sonnets of 'Master Shakespeare' in Latin? For a better knowledge of both languages and for a better appreciation of the poetry as well. And perhaps because it is becoming clearer day by day that — *the world wants Latin*.[41]

That the world needs Shakespeare and Latin in combination seems an odd idea today. That many parts of 'the world' need and use Shakespeare and the classics for prestige cannot be denied; but that the knowledge or possession of one or the other, or even of both, would improve its possessor is a notion that is too hard to believe, even if we may understand that Pavur, as a university professor of Latin and as a priest, still feels obliged to share this humanist creed with Barton and Harrower. We are more than

---

[41] For the URL see Bibliography, Pavur.

125.

Intereratne mea, si pars ego debita pompae
  Rebus in externis officiosus eram?
Grandia in aeternum mihi fundamenta locarem
  Luxuria fusis quae breviora fluunt.
Non ego perspexi, quos forma aut gratia movit,
  Pendendo nimium perdere quicquid avent?
Suavia non sincera sonant, praeque beati
  Deficiunt, oculis facta ruina suis.
Non ita, servitium cordis tu corde tenebis;
  Paupera de pura tu cape dona manu.
Non vili de pane fero, non arte parato;
  Me tibi, me donis pro tot, amice, tuis.
Hinc mendax delator abi; tua crimina veris
  Pectoribus minimum maxima quaeque nocent.

Nachtrag (statt auf S. 227)
Sonett/Elegie 125. Manuskriptseite von Alfred Thomas Barton.

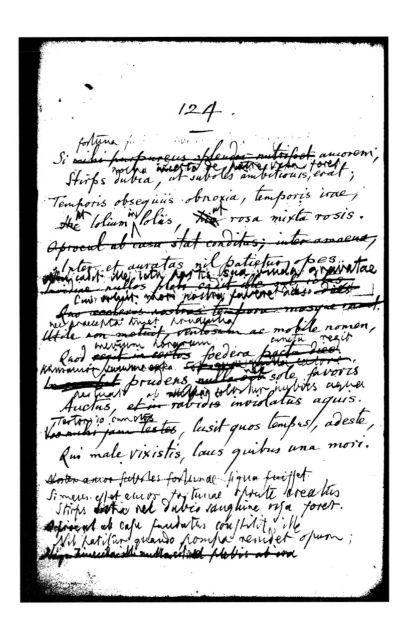

Sonett/Elegie 124. Manuskriptseite von Alfred Thomas Barton.

content with what Harrower calls only an insufficient reason for his publication, namely that Barton's translation is "a mere triumph of expression, a feat of verbal ingenuity", we are content with the pleasure (jouissance) that can be found in verbal artistry, in smooth expressions in a clear language. Shakespeare's sonnets as Latin elegies are for us just an amiable curiosity which reminds us of other curiosities of the Victorian age. There is some irony in Barton's choice of verse form: his sonnets are indeed *elegies* – swan songs to a time that still believed in such values.

MODERNE WERKE IN LATEIN /
SOME MODERN LATIN TRANSLATIONS

Bond, Michael. *Ursus nomine Paddington (A Bear Called Paddington);* tr. Peter Needham. London: Gerald Duckworth, 1999.

Browne, Dik. *Haegar terribilis,* München: Goldmann, 1986.

Busch, Wilhelm. *Maximi et Mauritii malefacta;* in Lat. conv. U. E. Paoli. Florence: Francke, 1960.

Busch, Wilhelm. *Maxus atque Mauritius;* tr. Alexander Lenard. 1962.

Busch, Wilhelm. *Max und Moritz auf Lateinisch;* tr. F. Schlosser. Stuttgart: 1993.

Busch, Wilhelm. *Plisch et Plum, versus iocosi Guilielmi Busch pictoris poetaeque de sermone Germanico in Latinum conversi* a L. Benning. München: Artemis und Winkler, 1976.

Carrol, Lewis. *Alicia in Terra Mirabili;* tr. Clive Harcourt Carruthers. London: MacMillan, 1964. Available: <http://www.gmu.edu/ departments/fld/CLASSICS/alice.html>(Dec. 05)

Dr. Seuss. *Cattus Petasatus: The Cat in the Hat in Latin;* tr. Jennifer Morrish Tunberg and Terence O. Tunberg. Wauconda, Illinois: Bolchazy-Carducci, 2000.

Disney, Walt. *Donaldus Anas atque nox Saraceni;* in Lat. conv. I. Recanati. Stuttgart: Klett, 1983.

Disney, Walt. *Donaldus Anas et actiones fiduciae;* in lat. conv. I. Recanati. Stuttgart: Klett, 1984.

Disney, Walt. *Michael Musculus et Lapis Sapientiae;* in Lat. conv. C. Egger. Stuttgart: Klett, 1984.

Disney, Walt. *Michael Musculus et Regina Africae.* European Language Institute, 1986.

Hergé, *De Titini et Miluli facinoribus: De insula nigra;*

(*The Black Island*, 1987)

Hergé, *De sigaris pharaonis* (*The Cigars of the Pharaoh*, 1990);
tr. C. Eichenseer, European Language Institute (ELI) and Casterman.

May, Karl. *Vinnetu Tomus Tertius* (*Winnetou III*);
tr. J. Linnartz. Bamberg-Radebeul: Karl-May-Verlag, 1998.

Milne, A. A. *Domus Anguli Puensis* (*The House at Pooh Corner*);
tr. Brian Staples, London: Penguin, 1980.

Milne, A. A. *Winnie ille Pu* (*Winnie the Pooh*);
tr. Alexander Lenard, London: Penguin, 1991.

Potter, Beatrix. *Fabula de Petro Cuniculo* (*The Tale of Peter Rabbit*);
tr. E. Peroto Walker. London: F. Warne, 1962.

Popeius. De circi mysterio (*Popeye*); tr. A. Pacitti. Stuttgart: Klett, 1984.

Rowling, J.K. *Harrius Potter et Philosophi Lapis* (*Harry Potter and the Philosopher's Stone*); tr. Peter Needham, London: Bloomsbury, 2003.

Sagan, Françoise. *Tristitia Salve* (*Bonjour Tristesse*);
tr. Alexander Lenard. Paris: Julliard, 1963.

Schulz, C. M. *Insuperabilis Snupius* (*Snoopy*);
in Lat. conv. G. Angelino. Stuttgart: Klett, 1984.

St Exupéry, Antoine de. *Regulus* (*Le petit prince*) ;
tr. Augusto Haury. Paris: Fernand Hazan, 1961.

Vicipaedia, libera encyclopaedia. <http://la.wikipedia.org/
wiki/Pagina_prima> (14.04.06)

BIBLIOGRAPHIE / BIBLIOGRAPHY

Baldick, Chris. *The social mission of English criticism: 1848-1932.* Oxford: Clarendon Press, 1983.

---. *Criticism and literary theory 1890 to the present.* London [etc.]: Longman, 1996.

Creizenach, W., ed. *Die Schauspiele der englischen Komödianten.* Vol. 23. Band. Berlin und Stuttgart: W. Spemann, o.J. (ca. 1888).

Dabrowska, Karen. "Shakespeare's Macbeth in Kurdish". *KurdishMedia.com united kurdish voice,* 2005. Available: <http://www.kurdmedia.com/articles.asp?id=10325>

Erckenbrecht, Ulrich, ed. *Shakespeare Sechsundsechzig. Variationen über ein Sonett.* Zweite, erweiterte Ausgabe ed. Kassel: Muriverlag, 2001.

Gutsch, Jürgen, ed. *„...lesen, wie krass schön du bist konkret".* *William Shakespeare. Sonett 18 vermittelt durch 154 + 1 deutsche Übersetzer.* Dozwil TG: EDITION SIGNAThUR, 2003.

Huxley, Thomas Henry. "A Liberal Education and Where to Find It (1868)." *Collected Essays III.* The Huxley File ed. London, 1893-94. Available: Charles Blinderman and David Joyce (eds). *The Huxley File.* <http://aleph0.clarku.edu/ huxley/CE3/LibEd.html>

---. "Letter on University Education", *Pall Mall Gazette* (Oct. 1891), in *Life and Letters of Thomas Henry Huxley.* Ed. Leonard Huxley. Vol. 2. London, 1900. 301f. Available: Charles Blinderman and David Joyce (eds). *The Huxley File.* <http://aleph0.clarku.edu/ huxley/ UnColl/PMG/PMGet/UnivEd.html>(14.04.06)

Jansohn, Christa, Annete Leithner-Brauns and Eymar Fertig. *Shakespeares Sonette in Deutschland.* Datenbank. Otto-Friedrich-Universität Bamberg. Available: <http://web.uni-bamberg.de/ split/britkult/links/sonettbiblio/index.htm>

Keinänen, Nely. "Shakespeare's Macbeth in Kurdish".

Online posting. 12 Aug. 2005. *SHAKSPER: The Global Electronic Shakespeare Conference*. Available: <http://www.shaksper.net/archives/2005/1331.html>

Marti, Markus. "Shakespeare Translations". *Sh:in:E – Shakespeare in Europe*. Department of English, University of Basel. Available: <http://pages.unibas.ch/shine/translators.htm>

Newman, Francis William. *Rebili Crusonis Annalium a F.W. Newman contractorum, Latine redditorum, ad pueros docendos accommodatorum*. London: Trübner, 1884. Available: <http://www.grexlat.com/biblio/rebilius/gl/index.html>

Pavur, Claude (ed). *The Sonnets of William Shakespeare with a Latin Translation by Alfred Thomas Barton. Edited, with a Prefatory Note, by John Harrower. Published at Fourteen Henrietta Street, Convent Garden, London by Martin Hopkinson and Company Limited MDCCCCXXIII*. St Louis University, 2004. Available: <http://www.slu.edu/colleges/AS/languages/classical/latin/tchmat/pedagogy/latinitas/dv/dv.html>

Quiller-Couch, Arthur. "VII. The Value of Greek and Latin in English Literature. Wednesday, February 6, 1918." *On the Art of Reading*. 1920. Available: <http://www.bartleby.com/191/>

Shakespeare, William. *Hamlet, Prince of Denmark (The Restored Klingon Version)*. 2nd edition ed: Pocket Books, 2000.

Shoulson, Mark. "The Klingon Language Institute". Available: <http://www.kli.org/>

Stray, Christopher. "Scholars, Gentlemen and Schoolboys: The Authority of Latin in Nineteenth- and Twentieth-Century England". In: *Britannia Latina: Latin in the Culture of Great Britain from the Middle Ages to the Twentieth Century*. Ed.: Charles Burnett and Nicholas Mann. Warburg Institute Colloquia, 8. The Warburg Institute - Nino Argno Editore, 2005. p. 194-207.

Stray, Christopher. "Curriculum and Style in the Collegiate University: Classics in Nineteenth-Century Oxbridge". (not yet publ.)

Taft, Deb. "The Victorian Education". 1999. Available: <http://www.gober.net/victorian/reports/schools.html>

Waquet, Françoise. *Le latin ou l'empire d'un signe : XVIe-XXe siècle.* Paris: Editions Albin Michel, 1999.

---. *Latin, or, The Empire of a Sign : from the sixteenth to the twentieth centuries.* London: Verso, 2001.

Alle Internet-Dateien: Stand 14.04.06

[Zusammenstellungen von Markus Marti]

Kurzbiographie von Ludwig Bernays

 Ludwig Bernays, geboren 1924, hat Musik und Medizin studiert und während dreissig Jahren eine Praxis als Arzt für Allgemeinmedizin FMH geführt. Nach deren Aufgabe Studium der klassischen Philologie an den Universitäten Zürich und Basel. Seit 1993 zahlreiche Publikationen zu philologischen Themen, insbesondere zu Horaz und zur römischen Elegiendichtung (Tibull, Properz, Ovid) in schweizerischen und internationalen Fachzeitschriften. Mehrere Aufsätze erschienen in einem Sammelband unter dem Titel *Ars poetica, Studien zu formalen Aspekten der antiken Dichtung* in der Reihe „PRISMATA, Beiträge zur Altertumswissenschaft" (Bd.9, Peter Lang Europäischer Verlag der Wissenschaften, Frankfurt am Main 2000, ISBN 3-631-34685-9). Ein weiterer unter Mitwirkung mehrerer europäischer und amerikanischer Forscher entstandener Sammelband ist O.F. Gruppe, dem Autor eines zu seiner Zeit bahnbrechenden Werks über die römische Elegie, gewidmet (*Otto Friedrich Gruppe 1804-1876, Philosoph, Dichter, Philologe,* hrsg. von Ludwig Bernays, Rombach Wissenschaften, Reihe PARADEIGMATA Nr.3, Freiburg i.Br. 2004, ISBN 3-7930-9377-8). Ein Aufsatz über Alfred Thomas Bartons lateinische Nachdichtungen der Sonette Shakespeares erscheint im Neulateinischen Jahrbuch 2006.

Mit Gedichtübersetzungen aus alten und modernen Sprachen, insbesondere mit Nachdichtungen der Sonette Shakespeares, hat sich der Autor seit 40 Jahren befasst. Einige dieser Übersetzungen erschienen in der Zeitschrift ‚Harass' sowie in den Sammelbändchen *Shakespeare sechsundsechzig* (Ulrich Erckenbrecht 2001) und *...lesen wie krass schön du bist konkret* (Jürgen Gutsch 2003). Ein 2002 erschienenes Büchlein mit 56 Sonetten nach Shakespeare und mit kritischen Bemerkungen zum überlieferten englischen Text, ISBN 3-908141-19-2, wurde u.a. in der Neuen Zürcher Zeitung und im Shakespeare-Jahrbuch lobend besprochen.

Kurzbiographie von Markus Marti

He studied English, German and Philosophy in Basel. The paper for his first degree (Oberlehrer) was on Arno Schmidt (in German Literature), his dissertation was an edition and translation of Shakespeare's *Timon of Athens* (1995) for the bilingual *Englisch-deutsche Studienausgabe der Dramen Shakespeares*, and he is now working on a translation of *Titus Andronicus* for the same edition. His interests include English drama and theatre, Romanticism and the Gothic novel, comparative literature and culture studies (e.g. Shakespearean influences on German culture, or: cultural, social and political influences of Mcpherson's *Ossian* in Europe). He is also teaching at the DMS2 in Muttenz.

E-mail: markus.marti@unibas.ch

LIST OF INDEPENDENT PUBLICATIONS

William Shakespeare. *Timon of Athens / Timon von Athen. Englisch-deutsche Studienausgabe.* Deutsche Prosafassung, Anmerkungen, Einleitung und Kommentar von Markus Marti, Englisch-deutsche Studienausgabe der Dramen Shakespeares. Tübingen und Basel: Franke 1995. 302 pp.
ISBN 3-7720-2342-8; 3-7720-2352-5
William Shakespeare. *Titus Andronicus. Englisch-deutsche Studienausgabe.* Deutsche Prosafassung, Anmerkungen, Einleitung und Kommentar von Markus Marti, Englisch-deutsche Studienausgabe der Dramen Shakespeares. Tübingen: Stauffenberg (forthcoming).

TRANSLATIONS

Anon. „Ein Lied". Übersetzung des Shakespeare zugeschriebenen Gedichts "Shall I Die, Shall I Fly?" (Preisausschreiben der Deutschen Shakespeare-Gesellschaft, 1. Preis) in: *Shakespeare-Jahrbuch*

134. Bochum: 1998. p.171f.
[http://www.unibas.ch/shine/texts2dt.html].
Shakespeare. William. „Sonett Nr. 66"; übers. Markus Marti. In:
Shakespeare Sechsundsechzig. Variationen über ein Sonett. Ed. Ulrich
Ercken-brecht. Zweite, erweiterte Ausgabe. Kassel: Muriverlag,
2001. p. 242.
William Shakespeare. „Sonett Nr. 18"; übers. Markus Marti. In:
Harass. Ed. B. Oetterli Hb.. Vol. 15/16. Dozwil: Edition Signathur,
2002. p. 249.
Collins, William: "The Passions. An Ode for Music", 1746 / „Die
Leidenschaften. Ode an die Musik". Deutsche Erstübersetzung.
In: *Harass.* Ed. B. Oetterli Hb. Vol. 19. Dozwil: Ed. Signathur,
1004. p. 109-119.

CONTRIBUTIONS
SHinE - Shakespeare in Europe, Markus Marti, editor
[http://www.unibas.ch/shine/] (editor of the webpage)
Compendium of Renaissance Drama (CORD), Brian Corrigan, editor.
2003
[http://radar.ngcsu.edu/~bcorrigan/COMPENDIUM.HTML]
(entries for twelve non-Shakespearean Renaissance plays for CD
database)

Non-Shakespearean Drama Database (NSDD) Gabriel Egan,
editor. 2001. [http://www.gabrielegan.com/nsdd/index.htm]

CONFERENCE TALKS
"Language of Extremities / Extremities of Language: Body
Language and Culture in *Titus Andronicus*". (7th World
Shakespeare Congress, short paper session 3.4: *Revenge as a
Mediterranean Phenomenon Before and After Hamlet.* Valencia, 2001)
[http://www.unibas.ch/shine/revengemarti.htm]
"Literary Fakes: Ossian", International Medieval Conference, Leeds.
1994.

Verlagswerbung der Edition Signathur CH-8580 Dozwil TG

signathur@gmx.ch · www.signathur–org.ch · Fax 0041 (0)71 411 00 91

◉ In der EDITION Signathur erscheint das Literatur-Magazin *HARASS* *– Die Sammelkiste der Gegenwartsliteratur aus dem Sängerland.* ISSN 1423-0984. Auch mit ISBN-Nr. Die Zeitschrift kann abonniert werden.

◉ In der EDITION SIGNAThUR erscheint die *Shakespeare-Reihe* mit bisher drei Publikationen:

(56) Sonette von Shakespeare. Mit deutscher Übersetzung und mit Anmerkungen zum englischen Text von Ludwig Bernays. 78 S. Zürich und Dozwil, 2002. ISBN 3-908141-19-2. 18 CHF | 12 €.

...lesen, wie krass schön du bist konkret! William Shakespeare, Sonett 18, vermittelt durch deutsche Übersetzer in 154 + 1 Versionen. Hrsg. und eingeleitet von Jürgen Gutsch, München; mit einem Geleitwort des Bibliographen Eymar Fertig, Bremen. 180 S. München und Dozwil, 2003. ISBN 3-908141-28-1. 24 CHF | 15 €.

Alfred Th. Barton: Lateinische Elegien nach den Sonetten William Shakespeares. Latin Elegies after William Shakespeare's Sonnets. Alfred Thomas Barton: GULIELMI SHAKESPEARE CARMINA QUAE SONNETS NUNCUPANTUR LATINE REDDITA (1913). Neu hrsg. und kommentiert, mit revidiertem Text der Sonette Shakespeares, von Ludwig Bernays, Zürich. Mit einem Essay von Markus Marti, Basel. 237 S. Dozwil, 2006. ISBN 3-908141-43-5. 24 CHF | 15 € | 18 US-Dollars.

◉ In der ED. SIGNAThUR erscheinen die *BLÄTTER AUS DER HINTERGASSE.* Bisher 5 Ausgaben; je 56 numm. und sign. Ex. mit Lyrik oder Prosa und mit Grafiken von Ch. Lippuner, Salenstein. 25 CHF.

◉ In der EDITION SIGNAThUR erscheint die Reihe *die kleine signathur.* dks 1: *Weise Worte des Vorsitzenden Wankelmuth aufgezeichnet von seinem gelehrigen Schüler Konfusius.* Aphorismen von H.P. Gansner. Mit einem Geleitwort von Fritz Reutemann. Zeichnungen von Sonja Hübscher, 52 S. 2005. ISBN 3-908141-36-2. 15 CHF | 10 €.

dks 2: *Fingerspiele. Sehnsuchtsgeschichten* von Ursula Heinze de Lorenzo, Santiago de Compostela. Mit Vignetten von Klaus Rothe, Ermatingen. 68 S. Dozwil, 2006. ISBN 3-908141-41-9. Je 15 CHF | 10 €.

◉ *Kommandier(t) die Poesie! Biografische Berichte,* von Eugen Gomringer. 168 S. 30 Abb. Dozwil, 2006. ISBN 3-908141-35-4. 24 CHF | 15 €.

◉ Weitere Werke von H.P. Gansner, Josef Good, Ernst Herhaus, Ch. Lippuner, B. Oetterli Hb., Johanna Plähn, Felix Schwemmer u.a.